THE PATH
of
PARENTING

THE PATH
of
PARENTING

Twelve Principles to Guide Your Journey

Vimala McClure

NEW WORLD LIBRARY
NOVATO, CALIFORNIA

New World Library
14 Pamaron Way
Novato, California

Copyright © 1999 Vimala McClure

Editing: Marc Allen and Chris Cone
Cover and text design: Mary Ann Casler

Library of Congress Cataloging-in-Publication Data
    McClure, Vimala Schneider, 1952–
    The path of parenting : twelve principles to guide your journey/ Vimala
       McClure.
      p.   cm.
    Includes bibliographical references.
    ISBN 1-57731-078-0 (alk. paper)
    1. Parenting — Religious aspects — Taoism.　2. Lao-tzu. Tao te ching.
    I. Title.
BL1923.M36 1999
299'.514441 — dc21   99-22342
                                            CIP

First printing, May 1999
ISBN 1-57731-078-0
Printed in Canada on acid-free, recycled paper
Distributed to the trade by Publishers Group West

10 9 8 7 6 5 4 3 2

This book is dedicated
to my children:
my best teachers

CONTENTS

—⚜—

Acknowledgments

———— ⋆ ————

N_o author gets to the end of a manuscript alone. My thanks go
to the many people who inspired and uplifted me during this
project, who helped me with their stories and points of view, and
who helped me finish when I thought I couldn't.

My special thanks to Marc Allen for his amazing ability to edit
so that what I say is said the way I want it to be, for his sense of
humor, and his kindness and dedication.

Thanks to Sue Thoele, my writing angel, who listened to me
when I needed a friendly ear.

And to those who have inspired me throughout this project and
others: Cheryl Clement, Mia Elmsater, DeAnna Wamsley Elliott,
Audrey Downes, Sylvie Hetu, Evelyn Guyer, Maria and Wayne
Mathias, Kalena Babeshoff, Helena Moses, Micki Riddle, Jharna
Morrisey, and others who I may have forgotten here but never in
my heart.

A special thanks to Dr. Judy Heller and Dr. Karen Leonard for
helping me keep my health together to finish this project.

Special thanks also to my sister, Sydney Reali, for listening,
holding me up when I was down, making me laugh, and for being
one of the best models of a good mother that I can think of.

TWELVE PRINCIPLES TO GUIDE YOUR JOURNEY

⌘

An entirely different picture of "family" is emerging in the new millennium. Most of the paradigms we have developed over the last millennium are no longer viable. Because our family structures, our values, and our experience of family will continue to change, it is particularly important for us to understand that being a good parent and raising healthy, responsible children requires us to be grounded in the deeper meaning of the role of parent. We need to be able to change beyond what may now seem possible to us, and the only way to achieve that is to develop a firm rooting in the spiritual dimension of parenthood.

What I know without any doubt is that bringing every gift I came here with, every iota of strength and wisdom, every drop of love and loyalty, everything I have, to the task, the mission, and the gift of bringing up two souls to live their own lives and fulfill their destinies is the most important thing I have ever done, or ever will do. I don't expect this singularity of purpose from others, but because of it I have been able to pay close attention to the dynamics, the secrets, and the lessons of real parenthood — much more closely, I believe, than many academic experts who observe interactions in made-up environments and offer theories on what is healthy or correct and formulas that rarely work. What I am attempting to do, rather, is to go deeper into the idea that parenthood is a mission, however large or small a part it plays in your life. From that perspective, everything you think about parenthood changes. It is no longer a series of problems to be solved; it is, instead, an important part of your personal growth, and even your spiritual path.

If there is anything I wish to do with this book, it is to help you, to encourage you, and to empower you to remember that you have chosen to be a parent because it is an important aspect of your purpose on this earth. In this book, you will learn that, rather than always trying to *do* the right thing as a parent, you will be more successful in your mission as you discover the right thing to *be*. Contrary to most books on raising children, this one will focus mostly on you, the parent. My assumption is that if you feel fulfilled, purposeful, aligned with your integrity, and satisfied with your role as a parent, your children will "turn out" just fine.

In fact, this book is not really about how they turn out. It's about how *you* turn out, and how your relationship with your children builds positively through the years. You don't need much in the way of how-to advice; each child is different, times change, and your family configuration and values will also change with time. What you do need is a firm understanding of the timeless nature of your soul's pledge to your child, and how that commitment plays out in your personal life, so that, when you reflect on your life, you can feel proud of who you are and what you learned by being a parent.

To do this, we need both a long-term, philosophical view and some short-term solutions. So I will try to provide both, with an emphasis always on the long-term. This approach won't, however, lead to an over-complication of the subject of "parenting as mission." Rather, it is a way to continually bring ourselves back to the simple truths that make the universe work and therefore can be counted upon to make our own little microcosm run smoothly.

The biological urge and the psychological need to bear children rarely help us look beyond pregnancy and birth. We may fantasize about what our baby will be like. We may form some opinions about home or hospital birth, breast or bottle feeding, and even about if or when we will put our children in day care. But few parents take the time to discover and define how being a parent fits into their lifelong mission. Few of us look ahead to how this new person will change our lives.

It's hard to imagine a new baby as a gap-toothed eight-year-old; a gangly, belligerent thirteen-year-old; a high school senior with expensive tastes; a college student experimenting with alternative lifestyles; or an adult with financial problems. We leap into parenthood, not realizing it is only the beginning of an ever-increasing expansion of our responsibilities. This new being will bring a long series of other people into our lives: baby-sitters, doctors, friends, teachers, boyfriends and girlfriends, pets, spouses, in-laws, and grandchildren. How we handle all of these relationships will have a profound affect on our children's lives, on their relationships, and on how they in turn relate to their own children. (Perhaps if we really thought about all of this, none of us would take the leap into parenthood!)

For the past ten years, I have studied ancient Taoist teachings, and have been struck by the depth of the principles these teachings are based upon. I also studied and practiced the martial art of Tai Chi, which has its genesis in Taoism. Tai Chi could also be called Taoist yoga. Like its counterpart in India, Tai Chi is a practice that quiets and focuses the mind with the goal of self-realization or union (yoga) with the Tao (pronounced *dow:* supreme consciousness or God).

A symbol often associated with Tai Chi is the *yin/yang.* The black area represents *yin* — passive, soft, open, yielding. The white

The *Yin/Yang* Symbol

area represents *yang* — active, hard, tight, assertive. The curved line represents the synthesis or synergy of these two aspects of consciousness. The black and white dots indicate that each contains its opposite. It is not possible, therefore, to separate them. Like two sides of a sheet of paper, both are intrinsic aspects of the Tao. Balancing these energies is the goal of Tai Chi practice. Striving for this balance is also the key to good parenting.

The twelve principles in this book are based upon the principles underlying the practice of Tai Chi. They are particularly appropriate for the journey of parenthood because they address issues of power, control, effectiveness, resistance, conflict, harmony, and longevity. The principles are, briefly:

1. Relax
2. Slow down
3. Empower
4. Be yourself
5. Be responsive
6. Avoid extremes
7. Flow and let go
8. Maintain continuity
9. Be present
10. Be attentive
11. Accept and validate
12. Harmonize

These principles are simple, interconnected, easy to apply, and their depth is beyond the scope of a thousand books. When you clarify your mission as a parent and begin applying these principles in your everyday life, I guarantee your family will experience an increase in peace, love, joy, harmony, and all the good things of life.

Sooner or later our children let us know they arrived in the world with agendas of their own. While we have a tremendous influence over the way they express and live out their agendas, we cannot mold and control them. They have as much to teach us as we want to teach them, and the wise parent realizes this early on. Because of this give-and-take dance, we sometimes feel out of step with our children and conflict arises. We may try to teach at a moment when we should be receptive. Our children may not be able to listen to us because they have not been heard. Therefore, the dynamic of opposition is always arising in these relationships. Tai Chi can help us learn how to dance with this flow of energy.

In Tai Chi, the goal is not to defeat an opponent. Rather, the Tai Chi practitioner learns to flow with the energy of opposition, assisting its movement toward its natural conclusion, which is exhaustion. The opponent then is defeated by his own momentum rather than by stiff resistance. Ultimately the practitioner's goal — peace and harmony — is reached without overt violence or force.

The principles of Tai Chi are based upon eternal truths: Tao is the immutable Being, the oneness toward which all beings are moving. Harmony prevails when we find harmony with the eternal flow of Tao. Strength is found in the persistent, gentle flow of the life force. Water is often used as a symbol of the kind of strength Tai Chi develops; the gentle drip of water on a rock eventually carves that rock as no brute force can. A river made the Grand Canyon; no bulldozer could create such a phenomenon.

In Tai Chi, you learn how to flow with the life force of the universe. You do not oppose an attacker's force, you step aside and permit the attacker's life energy to pass. As he is flying by, you give him a nudge to assist him to get where he is going more quickly. Similarly, Tai Chi practitioners learn to ground their energy into the earth in such a way as to have all the strength of the earth within their bodies. When this practice is mastered, they are unshakable. The strongest person cannot move them.

Once I saw a tiny, elderly Tai Chi master standing calmly in a pose. Several large men were asked, one at a time, to shove him off balance — even an inch would do. The young men were over six-feet tall, athletic, and robust. One by one they threw themselves at him, pushing for all they were worth, and he didn't budge even an inch. Finally, all five of them simultaneously lined up, pushing one upon the other. The combined force of five men did not move him even a fraction, and his face and body remained relaxed, calm, and serene. The men grunted, red-faced, straining against his upraised arm.

The wise parent learns to discover the life force within and move with it to guide his children. When met with opposition, he grounds himself in the eternal and allows the opposition to exhaust itself naturally. He remains calm, providing an immutable base for his children's growth. In this way, he teaches them how the universe works, provides a model of healthy parenting, and gains their trust and respect in the process.

Children need the same things in different ways at each stage of their development. Parents who know how to observe and learn can provide their children with the right kinds of respect, acceptance, encouragement, boundaries, assistance, understanding, affection, and — above all — unconditional love.

The experience of parenting is as instructive and productive for you as it is for your child. Children help us define and refine our character. They give us many opportunities, challenges, and tests along the way. If we look ahead to the coming years with, as Buddhists say, "beginner's mind," we can be excited about all we will learn. There is no guru or mentor that can give us greater or deeper teaching than our children.

Our kids mirror what is right or wrong in our lives. If we cultivate our ability to learn and perceive the deeper significance of our parenting experiences, we can correct our course as we go along. The perfect parent does not exist. Parenting is an ever-evolving school for all of us. If we continually clarify what kind of parents we want to be, we are better able to respond to new challenges with excitement and anticipation rather than dread. Discovering what is truly important to us is the first step.

YOUR MISSION AS A PARENT

Before putting these twelve principles to work, it is important to know what you are trying to achieve. In *The Seven Habits of Highly Effective People,* Stephen Covey says, "Begin with the end in mind."

Everything we do begins in the mind. First we create a mental picture, then the physical manifestation follows. The more clearly we can define our goal, the more quickly and accurately we can reach it. We are often caught up in the busy hustle of everyday life, reacting to everything that comes our way. We react automatically, based on what we have internalized — the "blueprint" of information we have from our life experiences. New parents are often surprised to hear themselves sounding exactly like their own parents. These internalized scripts are usually ineffective, sometimes outright destructive. Many people just go along reacting to everything in this way, not bothering to examine their blueprints and create something new for themselves — and then they wonder why their children are disrespectful, sullen, and rebellious.

In an article called, "Parenting for Pregnancy, Birth, and Infancy," doctors Eileen and Tom Paris say, "Looking back at our own feelings growing up will help us become more conscious and better parents. Did we feel close and attached? Did we feel understood? Were we treated as individuals even when we were little? Our own tender spots will reoccur with our babies. This is not to blame our parents, but we all have some bumps and bruises. Owning these tender spots, and separating them from our babies, breaks the chain. If our parents inadvertently hurt us, repairing the injury and not passing it on is just what they would want!"

We all have the power to change the scripts we have been given, to alter them so they accurately reflect our values and the timeless principles we decide to consciously embrace. The operative word here is *consciously;* it requires a deep desire and daily practice to change. We must examine our values with regard to our families, and to engage with our principles as passionately as we can. Only then will we have the requisite spiritual fortitude to communicate those values appropriately to our children. Covey says, "If you want to raise responsible, self-disciplined children, you have to keep that end clearly in mind as you interact with your children on a daily basis. You can't behave toward them in ways that undermine their self-discipline or self-esteem."

Children are experts at detecting hypocrisy. They know, even if it is at a subconscious level, when you are parroting sermons rather than communicating what you deeply feel and believe. They also know if you respect them. In over twenty years of working with infants and parents, it became very clear to me that even babies know if their parents respect them or not. Babies invariably become fussy and irritable when their caregivers are *doing* the right things but their minds are a million miles away. Nobody likes to be treated like an object.

Becoming aware of our deeply held principles and committing ourselves to living congruently with them is the means by which we realize our mission as parents. "Mission" may sound very big. But what is bigger than being a parent? What job or role is more important? What has a more direct and intimate affect on people, or creates a greater legacy for generations to come? When we think of parenting in terms of "mission," we begin to give this part of our lives the respect it deserves.

For good or ill (and probably a bit of both) you learned the most about being a parent from your own parents' example. Bringing both the positive and negative sides of these childhood experiences out into the open can help you clarify what you want and what you do not want. Sometimes we need to start with what we do not want, and this will show us the way to what we want. Being congruent with what we deeply want is the best insurance for happiness and success. *Being* what we admire in others engenders high self-esteem, perseverance through hard times, and joy for living — all important qualities to model for our children.

YOUR PARENTING MISSION STATEMENT

It's helpful to begin this book by writing a mission statement. Completing the following short version can help you write a paragraph, a sentence, or even a few words that will express the values you feel are most important to you as a parent. If you want to start with a more complete picture of the "end" you want to create, you can begin with the longer version that follows. If you prefer, you may skip this exercise, read the rest of the book, and return to this portion when you have finished or at any time while you are reading, to create a "parenting mission statement" that will be your compass to guide you through the beautiful, messy, calm, turbulent, and — always — worthwhile waters of parenthood.

The following exercises can help you clarify which aspects of your mission as a parent are most important to you. Set aside some time to complete them and commit yourself to total honesty. When you are finished, you will have a mission statement that can help you apply the twelve principles in the coming chapters. I have included, with permission, the responses of a friend who completed the exercise for me.

Short Version

Imagine that your children are grown and they have become famous. They are interviewed for television and asked, "How did your parents contribute to your success and happiness?" What do you want them to say?

> *Example:* I would want my children to say that their parents supported them in every way. I'd want them to say I taught them values of integrity and responsibility, that they were loved unconditionally, and that their parents' values and sacrifices made it possible for them to succeed. I would want them to smile when they think of me. I would want to see their love and respect for me shining in their eyes.

Now distill this into a paragraph, a sentence, or a few words that reflect, in present tense, from your point of view, what you want to be as a parent:

> *Example Parenting Mission Statement:* I support my children in every way to find their dreams and achieve them. I teach them integrity and responsibility by modeling these values in my own life. I love them unconditionally, and make sure they know that every day. I am willing to sacrifice, if neces-

Example:
responsibility
sacrifice
unconditional love
encouragement
quality time one-on-one

3. Now sit with your list for a while. Is anything missing? Think of other people you admire as parents. What do you admire most about them? If, as a child, you had been able to have anything you wanted from your parents, what would that be? Write down your answers to these questions. If you come up with tangibles such as more physical affection or a room of your own or a pet, think about what these things represent to you (love, respect, trust).

Example: I wish I'd had more one-on-one time with my mother. I wish she had helped me more, especially when I was a teenager, to learn how to be an adult. For example, I wish she had helped me learn how to balance a checkbook and take care of a car. I wish she had been more open about her own experiences growing up and that we could have had conversations about issues like sexuality and politics, rather than one-way lectures. I wish she had shown me more physical affection. I wish my mother had been able to request and elicit cooperation rather than demand obedience. The families I admire most talk a lot with each other, and they joke and tease a lot; there is laughter in the house and a feeling of warmth and welcome. My house growing up, because of our financial situation and other problems, was pretty tense. I wouldn't want that for my children.

4. Imagine that your children are grown, and they have become famous. They are interviewed for television and asked, "How did your parents contribute to your success and happiness?" What do you want them to say?

Example: I would want my children to say that their parents supported them in every way. I'd want them to say I taught them values of integrity, honesty, and responsibility, that they were loved unconditionally, and that their parents' values and sacrifices made it possible for them to succeed. I would want them to smile when they think of me. I would want to see their love and respect for me shining in their eyes.

5. Go back to your list of words or phrases from questions 1 and 2 that represent your values and the qualities you want to have as parents. Add the concepts you came up with in the last two questions. If a word or phrase from questions 3 and 4 is basically the same as one of the original words, underline it.

Example:
honesty
responsibility
respect
humility
sacrifice
cooperation
encouragement
unconditional love
quality time

Another example: Some people like to make an anagram from their list of positive attributes, such as SMILE:

Support
Mentor
Integrity modelled
Love unconditionally
Empower

6. Now write a paragraph in first-person present tense, incorporating the values you defined into a parenting mission statement:

Example Parenting Mission Statement: I love my children unconditionally and I demonstrate that love to them every day in
my words and actions. I tell them I love them every day,
and let them know I love them even when I am angry or
disappointed or disagree with them. I respect my children
and demonstrate that respect in my words and actions. I
allow them freedom of choice and respect their choices
even when they are different from what I would choose. I
am honest and open with my children, appropriately sharing with them my struggles and requesting their understanding and help when I need it. I continually seek out
information about healthy parenting skills and improve
myself as a parent as much as possible. I admit my errors
and make amends, and I allow my children to make mistakes and learn how to apologize and correct themselves. I
find peaceable ways to discipline my children, never resorting to physical or verbal violence. I listen carefully to my
children and treat their concerns with the same respect I
want for myself. I spend time with each child and encourage each child appropriately according to his or her needs.
I take care of myself and my own needs so that I have positive energy to give to my children. I try to demonstrate the
values I teach, knowing that my children learn primarily by
my example and that the combination of my words and
actions are what teaches them how to be a person of
integrity. I provide my children with deep roots in home
and family, and wings to fly away into new experiences,
knowing that love will always bring them home again.

The Value of a Mission Statement

A mission statement isn't just a collection of idealistic phrases.
It is a compass, a way to keep yourself on course as you handle all
the variables of daily life. When you read your mission statement,
it should make you smile and feel energized and inspired about the
future.

Some people develop lengthy mission statements such as the

one above; others need only a sentence or even a few words. Take time with this project, if it catches your imagination, and dig as deeply as you can into your soul to find your true purpose as a parent. You may want to revise and rewrite portions of your mission statement as you read this book.

If all this sounds overwhelming, don't worry about it. If you are reading these words at this moment, you're doing what you need to do. You can skip around in this book, and read and do whatever you feel like at the moment. You certainly don't have to go through it all and do every exercise before you gain something valuable.

I wish you joy on this incredible journey. It began with an act of love. With consciousness and some deep internal work, you can create a beautiful family whose love continues in forever-expanding circles, touching our communities and even healing the world.

Principle One
RELAX

The simple reason for relaxation is that it renews us, puri-
fies us, leaves us with a profound feeling of serenity....
In it, we are poised in our natural state.

— Deng Ming-Dao, *365 Tao Daily Meditations*

Relaxation, from the Tai Chi perspective, is the principle everything else is based on. For us in the West, relaxation is something we do on our day off, or when we get a massage or do yoga.
To us, relaxation implies being limp, flaccid, and empty. But to the
Taoists, relaxation implies fullness. As a practice, it can take years to
master and it is respected as a difficult discipline. But this is no problem — when you have children, years of mastering difficult disci-
plines come with the territory.

The word "yield" is often used to signify this principle. Again, it
has a very different meaning to the Taoists than it does in the West.
When we consider the word "yield" as more than just a traffic sign,
we picture surrendering to a stronger force — which in the West we
often consider to be failure. Yielding is done reluctantly, when there
are no other options. To Tai Chi practitioners, yielding is the finest
quality we can have. It means flexibility, clarity, faith, and surrender.
It gets the maximum positive result from the minimum effort, and
thus it is *efficient*, a much sought-after value in the West. Relaxation is

a state of openness, allowing space for listening and receptivity. The Taoists consider it a discipline because it takes a conscious intention to learn and practice it. We must decide we want to relax, and we must know if relaxed is truly what we wish to be.

Water Can Teach Us

Taoists say that water is the most yielding of all things, yet it can overwhelm that which is most hard — rock. The three aspects of water that are particularly useful to us as parents are those most closely identified with the Tao, or God.

First, *water nourishes without needing to be nourished.* Like water, which nourishes all things without discrimination and without needing anything in return, good parents give selflessly to their children. They provide for their children's physical welfare, intellectual growth, emotional security, and spiritual connection without expecting anything in return. They are willing to sacrifice, if necessary, so their children may grow and prosper. The "martyr" parent, who exacts payment in guilt for every sacrifice, is not part of this paradigm. We remember that every principle contains its polarity in seed form, and we can catch ourselves before fatigue or frustration goad us to shame our children for requiring so much of us.

Ideally, marriage prepares us for the bigger sacrifices required when children come along. We have the opportunity to practice selfless giving, to test and stretch ourselves, and to explore our programming. We may consider ourselves giving people, but sometimes when confronted by the stress of another's need we discover how limited our patience can be. We may find ourselves doing and saying things that precisely echo the voices of our parents' mistakes. But how do we then think and act to correct our course? It is exactly at those moments when we are most un-Godlike that we have the opportunity to choose to grow toward oneness rather than separation. So, the idea is not to suddenly (or ever) become the perfect parent; rather, it is to use parenting as our path — and discover, along the way, the excitement of a journey that gives us real opportunities to become what we wish to be.

Where do we get all this strength, if we are to endlessly give and provide? Again, water is our model. There is an ocean of consciousness from which all things are created. Some call it God or Goddess, some call it the Great Spirit; Tai Chi practitioners call it the Tao or the Way. Yielding like a cup of water yields to the ocean, we merge our consciousness into the great, eternal consciousness that creates and maintains all things, forever. Thus our strength is omnipotent, our well never runs dry. Wise parents take time for personal spiritual renewal so that the strength upon which we rest is that of the infinite source of our being.

Second, *water flows into places where there is seemingly no room.* Rigid things can't do this. Only that which is relaxed, yielding, and fluid can go into places of seemingly no space and be effective there. I have discovered this principle over and over again in my mission as a mother. To discover what my child needed, a deep, yielding receptivity was vital. The temptation is to become more and more rigid — and when you do, the less you understand. The frustration of not knowing how to fill a need that cannot be articulated can be overwhelming. Often we direct the rage that stems from that frustration toward the child, and that serves to distance us even further, making it impossible for the child to open up to us.

To get to this type of receptivity, a practice of conscious relaxation is a must. The single most effective thing most of us can learn is simply how to breathe deeply into our bellies and relax for a moment. To know how to belly breathe, to relax each muscle group, and to sink your mind into your heart are techniques you can use to change from a rigid to a fluid state. This allows you to be able to flow into the cracks and crevices of a child's hurts and anger, to soothe, to heal, to allow the child to find wholeness again, and, best of all, to allow the child to claim the finding of that wholeness for him or herself.

The third aspect of the Tao that we can learn about and use is *its immutable nature.* While all things animate and inanimate are "made" of Tao, it is impossible to truly separate it from itself. Therefore, there is an aspect of being that is unchangeable and is not separate — between you and your child, the dog or cat, or the rocks in your driveway. All is one. The ability to sink into this awareness on a conscious level is *empathy*. The occasions to use this awareness are innumerable, and the more you practice it, the more you feel the limitlessness of your own being. So rather than contracting into a hard, little "I"-ness that has no common ground with, say, a teenager with green hair and piercings (or whatever the passing show of seeming separation requires for costume at the time), we expand into an awareness of oneness that includes it all.

We learn to acknowledge the game of hide-and-seek the Tao is playing with itself. How different can we be? How many pieces can we break into and test this knowing that all is one? This is why holidays like Halloween can be such fun. We play God and Goddess, creating ever new and interesting creatures, dancing and singing and doing naughty things in these disguises. We pretend, and we help others pretend, that these disguises are real. But the knowing is there; it need not be spoken. Some Halloween enthusiasts are so good at it that they can fool their own mothers. But that does not alter the truth of who they really are. At the end of the day, the costumes fall away and here we are, the people we have been all along. When we can recognize that we are one, and bring that realization to awareness during times of conflict, things that seem important within a consciousness of separateness are no longer as critical. We find it easier not to "sweat the small stuff" and to recognize the small stuff when we see it.

When an individual dipper of water is placed into the ocean, it merges with the ocean as if separation never existed. Studying the qualities of water can give us important clues about how to relax and yield in the Taoist way.

The type of strength we need as parents is that of water, not rock, for the challenges we face are numerous, repetitive, and long-term. We need the kind of strength that flows over obstacles, rather than that of the sledge hammer. If our strength is rigid — authoritarian — there is no space for our children to develop their own strength. Rather than exercising their mental and emotional muscles, their will is broken and the result is failure. Children with no inner strength either become passive victims of others or they lash out at authority in a desperate attempt to reclaim their sense of self. Some people spend their lives alternating between the two, tortured, never feeling the sense of security that comes from a solid sense of one's power. The only way to give that security to our children is to be flexibly strong, like water. Children need to know that nothing they say or do will break us, make us snap. And the only way they discover this is to test us. When they know our strength, they relax into it, and they develop that kind of strength for themselves. Respect for us arises out of their confidence in our strength; eventually, they want to be like us.

THE OPPOSITE

Often, to deeply understand a concept like this, it is helpful to examine its opposite. In Tai Chi it is essential, because everything contains its opposite within it; we must understand its antithesis in order to truly understand anything.

Where there is pain there is tension, and that tension creates more pain. Therefore, tension is the opposite of relaxation. When we apply relaxation to pain, it diminishes. Underneath tension is its root — fear. Now we get to the key, the essence of the discipline of yielding: the release of fear.

Fears and worries assail us at every point along the path of parenting. If you are beginning on that path, let me tell you the truth: it never ends! Until the day you die, your children will be producing, in a never-ending stream, the triggers that create anxiety in you. Some of these fears and worries are justified. You can't predict your children's lives or destinies, and if you love them you will always be there for them. You will be a better parent, a healthier role model, and a happier person if you learn how to relax.

Fear hardens us as we try to hold on to the familiar. If we are fearful, we want to stop the flow of time and change. But the cessation of change is called *death*. Acting out of fear, our inner "juice" slowly dries up and, like a dead tree, we are easily broken.

Relaxation — yielding to the flow of change — is, then, essential for life. If we wish to continue to be full of life, we must learn to relax and yield, to flow. Like the young tree, we will be flexible and strong, ever growing, with abundant youthful energy. If we cannot relax, we cannot listen to and truly hear our children, and we miss their messages to us, misinterpret their needs and wishes, and lose touch with who they are.

Like yoga, Tai Chi begins with slow movement and breathing. The combination of breathing and flow creates strength and flexibility. Breathing slowly and deeply increases our intake of *prana* — the life energy the yogis say is all around us. *Prana* is essential to our vitality. It is why we instinctively take a deep breath when we smell rain or the fragrant forest; these natural wonders are laden with prana, and our bodies crave the vital energy produced by them.

CONTROLLED BELLY BREATHING

Slowing down your movements and breathing deeply are two easy ways to bring yourself into a relaxed and flexible way of being. You can teach yourself to go to these tools when you feel the tension of anger or fear hardening your heart and stiffening your body and mind.

If you do not practice meditation or deep relaxation on a daily basis, there is an even easier method that can be incorporated into your daily routine with little effort. When children come along, you can include them in the practice, either doing it in front of them or teaching them to do it with you. I found with my own meditation practice that my children became curious about what I was doing, and that curiosity led to many interesting and intimate conversations about God, nature, life, death, and miracles.

A simple — and effective — practice is called *controlled belly breathing*. For this method to come in handy when you really need it (that is, when your child's behavior has you one step away from saying and doing all the things you may regret), it helps to practice it every day, twice a day. It only takes three minutes, so it is easy to fit into your life.

"B" Is for "Be"

I've developed a kind of shorthand to remind me to do it. In my life, most of the time the plans that have not been thought out with my mission in mind do not happen. I've come to label these plans as *Plan A: My ego plan*. The plan that ultimately happens, the response that always works, is God's plan (or my higher self's plan, however you wish to put it). This is *Plan B*. I can always count on Plan B turning out so much better than Plan A that I've learned, and continue to try to learn, to bypass Plan A altogether. Controlled belly breathing is a way to get you out of Plan A and into Plan B; thus the "B" is my reminder. "B" is for belly, "B" is for breathe, and "B" is for be. This short little practice accomplishes all of those things so that Plan B can unfold immediately.

You don't need any special time or equipment to practice controlled belly breathing, though it is helpful to have a clock nearby to time yourself.

How to Do Controlled Belly Breathing

1. Sit in a chair and place your hands over your navel. Relax your body as much as possible.
2. Blow out as much of the air in your lungs as possible, and imagine your tension going with it.
3. Slowly breathe in through your nose, counting 1-and-2-and-3-and-4, feeling your belly rise as air goes to the very depth of your lungs, expanding your diaphragm.
4. Slowly breathe out through your nose, again counting 1-and-2-and-3-and-4. Make sure all the air is expelled without tension.
5. Repeat this sequence for three minutes. You will notice a slight natural pause (not holding your breath) at the upper and lower end of the breathing cycle. Let it be there. Keep your body as relaxed as possible, and your mind engaged in the counting process and in relaxing your muscles.

I suggest you use this technique very consistently, upon waking and right before sleeping, each day for a month. Then you can practice under duress: during a traffic jam, a long elevator ride, waiting in the dentist's office, or on the subway.

After you have mastered and assimilated the technique, begin using it when you feel your emotional temperature rising with your spouse or children. You can excuse yourself (I like to go into the bathroom) or you can do it right then and there. You will feel Plan A turning to Plan B; you'll calm down, center and focus your energies, and automatically use better parenting and partnering skills.

As the ancient Tai Chi master Liao said,

> The only condition for allowing your internal energy to develop, grow, and become strong is that you must relax yourself and yield to the universe. When you become soft and pliable, your internal energy will gradually begin to develop and accumulate. Eventually you will have the ability to become extremely hard and strong, when it is necessary to do so.

When faced with a child who is testing your resolve, relax and yield in the manner of water. Absorb the child's energy without moving. Sink your strength into the earth with the relaxing breath. Allow the child to bounce off your energy, discovering without harm the nature of your power.

Ron Sieh, a modern Tai Chi teacher, advises students,

> Let everything you have — mind and body, thoughts and reactions, plans and avoidance of plans — sink with gravity into your feet to beneath the earth. Relax your intention. Put everything underground where it can support you. Strewn anxiously through your body, it can only distract you.

This is called *sinking power* — and it's a good power to develop. It can help us master all the principles in this book.

PARENTING WITH PRINCIPLE ONE

Each set of parents is different in their lifestyle, their history, and their approach to the concepts covered in this book. It is not my intention to teach parenting in all its detail. Rather, I'd like to give you some ideas to get you thinking, some examples to show you how it *can* go, and some insights that may help bring you back to your own center when times are challenging. Principles are the never-changing polestars we can use to guide ourselves to smooth waters. Practices, on the other hand, change with time, place, and circumstance.

Keep in mind that I use practices as a way to reconnect with principles, not as an end in themselves. Your practices may differ; it is the deep seed, the core principle, that is the most important focus of this book and, I hope, the focus of your life as a parent.

Principle One in Pregnancy

Pregnancy is a great time to teach yourself controlled belly breathing and other relaxing techniques. At the same time, with or without massage cream (better with), you can rub your belly for a few minutes each day, loving yourself and the new being growing within. Massaging your belly not only helps prepare it for the stretching to come, but directly communicates to your baby your feelings and maybe even your thoughts.

Partners can participate together in this practice, too. After the baby is born, hopefully massage will be as much a part of your daily routine as changing diapers, so now is a good time to slow down and make that time. It is the beginning of your conscious choice to make spending loving, listening time with your child your day's most important priority.

The Prenatal Environment

Dr. Bruce Lipton, in an article on maternal emotions and the development of the prenatal infant, says,

> The information relayed by the mother to the fetus concerns the status of the environment. This status is conveyed in the mother's perceived attitudes about life. The mother's emotions, such as fear, anger, love, hope, among others, can biochemically alter the genetic expression of the offspring. . . . The mother's blood-borne emotional chemicals cross the placenta and affect the same target cells in the fetus as those in the parent.

An article in *Science* magazine in 1996 reveals that parents pass more on to their infants than their genes. Studies revealed that maternal emotions can profoundly enhance the baby's chances for thriving and even influence its ability to adapt to the environment. Recent evidence suggests that even though a child may be affected by specific genetic defects, such as Tourette's syndrome, the degree of severity of the gene's defect is modified by nongenetic factors, including the prenatal environment.

More and more, we are finding that babies are affected by their parents even before conception. For example, a father who smokes damages his sperm and passes a higher risk of childhood cancer to his offspring. Research consistently supports the idea that even prior to birth an infant is profoundly affected by its parents' activities and emotions. Being as relaxed, happy, well nourished, and stress free as possible gives your baby the best possible start in life.

Preparing for the Birth of Your Baby

Taking a childbirth education class together can help both you and your partner prepare for the baby's arrival. Practicing the relaxation and breathing techniques at home can slow you down enough to begin talking about the deeper issue of what each of you feel is important that this child receive. You may each want to do the parenting mission statement we discussed earlier and compare notes, combining your work into a new mission statement that encompasses both.

Long warm baths, massages, and periods of deep relaxation each day can help you sort out all the information coming your way and to feel what it is this baby needs and what your soul has chosen to learn by being a parent. Try to imagine different scenarios and how you might handle them. For example:

- What if your baby hardly ever sleeps through the night?
- Are you going to nurse? If so, how might you change your diet to help support a balanced state of mind and body?
- Are you going to have someone else minding the baby? If so, look closely at the character of that person. Is he or she

the kind of person who easily adapts to changes of mood, who easily incorporates babies into the world, who is unruffled by noise and chaos? Can that person relate to the deeper issues we are discussing in this book?

- What if your baby needs to be held much of the time? Are you and/or your partner willing to cooperate in using a baby pack?
- Who will massage the baby, and when? Read books on the subject and discuss them with each other — not just logistics, but the concepts they encompass with regard to your family's future habits of interaction.
- What if the baby has health problems that change your plans? How can you still hold to the principle of relaxation?
- What if you find yourself suffering with postpartum depression? Do you have a psychiatrist, therapist, or alternative healer who could help you with this?

Very few parents take the time to reflect on these things — and yet discussing things like this can be tremendously helpful in the months and years ahead.

The Qualities of Water

Using the Taoist meditation on the qualities of water helped me throughout my parenting years, but especially during my pregnancies and the first year of life. I was lucky to be a homemaker and to have the opportunity to be my children's main caregiver and teacher. During my pregnancies I spent a lot of time in warm water, relaxing and floating, getting in touch with my infant on a deep inner level and relaxing my body through the weightlessness. I thought about the water's fluidity and flexibility, and how when a bit dripped from my finger, not only did it join the whole, but it made ripples that spread outward to the limits of the water. I knew, with a deep inner certainty, that I had the power to be that "drop" in my children's lives and thereby affect the world.

Because of some birth defects of my own, I had to give birth by cesarean section and, back then, my choices were few. But I was able to remain awake and alert during their births and to hold and nurse them right away. Getting home as soon as possible was important to me, to get my babies into the kind of atmosphere I wanted for them right away. I encourage you to explore all your birthing options and choose those that feel right, comfortable, and good for you. Also consider that fate has a way of intervening, and that if things don't go exactly as you wish, you still have plenty of time, choices, and opportunities to follow through on your principles.

Principle One with Babies

Remembering the principle of relaxation, design your baby's room so that it is as low maintenance as possible. Imagine the toddler's curiosity, not the cute little bundle with matching *everything*. Large plastic storage bins allow toddlers to put their toys away without special skills of manual dexterity. A warm place for massage gives the child a place both you and she associate with relaxation and to which she can go for massages or naps as she grows older. Easy-to-clean surfaces help save you time that you can then give to your baby. Forget knickknacks and clutter; help your baby connect with the natural world rather than the commercial world with its endless array of "things" that are forced upon the child by media and culture.

I've always said, as the Taoists believe, that the best mobile is leaves dancing on the branch of a tree. The best toys are large wooden spoons, plastic bowls from the kitchen, water, a cardboard box, or puppets made from socks. My kids would go for these over the colorful and noisy commercial toys every time, even though when they saw the commercial toys on television or in the toy store, they wanted them with the kind of greed stimulated by modern advertising. They had some of each, with an emphasis on the simpler things. They didn't grow up mentally deficient in the least. In fact, one is a writer with two college degrees, and the other is an artist, and both have the creativity of thought and heart that can come from such an upbringing.

The first few months with a new baby in the house can be magical and also challenging. Consider all the factors at play: a new lifestyle, with perhaps one parent at home with the baby and the other working hard to keep the finances in balance; a new mother's hormones, which rearrange themselves daily; and sleep deprivation, which affects the parents' emotions, patience, and ability to concentrate — particularly the mother if she is breast-feeding and getting up at night to do so. Each stage the baby goes through brings up a whole set of needs in terms of paraphernalia, from carseats to strollers.

If it is possible, I suggest both partners go over their parenting mission statement together once a week, and talk about the issues that have come up during the previous week, resolving areas of stress before they become long-held resentments. Both parents must realize they are being called upon to stretch the boundaries of what they previously considered to be their limits. Partners who work outside the home may no longer be able to come home and just relax and have a quiet meal. Partners who stay home with the baby may suffer loneliness for other adults, may miss recognition in their jobs, and self-esteem may suffer if they don't get enough recognition and support for the difficult job they've volunteered to do without a paycheck.

Time Out for the Full-Time Parent

I remember when my husband walked in the door at five o'clock or so, I'd practically throw the baby at him, and run toward a hot bath, yelling, "Your turn! I need a break! Leave me alone!" Well, he needed a break too, but was willing and eager to do his part. Finally we worked out a system. He would arrive home from work, sit down for fifteen minutes with the paper or whatever, as I kept myself and my temper under wraps. Then I would hand the baby to him, take my hot bath or a walk to the park, breathe and meditate. When I returned he would have changed the baby, and if I hadn't had a chance to begin dinner, he would have strapped on the front pack and started the meal (our first baby needed tons of in-arms time). Then we'd all sit down to eat together, literally, as my baby was a demanding breast feeder who wanted to nurse whenever he smelled food. There were times I'd use my hot-bath time to cry or write my stress away; other times I'd take a book with me for inspiration or entertainment during the first and only time all day I could call my own.

My husband took charge of bedtime while I used the time to clean up the house, do dishes, and so on. Our roles fell into place. I had to do most of the nighttime getting up, since we were nursing, but having a "family bed" helped me get much needed rest in the meantime. At night when the baby was inconsolable from colic, often my husband would get up and do a massage routine to relieve the baby's colic and then lull him to sleep in the front pack, walking the living room floor. I'd wake in the morning to see them both asleep on our giant beanbag chair, the baby snuggled into the pack on my husband's chest. The gratitude I felt at those moments is beyond words.

Part of our mission was to bring our children up in a relaxed, easy-going household in which they were loved, valued, respected, and "spoiled" in the best sense of the word. That is, they would be given all the love and understanding we could possibly muster, and we would release, at least temporarily, the need for the kind of control that leads to tension (such as needing the house to be perfect). One father, whose wife had died, said he thought he had been very involved with his children before. But he said, "I didn't know how removed I was until I had to do all the thousands and thousands of things it takes to raise a child."

When Baby Keeps Crying

When the baby keeps crying and you feel you can't handle it any more, if possible ask someone else to hold the baby while you do your relaxation exercises. Even five minutes of controlled belly breathing can bring you back to center and get your mental faculties working again. Think of an affirmative thought, such as, "I release fear and tension and go with love to comfort my baby. Crying is just crying."

Like all of us, babies have many different reasons to cry. Much of the time, it is the only means of communication they have available to them and, because they can't talk about it they cry. Unfortunately, we have lost much of our capacity to intuit their thoughts and feelings. Most people are able to recognize a sharp cry of pain, but our interpretation of other cries and fusses are filtered through the veil of our own insecurities and projections. It may be easier to adopt a mechanistic philosophy, whereby we always respond in the same way — either to ignore or to hush. But babies are not interested in philosophy and are unable to attend to their parent's or anyone else's comfort. They need the response of clear thinking, caring, centered adults to help them find a way through this world of unknowns.

A trip to the store or a friend's house can bring on a crying spell after the baby is home and safe. Allowing some venting and responding with compassion and not alarm is the best and easiest way to let your child release the stress these new encounters can induce. Gradually, the baby gets the message: it's okay to cry, it's no big deal. I am still loved, and I feel better now. What is required of parents is a conscious effort to raise their own stimulation threshold, to tolerate more noise, and to take it easy.

If infants can be helped to raise their own stimulation threshold and to use relaxation techniques as a way to slowly vent stress instead of letting it build to explosion, they can carry these ideas with them into childhood. Massage time, in the beginning, may not be all smiles and sleepiness; many babies fuss through their massage, venting the stress that has built up in their bodies. After a massage, however, their sleep will be deeper. Gradually fussing will diminish as the stimulation threshold increases and the baby's body learns how to release stress gradually throughout the day rather than having it build up.

What Crying Means to You

To begin to develop a more centered awareness, observe yourself when your baby (or someone else's) cries. When you understand your reactions, you will be able to begin to understand the baby. Notice what a crying baby stimulates in you. Breathe deeply, relax your body, do your exercise. If it is someone else's baby, imagine that it is you, and picture yourself, as an adult, soothing (not hushing) yourself as an infant. It is not necessary to overanalyze yourself or your baby. Just take some time to think about how you respond to your baby's cues. Eventually you will find the intuitive bond growing between you and your infant, and your confidence in understanding his needs increasing day by day.

Daily massage can be a tremendous aid in this process, because it helps you to literally keep in touch with your baby's body language and nonverbal signals. It also helps to slow you down, to relax you. It allows your baby to learn how to relax himself, and teaches him that relaxation is an important part of life. I can't emphasize enough how helpful the first six months of massage can be in developing your lifelong relationship of relaxation, communication, and openness with your child. Nursing is another time when controlled belly breathing can slow you down and relax both you and baby.

Another exercise that is helpful in learning how to relax as a parent is to listen to your baby. When I begin to talk about infant conversations in my infant massage seminars, I like to start with an analogy, usually acted out by the participants.

Imagine you have just been through a traumatic experience, something that disturbed you deeply. You feel yourself on the verge of tears and unable to relax or concentrate, and you go to your spouse or a friend for help. You begin to talk about what happened to you and how you're feeling about it.

After a moment of sympathy your friend begins to shush you, saying, "There, there, never mind. Please don't cry. I can't stand it when you cry. Come on, smile for me now. Let me get you something to eat. Maybe you should go to a doctor." You will probably dry your tears and internalize your pain in order to preserve this relationship because your friend's responses have told you it is not safe to be yourself in her presence.

Now imagine yourself in the same situation, but with a different response from your friend. You begin to talk about what happened to you and how you're feeling about it. Your friend looks you in the eye. She leans forward and holds your hand. She says, "Tell me all about it. I can see you're really hurting, and I want you to know that I love you and I want to help you through this."

She puts her arms around you and you relax into deep sobs in the safety of her presence. You ramble on, sometimes incoherently, and she's there, saying, "Tell me more. And then what happened? That must have been so painful." You feel her genuine support, and that trust enables you to really unload and, finally, to come back to your center again. Your relationship with her is stronger; she feels good for having been there for you, and you are better able to go on toward healthy functioning. Friends like that don't judge you for these moments of "weakness," they have confidence in you, they respect you, and they allow you to be human.

Babies Need to Be Heard

Infants need to be heard as much as anyone. I have seen many remarkable instances in which an infant's responsiveness and general disposition has completely changed after being truly heard.

Doctors Eileen and Tom Paris contend that part of creating a healthy relationship with our children is owning our feelings and expressing them as our own. They say, "For example, telling a startled newborn, with kindness, 'I see you got startled when Mommy and Daddy yelled and had a fight. Grownups get angry sometimes, especially when we are tired. You're okay, we love you,' mitigates the effect of the fighting. Even though it is true that adult fighting stresses children (even in utero), never feeling angry is an unreasonable expectation for either ourselves or our children."

We begin, as soon as our baby is born (and even before) to show him the respect he deserves as an individual human being with his own feelings, memories, and experiences. We can help and teach our babies to "talk out" their stress and thus enjoy a more relaxed and productive life.

I was demonstrating some massage strokes on a baby in one of my seminars. The baby had been premature and had undergone the additional trauma of an injury to the skin of her chest that caused some scarring. Her mother said that she enjoyed being massaged, except she could not tolerate having her chest touched.

The baby responded well and accepted the massage for her legs, feet, and stomach. But when I reached the chest area, she began to cry. Rather than stopping and shushing her, I continued to gently mold my hands to her chest in what one of my instructors calls "a resting hand." I started to actively listen to what she might be saying through her tears. "Yes, you've really been through a lot of pain," I said. "Tell me all about it, I'm listening." She cried hard, and after a moment her mouth began taking on a different quality. She moved her mouth as if talking, though she was crying. She looked at me intensely, as if she was trying to tell me something very important.

"You were very brave, and I know your mommy is very proud of you," I said. "And when you're ready to let go of that pain, she's here to help you. We all love you very much." I continued to gently hold her chest as she cried, and let her know I was listening to her. After several minutes, her cries decreased and her mother picked her up to comfort her.

The next day her mother brought her again for a demonstration. This time, when I began massaging her chest she opened out her arms and smiled at me. Her mother turned to me with tears in her eyes, saying this was the first time the baby had ever been able to accept someone touching her chest area. Later, the baby's mother reported that she loved being touched and fully accepted a complete massage.

Actively and compassionately listening to an infant isn't much different than listening to a child or an adult. It requires empathy, genuine love, and respect for the infant's experience. I believe that the reason it is so difficult for us to listen to our babies is that our own infancies may have been full of frustration and unheard feelings. When we hear our babies cry, rather than truly listening to what they say, we superimpose our own inner infant. Our overwhelming impulse is to quiet *that* baby.

How to Listen to a Baby

I go through a three-step process when a baby I'm with begins to talk, to fuss, or to cry. First, I take a long, slow, deep breath and relax my whole body — controlled belly breathing. This directly counteracts the tendency to hold the breath and tighten up.

Second, I set aside my own inner infant for a moment, recognizing that in order to truly hear this baby, I must clear myself.

Third, I connect with the baby, looking her in the eye if possible. If the baby avoids eye contact, I place my hands gently but firmly on her body and connect through my hands. I let my energy go to the baby, and tell her with my voice, my eyes, and my hands that I would like to hear what she has to say.

Then I stay with the baby, keeping myself in a very relaxed and receptive state. I listen and respond, and observe the baby's body language. I watch her mouth and what she says with her eyes. I have noticed over and over again that, when the baby is intently listened to in this way, her crying takes on a different quality. The baby's mouth will begin to move as if she is talking, moving expressively. The baby's eye contact may become very focused, as if she intensely wants to communicate. When I am sure the baby feels heard and has said most of what she has to say, either I or her caregiver offer her the comfort of rocking, walking, or patting if the baby needs it to help her get sensorially organized again. Invariably, a baby who feels heard will sleep more deeply afterward and will further extend herself in trust the next time I see her.

When we truly listen to our infants we fulfill all of their psychological needs. The underlying message is, "You are worthy of respect. You are valuable just the way you are." The baby is biologically driven to agree, and she grows in confidence, feeling her place in the world. Her sensory receptors take this message in and her whole body relaxes.

The chalice of this infant's heart is filled to overflowing, and as she grows she will seek opportunities to share her love with others. And how will she do this? By following the model she has been given. She will be there for others in the way her caregivers have been there for her.

Principle One with Young Children

When your baby begins to crawl around by himself, you can be assured of a devoted follower. Bathroom doors are no longer closed, and every task that has to be done requires a creativity you may never have thought you had. Two of the most important characteristics you can develop to help you stay relaxed are keeping a sense of humor and understanding the impermanent nature of childhood stages.

When your child gets on his feet, the roles reverse. You become your child's devoted follower, for heaven knows what he is going to get into next! A "childproof" house is essential, so that you can be assured there is not much in harm's way. Great playthings, as I mentioned before, include household items without potential for harm. At this later, toddler stage, you can add other creative options. Young ones love to emulate you, so miniature versions of your household cooking and cleaning objects can be helpful; while you're making dinner, the little one can be at your feet stirring his own pot. You can get huge buttons and sew them on pieces of felt, cutting buttonholes in another piece, and let your child play with buttoning things. Plastic bowls that fit inside one another make for hours of fun, as do the same kind of containers with easy-fit lids, which the child can practice with, putting things in and taking things out. Big boxes from moving companies with holes cut out for windows make great disposable playhouses. Paper towel tubes can make marvelous toys, as can large paper bags and other items that are free, disposable, and don't present a hazard to your little one.

Of course, at this age constant supervision is a must. Read up on all the potential hazards around the house and make sure that the environment and anything you give your child to play with is safe, and that your toddler is supervised at all times. Observing your child interact at this stage is fascinating and can teach you a lot about being present. See how totally in the moment he is, how complete his concentration can be when he is involved in an interesting task. At this point, he will often wander back to home base (you) to touch in, making sure that you are still there, that continuity and safety are maintained as he begins to widen his interest in exploring his environment.

These are the months and years of practicing what in the great spiritual tradition of India is called *madhuvidya,* or "sweet knowledge."

This means simply the realization that all is one; no one activity, person, or time is more important than another. This may be the only period in your life, for a very long time, when you have the chance to learn about this, for as your children grow, all of you get busy with worldly life and with others.

When you realize that in some sense you represent the Tao to your child, you can begin to deepen your own relationship to your spiritual base. Thus, your observation of the relationship between yourself and your child can teach you a lot about Oneness. What kind of God do you believe in? How do you want God to relate to you? Is God all-loving, all-forgiving? Does God care for you unconditionally? Do you want to be lifted up when you fall? Do you want your prayers answered? Do you want help to find and empower yourself, your destiny, and your dreams? Do you want your Higher Power to listen to you patiently and comfort you, not leave you alone to tough it out? That is what a parent needs to be for his or her child.

As you practice being that way, you begin to realize you have a greater — some say higher or deeper — power in your life that cares for you in the same way. So, to practice being the Tao for your child every day brings you closer to God, and also helps your child stay connected to the spiritual source he has just come from.

Help Yourself with Relaxation

The precious toddler years are a time for this level of spiritual learning for the parents. Often your toddler needs you to simply witness him play; you may sometimes feel like you are doing nothing, wasting your time, and impatience can set in and grow. In many other countries, this is when grandparents come in to provide the patient, observing, teaching witness the child needs. In western countries parents are required to be both this slowed down, tranquil, in-the-present witnessing "master" and the busy manager of the family; it's a daunting job. But for the sake of your child and your own spiritual growth, take time every day to be in the present with your little one. It is more important than the seemingly urgent things that call you away. Believe me, when you are old, these seemingly empty moments are what you will remember as real. Remember, as the Taoist masters do, that relaxation is fullness, not emptiness. As they say, what is real remains, the rest falls away.

As children grow, and especially if more children come, life gets more hectic and relaxation takes on a different quality and meaning for parents. In my circle of friends, I noticed that the most relaxed parents were the ones who had four or five kids! By then, they had surrendered. While their households were messy and noisy, and one or the other parent was always in the car, driving kids to various practices and functions, there was a kind of flow to the chaos. Perhaps these parents, who also happened to have practiced meditation for years, had found the "zone," where one thing just flowed into another, where all was included, and they realized it was useless to sweat the small stuff. I studied these parents to learn that art, knowing my family was to grow no larger than the two children I had.

Somehow the parents always found time for their own relationship, and each of them had outside interests they continued to cultivate through it all. The only way they were able to do this was to have a strong sense of mission, to understand the importance of balance and role modeling, and to consciously, each week or month, make decisions as to what they would and would not do, what they were willing to forego in the short term for their long-range mission: a happy family.

I also knew busy, stressed-out parents who never took time for themselves and each other, and who had more and more children just so they could put off the inevitable empty nest. Creating a happy family takes parents committed to a certain kind of mission and lifestyle, and often, while we start with the best intentions, at some point we lose focus, drift apart, allow betrayals to fester into permanent rifts, and divorces to happen. Some people are better partners than they are parents, and vice versa. Some can do both smoothly. The Tao teaches us to accept it all, and try to attain a level of relaxation through all the changes life brings our way.

If you are on a path of spiritual attainment, it is bound to bring you changes you are not at all comfortable with, changes that naturally tighten your defenses. The practice then is not to ward off change (which is impossible) but to notice when change is causing you to tighten. At those times, consciously allow your body and mind to relax and slow down enough to make better decisions. Let your children know this is what you are doing, and you can help teach them to relax as well.

Help Prepare and Heal with Relaxation

When my children were school-aged there were many opportunities to help them learn how to relax their bodies and minds. On one occasion, my eight-year-old son was to have surgery within a week, and though I knew it was important for him to talk about his feelings, I hadn't yet been able to get him to open up. The evening after we had met the nurses at the hospital and taken a tour of the children's ward, he was a little tense, so I offered a rubdown at bedtime. I used a nice oil-based lotion and gave him the "sports special," gently massaging his calves, knees, and feet. Within five minutes he relaxed and began to talk and talk and talk! He had several questions about the hospital and his surgery and was finally able to get the reassurance he needed but didn't know how to ask for — that I would be there with him, that he wouldn't wake up during the operation, that he would be able to talk after his tonsillectomy.

The operation went smoothly, and I remembered to use the soothing power of touch relaxation with him throughout the entire experience. A foot or hand massage now and then helped us *both* relax and let go of scary feelings. Prayer to our "guardian angels" always provided some spiritual connection for us, so we added that, too. As Polly Berrends says, "You need to understand what the fears are, and your child needs to know that her fears are understandable — not something the matter with her. Then you can pray together, opening your minds to a source of light and reassurance."

I was presented with another opportunity to bring the healing effect of slowing down into practice when my son was hit in the head by a swing at school. The cut on his head was deep and long enough to require stitches, so we had to meet his pediatrician in the emergency room. I had someone else drive, and sat in the back seat with my son, holding a cloth tightly over the cut. With my most soothing voice I helped him to stop crying, slow down, and relax. The cut bled badly, soaking the cloth as I held it. I asked him to imagine that a beautiful purple light was moving around the cut, healing it effortlessly and taking the pain away. He closed his eyes and began repeating "purple light, purple light," as I continued talking him through the relaxing visualization. When the two doctors cleaned his head and prepared it for stitches, they looked at each other, then at me.

"Uh, well, your son has really good healing powers," one of them said. "This cut has completely closed. It should need stitches but it really doesn't. Are you sure this happened today?"

In Taoism, it is very important to keep an awareness of emptiness. That is, what is *not* there is as important as what *is* there. The *t'ui sho circle* is a calligraphic meditation on this subject, in which the student makes a circle with a calligraphy pen and meditates upon it. Without the emptiness of what the circle contains, there is no circle. So it is important to pay attention to what is *not* happening as well as what is. A child's silence does not necessarily mean he has nothing on his mind. Make a physical connection through a massage or relaxation technique at bedtime to facilitate talks with an older child. Even now, in their twenties, it is easier for my children to express their feelings if I touch them. If your child, even a grown one, needs to cry or express fear, let him, assure him that what he feels is natural, that he is always guided and protected, and that it is okay to cry sometimes, to let out our tension, frustration, fear, or grief.

Help Calm Your Child with Relaxation

When my daughter turned eight years old, it was her turn for a relaxation lesson that was of great benefit to me, too. She was to have eight teeth removed at once in preparation for braces later on — a scary proposition for both of us. At first I tried the normal route, having discussed the procedure the night before and prepared her well for it. I sat in the waiting room after getting her settled. When I heard her begin to scream and cry in pain and fear, I, in full lioness mode, went charging back into the operating area, fully tense and ready to yank her out of the dentist's hapless hands. Then I stopped. As he and his nurses blathered on about how normal this was and how I should just go away for a while and everything was under control, I stood, letting my energy sink into the earth where it could hold me. I took two or three deep belly breaths.

I explained to the dentist that I had massaged my children all their lives, and I could probably help my daughter calm down and get through the procedure relatively painlessly if he would allow me to stay with her and talk/touch her through it. Reluctantly he agreed, seeing that most likely the alternative was that I would get her out of there. I sat near the dentist and talked to my daughter about relaxing her body, "just like we did last night." She nodded in comprehension, and we both took a deep breath together. I quickly took her through a relaxation sequence, gently touching each area to be relaxed, breathing away the tension, from head to foot. Then the dentist began his work. I asked her in my soft "mommy voice" to keep her eyes closed and listen to me. I talked her through relaxing each part of her body.

I asked her to create a picture in her mind of her cat, Blackie. I helped her imagine Blackie in every detail, including how soft she was and how much she loved my daughter. Then I said, "Each time you feel scared or it hurts, imagine Blackie is rubbing against your leg, and when she does, your whole body relaxes. Can you do that?" She replied, "Mmm-hmmm." I hummed a favorite tune, kept my breath deep and slow, my body relaxed, my feet planted, and imagined her fear and pain draining through my feet into the earth as I held her hand in mine. When I felt a tightening, I would whisper, "Here comes Blackie!" and gently rub her hand. I felt her body relax as her mind went to the soothing imagery of her beloved pet coming to comfort her. The surgery went faster than expected, and she healed faster than expected, as well.

The dentist asked me to come to his office and give a class for his young patients' parents on how to do what I did, as it made his job easier and everyone felt so much better in the end. These days, "Here comes Blackie!" is still a code between my daughter and me that makes both of us smile and relax. I wouldn't be surprised if, when my daughter has her own babies, she uses Blackie's healing energy to focus on during labor. You can use times like this to actively practice relaxation and teach your children how to do it for themselves and provide lifelong benefits for the entire family.

Principle One with Teens

When children reach adolescence, it is essential to practice Principle One. It should be the first thing you do before responding to anything your teen does or says. Belly breathe, use the exercise below, and follow up with other principles that are appropriate to the situation. If you allow yourself to tighten and react, you will accomplish nothing but more and more distance between the two of you. Some people say this is natural. It is not. We accomplish much more from a smooth state of relaxation than from the jagged edges of stress.

Exercise for Principle One

1. Sit comfortably, close your eyes, and relax each part of your body.
2. Take a deep belly breath. As you inhale repeat, "re . . . " and as you exhale repeat, ". . . lax."

Principle Two
SLOW DOWN

---

*Muddy water will become clear if allowed to stand
undisturbed, and so too will the mind become clear
if it is allowed to be still.*

— Deng Ming-Dao, *365 Tao Daily Meditations*

"Slow down" is more similar in meaning in the East and in the West than "relax" and "yield," but Tai Chi deepens its significance. In the Taoist way of thinking, slowing down brings us the ability to perceive the more subtle, or unseen, aspects of a situation. It also brings awareness to those things we may forget or ignore when rushing to get something done, settled, over with, or achieved.

Slowing down helps us immensely to remember and practice Principle One because it is difficult, if not impossible, to relax in a hurry. When you have mastered the art of living in a relaxed way, you know how to move quickly in a way that does not tighten and harden your energy. That type of mastery takes years of conscious, everyday practice, yet it is possible for parents to achieve at least enough of this quality of slowing down in the midst of hurry to reap its benefits.

Surrender Your Limitations

In Tai Chi, slowing down helps to create an awareness of all that is going on in the moment. One is able to step into a place that is purely present time, in which the past and future do not exist. A passage I interpreted from Lao Tzu's *Tao te Ching* in my book, *The Tao of Motherhood,* captures the moment I understood this principle in my life as a parent:

> *Everything that endures can only do so because Eternal Consciousness gives it sentience.*
>
> *A mother who gives herself completely to her infant meets herself in the dark and finds fulfillment.*
>
> *In the hours between midnight and dawn, she crosses the threshold of self-concern and discovers a Self that has no limits. A wise mother meets this Presence with humility and steps through time into selflessness.*
>
> *Infants know when their mothers have done this, and they become peaceful.*
>
> *Who, then, is the doer? Is it the infant who brings its mother through the veil of self-concern into limitlessness? Is it the mother, who chooses to hold sacred her infant's needs and surrender herself? Or is it the One, which weaves them both through a spiraling path toward wholeness?*

You can sit and meditate while
your baby cries himself to sleep.
Or you can go to him and share
his tears, and find your Self.

The ability to do this — not all the time, but at appropriate times — increases the energy you have to give to your children. Why? Because the present is, literally, the heart of God or Tao. We find a second wind when we slow down enough to really be present, even for a few moments.

Tai Chi teacher Douglas Lee talks about *kinesthetic perception* in relation to the benefits of slowing down. Especially during the period of time from the beginning of pregnancy until your child is fully able to communicate with words, this ability to perceive on a subtle level is valuable to every parent. It enables you to tune in to the body language of your baby and respond accordingly. It also allows you to learn how to listen to your own body and your own intuition or inner sense of what is best for you and for your child. You pick up the signs of stress before they have turned into full scale alarms, and you have the opportunity to de-escalate, to take care of your needs appropriately, at the appropriate time.

Many health professionals these days talk about "cues" — sensory signals babies give that mean they are experiencing one thing or another. It is very good that the medical profession finally acknowledges the need to respond to babies as more than just unfeeling objects. (When I had my first baby, scientists were still saying babies didn't feel pain!) As a parent, you are the one best equipped to learn your child's cues or body language, not only because you've carried the baby around for over nine months and are intimately, cellularly connected, but because you live with your baby twenty-four hours a day and can translate all those signals much better than a stranger. (We'll talk more about this in Principle Five.) To access this knowledge you need to slow down, observe, and receive what your baby wants to communicate.

In a society like ours (and increasingly in societies around the world) slowing down is perceived as being tantamount to growing old, being depressed, dying, or inviting failure. We are afraid of falling behind; we have lost respect for the slow wisdom of our elders and the natural ebb and flow of the life force. So we literally wear ourselves out, and in the meantime we miss so many of the most valuable treasures of our lives.

Remember the American cartoon character Roadrunner? We admire the roadrunner figure; he is always faster, way ahead of the crafty coyote. But if you think about it, that style of life, while bringing certain kinds of success, eliminates any possibility of *being*. As a parent, this style is disastrous, because the things we miss in our frantic race to beat the odds, or the next person, or to reach a goal, are the things of which life is made. We rush toward hardness and death having never enjoyed the very thing we are rushing to secure — the soft, juicy stuff — our children, our families, our lives.

Perseverance Furthers

Like the fable of the tortoise and the hare, we ultimately find that, as the Taoists say, "perseverance furthers." Rather than bringing into being all the things we fear, when we slow down we're given the tortoise's endurance to outlast the speeding rabbit, the endurance to face our fears courageously and master our challenges.

While a rushing stream may push obstacles out of its way, a lazy river will flow over, around, and through all things in its path. There is harmony and serenity outwardly, and great power underneath, where the current is very strong. All rushing streams end up in lazy rivers that follow their nature to merge with the great ocean. Similarly, when we slow down, we find the great internal strength available to us, and we begin to both communicate with and follow that deep tug of the "ocean" — the Oneness of all things, the Tao, the natural order of things. Outwardly, we appear calm, relaxed, and we seem to be doing little. Ambitious strivers rush past us with a look of disdain.

Perseverance is definitely a quality of Principle Two. In *365 Tao Daily Meditations*, Deng Ming-Dao says,

When it seems as if nothing encouraging is happening to us, it is important to remember such perseverance. Work may be drudgery, maintaining a home may be routine, and we may find our goals quite distant. But we must persevere and prepare nonetheless. That will bring a steady pace toward our goals, and buoy our faith in rough and threatening times.

In the anthology, *Vitality, Energy, Spirit: A Taoist Sourcebook*, Taoist master Huai-Nan-Tzu said, "How could the vital spirit be forever rushing around without becoming exhausted?... When the vitality, spirit, will, and energy are calm, they fill you day by day and make you strong."

THE OPPOSITE

When you forget to slow down, you react to whatever comes your way according to how you feel at the moment. You rush through your days, trying to be the thousand-armed Goddess or the unstoppable Hercules. You yell at your children while you struggle with your pantyhose or shave, because you are late for work or school, the phone is ringing, and you need to remind your spouse to pick up the dry cleaning; you throw food toward the dog's bowl, clothes in the washer, and then forget your keys — and that's only the start of your day.

You are always doing several things at once, with a nagging feeling that your soul, your spiritual being, is waiting on "hold," and a festering fear that it may finally give up and hang up on you. Any spare moments are spent worrying about the future (that doesn't exist) or fuming about the past (that no longer exists) or making lists of how to make tomorrow even more stress packed than today, so that you can finally get it all done and relax. But you are operating under the fallacy that it will all get done, and deep down inside, you know it.

In your heart, you may be terrified of relaxing. What if all those things from the past and future come up for review, tighten you up, and destroy your relaxation and connection to Spirit? So, to convince yourself you are relaxing, you schedule a grueling weekend of sports, yard work, projects, or entertaining that completely wear you out, just in time to start all over again Monday.

This may be an exaggeration for some people, but for many, unfortunately, it is not. Even if it is only partly true for you, the concept of what is *not* Principle Two is within your reach, within your own experience. Something I heard once has always stayed with me: If you are *trying* to do or be something, you are not actually doing or being it. So forget trying. Slow down. Literally. It is not a metaphor.

See what happens if, just for one week, one day, or one hour, you slow down as if your personal movie — including your thoughts, emotions, and speech — has gone into slow motion. This slowing down has nothing to do with depression, or low energy. Just slow the pace while keeping your energy positive and your head up. Allow people to notice how slow you are, and even to get impatient with you. See what happens.

Keep a journal at night, documenting the times when you slow down. At first, they may bring pain, inconvenience, and confusion. But toward the end, you will realize more about how you can incorporate this principle into your life. If you can find time to just sit alone, without fretting, and simply be who you are and face the fear that aloneness and quiet may bring, you have gotten it.

Principle Two is *not* rushing through the grocery checkout lane without noticing the clerk who is working hard to provide you with food and who may not be having such a great day. It is *not* "road rage" — the internal emotional combustion of being behind a slow-moving vehicle and wishing harm to the driver. It is *not* diapering your baby without making eye contact. As someone once said, *"Accept the limitations of the day."*

The Consequences of Rushing

Another way to increase your understanding of Principle Two is to look at your life for a week — say, the past week, if you weren't rushing so fast you don't remember it — and list all the elements of it that are *not* Principle Two. Then list the potential consequences of those things. For example, the potential consequence of road rage is an accident, which could cost you even more time, energy, and resources, and possibly physical, mental, and emotional pain. The potential consequence of not making eye contact with your baby is that your child will grow up unable to connect with others, and may distrust you, having never felt the love in your eyes, the windows of your soul, during the most intimate moments of your child's infancy, at the time when all imprinting occurs. Again, the loss of this connection costs you both more time, energy, money, and physical, mental, and emotional pain down the road.

Observe an expert doing Tai Chi. Notice the slowness and deliberation of the movements, and the awareness that encompasses every movement. How can this type of awareness be brought to your everyday life?

SLOWING THE SPEED OF YOUR LIFE

Now that my children are grown, I occasionally indulge in my dubious but relatively harmless pastime of watching talk shows — most of the time listening, watching out of the corner of my eye as I work on a new art quilt. I'm not talking about the shows that gossip about celebrities, or where the guests throw chairs at each other, but the middle-of-the-road ones that peek into the lives of somewhat interesting, sometimes slightly deviant people and families. What interests me more than the guests are the audience members — their reactions to and opinions about the information they get. I think these shows can give us a good look at how quickly we size up situations or people or relationships, judge them, stamp them good or bad, and react based on the prevailing agreement of what is "normal." How easily we demonize that which is different. How little compassion and love we bring to our judgments, how easily we bend to the mass or media psychology instead of taking the time to reason out what is right, or how a "deviant" or "evil" person got that way.

One talk show that I remember well was about young spouses who were complaining that their mates didn't have jobs. On the stage were several couples in which the men stayed home relaxing while their wives worked to provide all the necessities of life, and there was also a couple in which the man was working and his wife didn't have a job. This was the only couple with a child — a three-month-old baby. The audience reacted to this young mother, staying at home raising her infant, in the same way they reacted to the able-bodied unemployed men — that she was a "bum" who should get a job, because that is the type of life deemed appropriate in American society, applying to all, under all circumstances. There was absolutely no recognition of what it takes to have a baby and raise it, or that parenthood and being there for our children may be a valuable and important occupation in itself.

Choosing the Speed of Your Life

In American society today, and in many other societies around the world, from the moment a child is of an age to do so, he or she is trained to rush, to hurry, to do, to produce, to win, to excel, to achieve. Many of these things aren't bad in themselves. It's when rushing, hurrying, and achieving become *requirements* of life that we must question why. It's when *earning* one's very place as a being on this earth, regardless of personal tragedy or hardship, is normative, that we must begin to rethink what it means to be here.

Think about the speed of your life, and whether it feels comfortable to you or not. Each person has a different comfort zone. Some need more stimulation than others. This is the difference between Tai Chi and aerobics. In an aerobics class everyone moves together, one-and-two. In Tai Chi, the key to finding *chi*, the flow that makes it possible to do the movements correctly, is to find your own rhythm, your own internal pace and power. It is a continuous flow. A group of people doing Tai Chi properly will not be in perfect synchronization. The idea is to ask yourself if there are times in your day when you can slow down. Controlled belly breathing, morning and night, can help, and increasing our awareness always helps us to control our behavior.

It Takes Practice

When you get some time to yourself, practice slowing down. Relaxing (Principle One) and slowing down (Principle Two) are natural mates, so both can be accomplished at once. Some ideas:

- Do gentle, slow yoga regularly.
- Practice Tai Chi if you can.
- Use traffic slow-downs to help slow you down internally.
- Wake up slowly. Get a tape or CD player that will automatically turn on and play music or sounds to wake you up gently and remind you to do your breathing, prayer, or meditation, and to move slowly. It is worth getting up ten or fifteen minutes earlier, if that's what it takes, rather than jumping out of bed and rushing off.
- In some parts of India, bathing is a slow-down ritual. After bathing, a prayer or song is given to the direction of the sunrise. Try it. See if you can come up with an after-shower ritual that feels uncontrived and helps you slow down and acknowledge your connection with the larger universe before beginning your day. Perhaps an affirmation or prayer, followed by greeting your sacred self in the mirror with something like they say in India, "Namaste" (meaning, "I bow to the divinity within").
- Use cooking time, if you cook, to slow down. Chopping vegetables is a great mini-slow-down break.
- If you have a baby, use diapering or massage as slow-down time, and connect emotionally with your child. With older children, a bedtime ritual is often the best slow-down time you have. Light a candle, say a prayer, look into the eyes of your child and say "I love you" in your own special way. This is not necessarily for your child. It is for you.
- Use one of your breaks at work for a slow-down ritual such as Tai Chi, yoga, or simply sitting in the bathroom behind closed doors, doing five minutes of controlled belly breathing. Rather than making yourself stop moving, consciously *allow* your movements to subside and your body to relax.

It is my hope that Principle Two will stay with you and give you a refuge to go to during times of stress. It can prepare you for the natural slowing down that comes with growing older, and, rather than creating a sense of being useless, slowing down will bring you an experience of peace and oneness that many monastics strive for all their lives.

PARENTING WITH PRINCIPLE TWO

Slowing down seems contradictory to family life in Western cultures, especially if we have more than one child. But if you can learn to consciously slow the pace when you feel it going out of bounds, your family life will be easier, more fun, relaxed, and happy.

Principle Two in Pregnancy

For a woman, from the beginning of pregnancy, slowing down is a must; the energy you produce within your body is going directly *through* your baby's body via the placenta. What I mean by "energy" is the life force, which the Chinese call *chi* and the Indians call *prana*, that circulates throughout your body — both your physical body and your more subtle psychic or mental body. The energy flowing through your body helps to regulate your glandular system, which produces hormones through your endocrine system. The more rapid, harried, or frenzied your energy, the more stress hormones you send through your body. If that type of energy is chronic, you are likely to chronically stress your baby, to the point where the baby's body recognizes this type of energy as normal, and will continue producing it after birth.

Noted physicist Dr. Bruce Lipton says,

It is important to note that individual events of parental anger and fear do not necessarily distort the physiology of the developing child. It is specifically chronic, or continuously held emotions that prove to be detrimental during pregnancy. For example, women who sustain physical and emotional abuse during their pregnancy represent situations where adverse environmental cues surrounding the birth of the child can be passed on to the offspring. These are cases of repeated, or patterned, abuses which is entirely distinct from parents that express a transient occasional spat or emotional peak.

Dr. Lipton's work has focused on how a mother's emotional experiences affect an unborn baby's development via biochemical "signal" molecules that are released into the blood (which passes through the placenta) and activate specific receptor proteins on the surfaces of cells in tissues and organs. These serve as molecular "switches" that adjust the metabolic system and behavior of the infant. So it is important that prospective parents realize they are "programming" their baby, even before birth, through the chronic emotional states they experience.

Stress hormones chronically circulating throughout the body eventually have devastating effects on physical, mental, emotional, and spiritual health. As women, we must understand the importance of how our energy affects our infants. To stay in what may be our own addiction to stress and drama is to deny this connection. As Dr. Lipton says, "Sustained parental anger and fear compromise the child's development and health, as the emotional stresses chemically impact the fetus."

If there truly are circumstances we cannot control that put us in emotional situations, such as grief over the loss of a loved one, the key is to be sensitive to the fact that both you and your infant (I won't say "fetus" because I believe in this context it depersonalizes your baby) are going through this process together. Both of you need care, attention, and the awareness, not denial, that this stress affects both of you, and measures should be taken to slow it down and bring healing energy to it as much as possible. As Dr. Lipton says, "It should be noted that behavioral consequences of children exposed to negative or destructive attitudes during their prenatal development can be psychologically reversed, once the issues are recognized."

The job of the baby's father (or your partner) is to help you slow down and relax. This requires a lot of communication about what these concepts mean to each of you, and what is helpful and what is not. For example, criticizing a woman for *not* slowing down is usually not helpful. Asking if he can do tasks she usually does to help lighten her load is helpful. In addition, learning to slow down is very helpful for the baby's father if he is to be an integral part of his child's life. In order to truly be with children of any age, we all must have the ability to slow ourselves down and relax into the present moment, because that is where our children live.

Practicing controlled belly breathing every day during your pregnancy will help. A childbirth education class should also help you, provided your teacher is aware of the more spiritual aspects of your new journey and your "coach" is a willing participant who is capable of helping to both calm and empower you. If your male partner has a hard time doing this, consider getting a birthing coach. If you choose to do this, take care not to disempower the father, and be sure to include him as a member of the team, so that all the bases are covered. Dad could take the role of family communicator and picture taker, getting ice chips, holding the mother's hand, and so on. Dad and the birth coach could take turns. Make the decisions together, so everyone feels good about them.

If you are a soon-to-be father, be sure to slow down and relax yourself so you can help your partner get through the birth more smoothly. If you can remain unruffled, and not take your partner's expressions of fear or anger personally, you can be her rock — and believe me, she will be very grateful for it later.

Slowing Down Your Body

To slow down your body during pregnancy, do stretching exercises and squats, deep breathing, meditation, or prayer. Maintain a diet of fresh, life-enhancing foods, and practice deep relaxation to help slow down the body and mind. These are all part of your job as a "grower nursery" for this new being, and will also help prepare you for the experience of giving birth. You will learn to nurture yourself and to take care of your body, mind, and spirit in a better way than before — in other words, you will have incorporated Principle Two into your life.

Pregnancy can also help you learn how to deal with day-to-day change. Your body changes, your relationships change, what you think about and are interested in changes. Tai Chi teacher Chungliang Al Huang, in his book *Embrace Tiger, Return to Mountain*, says,

> Part of our everyday conflict is how to cope with change and how to be happy with the constant. We are usually bored with the constant and frightened by change. Moving slowly, breathing slowly, turning everything into slow motion for a few minutes each day helps us remember the balance of these two seeming opposites.

Principle Two with Babies and Young Children

If you have learned how to slow down by the time your baby arrives, you will have the time of your life. Your baby's infancy will be filled with magic, with moments that turn into hours, just watching him or her being. But there are a lot of responsibilities that come with a new baby in the house and, particularly if you also have other children, life can get even more action packed after all the drama of childbirth has passed, the relatives have gone home, the spouse has returned to work, and hormones begin adjusting once again to a new body structure, nursing or not.

Fathers can play an integral role in learning to practice Principle Two with a new baby. Dads, don't wait for an invitation to get involved with the care of your baby. At the hospital or birthing center or at home, during the first few days, allow the new mom to rest. Don't let well-meaning aunts or grandmothers push you out of the way. Ask the nurses or midwives or grandmothers how to change, burp, take the temperature, and bathe your baby. If you and your partner have agreed, learn how to feed the baby (even breast-fed babies can occasionally accept breast milk from a bottle). If your partner complains about the way you do things, don't be defensive. Ask her to show you how she does it, and thank her. As one dad said, "After a while she'll get tired of being the 'baby boss' and will relinquish more and more control to you." Studies have shown that a father's sensitive caregiving leads to a secure bond with his infant and that a warm, gratifying marital relationship supports a father's involvement with his baby.

Fathers can walk, rock, sing to, dance with, read to, and massage their babies as well as do maintenance activities like feeding, changing, and bathing. Many people don't realize that fathers, too, have "parenting hormones" that are activated by close contact with their infants. I urge you dads to get fully involved with your babies, for your own well being as well as theirs.

As your children grow, there are plenty of opportunities to practice Principle Two, to the benefit of both you and your children. For instance:

Slow Down while Getting Dressed

Often, getting everyone up and out in the morning means the day begins with stress, chaos, and hurry. Wouldn't you rather start your day with connection, joy, and relaxation? Try making the morning ritual as easy on yourself as possible. You can minimize the struggle with pre-schoolers, either the night before or when they get up, by offering them choices so they feel in control. Often power struggles over food and dressing come from the conflicting needs of the parents who have time constraints and the child who is beginning to try out her autonomy by saying "no" at every opportunity. Offering choices usually helps to head off a conflict: "Do you want to wear this outfit, or this one?" It does sometimes require some grounded parental power (which we'll talk about as we go along) so the child knows you mean what you say and that there are no other choices.

With breakfast, again, choices can be offered such as juice or milk, this cereal or that, hot or cold, and so on. Choosing is fun for kids, so often it can keep them preoccupied and their minds off the need to control their environment by saying, "No!"

Having a morning ritual that is the same every day can help, too. Make it a slow, easy ritual, perhaps accompanied by music. (By the time my daughter was in high school, we had to part ways on this one — she needed "pump-up" music, I needed meditative, harmonious tunes. So we agreed: she could have her rap music in the car if I could have my morning New Age melodies at home.) Maintaining a morning ritual may mean getting up earlier, so everyone can feel the support and enjoyment of family before going their separate ways. Again, making some of these choices the night before can be part of the bedtime ritual, and make mornings easier.

Slow Down in the Car

One of the things I dreaded most was driving with my children in the car. Even with car seats, they sat in the back and fought incessantly. Once, we even got into a minor accident (we hit a parked car!) because the loud fighting and crying in the back was so distracting. I discovered this was *my* problem. No amount of yelling, cajoling, bargaining, understanding, or pleading changed the situation. I even, regretfully, resorted to spanking my son after one such ride; it made no difference at all.

One day I was on my way to teach a class, kids in tow. The fighting started. I pulled to the side of the road and sat.

Slowly the children became silent and the oldest asked, "Mom, what are we doing?" I said, "When you two fight it distracts me. I can't drive safely so I am putting us and other people on the road in danger. I won't drive under those conditions. We'll sit here until you are quiet." So, they were quiet. We started out again. The fighting started again. I pulled over again. I repeated my speech, neither adding nor subtracting a word, but adding a minute to our five-minute break. We began again. Now it was time to test Mom. Many parents, at this point, knowing they are going to be terribly late, might give up just to meet their objective. I stopped at a phone, called the place I was going, explained I was having some "kid trouble" and said please forgive me but I'd be late. If necessary I would cancel the class. Then I called a fellow teacher to see if she could fill in if necessary — but she couldn't. Talk about stress!

Each time they began to fight, I pulled over and added time. No radio, no air conditioning (it was dead summer), just total silence.

My feet were planted, and you can bet I was practicing controlled belly breathing. After a while, the kids began to get bored with this game. It was hot. Being confined in their car seats was not fun. But I've got at least one boundary tester, so I knew we were in for an ordeal. I called and canceled my class with great regret. I told the kids this was what I was doing, and that it really felt bad to me and would reduce my income so that treats would be out of the question, and stopping at the toy store would be impossible. We spent around two or three hours at this. Eventually, it definitely was no fun any more.

They could feel my resolve, and from then on there was no hitting or yelling. They knew I would sit in that car, bored and sweating, all day if I had to. They also knew, though it hurt me, I was willing to give up my objective to teach them something. Not only did they see this type of parenting clearly modeled for them, they also, deeply, unconsciously, got the message that they were my number one priority. I was willing to slow down and sacrifice in order to teach them right from wrong. The next week, I explained this to my class, and apologized to all of them for the inconvenience. But they benefitted, too. As parents, they could see that I walked my talk, and they respected me for it.

Slow Down at the Grocery Store

If you decide to take your children to the grocery store (and I recommend against it most of the time), try to think of ways to apply Principles One and Two. With babies between the ages of six and eighteen months, you have to be willing to handle it when your child cries, fusses, grabs, wiggles, and wants. Our culture frowns on crying in general. If your baby cries in the supermarket, some people will be annoyed and glare at you as if you should control your child. But most are much more sympathetic than you would imagine. Often they will take their cues from you.

If you smile, shrug, relax, and treat your child with love and kindness, that energy is contagious — others smile at you in sympathy, especially parents. I remember standing in line at a grocery store with my eleven-month-old daughter in the cart, and she screamed and cried because she wanted to get down. It was not physically possible to allow it at that moment, and I explained why rather loudly to her. I kissed her and said, "Mommy loves you even when you misbehave," and I smiled and shrugged at the others in line. "This can be very embarrassing," I said, to no one in particular. Everyone relaxed and smiled together knowing, hey, it's just a baby. Sometimes intolerant people will glare no matter what you do. Breathe deeply and ignore them.

With older children, allow plenty of time so grocery shopping can become a teaching expedition and an adventure in making choices. Give each child an opportunity to choose between one style of beans and another, or show them how you read the labels and compare the prices, or how to choose the freshest produce. Let them pick out some of their lunch items and treats for the week — again, using specific choices so that you are ultimately in control of what gets chosen. I suggest you allow the occasional forbidden treat to de-emphasize its importance in your child's mind. Later, we'll talk about how to use these times to show the consequences of dietary choices in order to help your child choose foods that are nourishing.

Allow the child to pick out items for others in the family, like presents. Above all, try to prevent grocery shopping from becoming associated, in the child's mind, with pain, challenge, and power struggles. Don't use treats as rewards, but save them to use as fun snacks for the movies or some other occasion. Listen to your children tell you what other kids have in their school lunches, and try to include some of these items, even if you don't technically approve of them. Supporting their emotional needs is just as important as nourishing their bodies properly, and as long as they are getting the kinds of food you want them to have at home, a "no-no" here and there won't do any harm. You don't want your child to eat alone and be made fun of because she is the only one with a seaweed sandwich. On the other hand, you do want to slow down enough to take the time to educate your child about food.

We are vegetarians, and, while you may or may not agree with my choices, I think you can get an idea about the importance of teaching your child about food from the following example and find ideas you can apply as a parent in other ways. I made sure my children knew from day one that they were vegetarians and most of their friends' families were not. I let them know it was a matter of choice, and didn't mean people were bad or weird because they chose differently. But I also wanted to make sure that well-intentioned friends and family would not feed my kids meat when I wasn't around.

So I simply told my children the truth, right from the start — the truth about what a hamburger, hot dog, bologna, "nuggets," and so on really are: dead animals. I didn't give them a lot of detailed explanations, though that came later as they began to ask more sophisticated questions. I used opportunities such as commercials advertising ham, steak, and "Buffalo wings" that showed pigs or cows or chickens to point out what the truth was, and ask the children what they thought. Did they think the pig, chicken, or cow really felt happy to be slaughtered and eaten? We had farmer neighbors who named their livestock, treated them wonderfully, and then killed them by hitting them over the head with an iron mallet, so these questions were really not so far off base as some meat eaters may think.

As the children grew older, I encouraged them to use the opportunity of having to do speeches and school papers to find out more about these issues, so they felt educated about why we were vegetarians and could answer other kids' questions. In addition, I wanted them to make their own choice about it when they were old enough, and I wanted that choice to be an informed one.

Principle Two with Teens

When my daughter was in high school and editor of the school paper — and mind you, this was a rural, midwestern, small town high school whose graduates were 60 percent farmers — she used the opportunity to have an editorial debate on vegetarianism with a meat-eating friend. It was great! It turned out to be a very positive experience that gained her respect at the school. Kids came up to her and said, "Wow, I never knew that!" Of course, others took the opposite side and sometimes teased her about it, but her editorial was so well written that none of them could bring themselves to make much fun of her. She learned that sometimes knowledge truly is power.

I had to slow down enough to make this issue important and help my children do their research. Another added benefit was that I could show my kids how to research their questions, find facts, statistics, and anecdotes to back up their theories and opinions, find out why the "other side" thought the way they did, and expose false information as fraudulent. (Teens love that!) If you want your children to embrace certain values, you must slow down enough to teach as well as parent, and to back it up with more than just your opinion or experience.

We rarely have grandparents, as many indigenous cultures do, who can do this educational part for us while we go out there to make a living. It does require some sacrifice. But it is a short-term sacrifice, because children are not children for long. And believe me, the time spent is well worth it when you look back on it after they are grown. The children not only have the benefit of being educated about what you want them to know, but they understand, in their very bones, that you love them enough to give your time and energy to the process, over and over again. What you get is a great feeling of pride in yourself for being the best parent you can be, leaving a positive legacy that will last for generations, and learning a great deal in the process.

Slow Down During Meals

These days, few families take the time to have meals together, and I believe this is a great loss. Having at least one meal together every day has always been high on my family priority list, and though my children sometimes complained when they were young, wanting to be like their friends and eat on the run, now that they are grown we eat together one night a week, and they complain if we don't!

Humans are built for ritual. It is the ritual celebration of what is good in our lives, of our connection to each other, that makes life rich. So, if you don't do it already, I'd like you to consider having at least one meal together every day as a family. Responsibilities for cooking, cleaning, and atmosphere can be rotated or divided up. Keep it light, let the kids have a little fun, and try to find some jokes or funny stories to tell. It's wonderful to start the meal by saying grace, if that's comfortable for you, or just thanking creation for food and togetherness. For us, at first it wasn't really comfortable (it seemed a bit contrived), but with time it became a ritual that seemed just right.

Especially now, when we eat together only once a week, holding hands and giving thanks for our connection, our safety, and our food is important to us all. After dinner, we sometimes watch a video or play board games or just sit around and talk for a while. The kids' friends and sometimes one of my friends or family members are invited and treated with the relaxed acceptance of family. It gets our week started in a way that makes us all feel part of something bigger, and reminds each of us how lucky we are to be so loved, regardless of what else is going on in our lives. Small children like it when the same blessing is said every night. For children, ritual means safety, stability, and continuity. Having table decorations to celebrate holidays or the seasons adds festivity and remembrance to the meal.

When the kids were adolescents, naturally rebellion had to come out around this ritual. The kids would refuse to say blessing, or when it was their turn, say something silly. The boys would find some way, at some point in the meal, to start talking about something gross or disgusting to the adults. At first we tried to stop and control it, but that just led to a tension-filled meal that was no fun. Finally, we just let it go. Now it is a kind of family joke. As the boys grew older, they'd wait until the very end of the meal to bring up something totally tasteless, just to let us know they hadn't forgotten — and we'd all laugh. Eventually, that little "tradition" went by the wayside as they grew up and got more interested in the food and the positive energy of our family being together. By taking the long-term view, keeping the end in mind, I allowed them to work through this period in their lives. Sure enough, it eventually just died away.

Tai Chi teacher Chungliang Al Huang says,

One of the best images of Tao is to be like bamboo, or a bow. You can feel the weight here on your shoulders. But instead of resisting, you bend like a bow and then spring back when the weight releases. Instead of resisting the energy, you store it up and use it as you recoil.

You may not use all these opportunities to slow yourself and your family down. However, I hope these ideas will encourage you to think about a few places where you can start, and to experiment to find the right pace for you. If and when anxiety and tension build, consider these first two principles and how they can help you get back into the moment.

Remember, the past is gone, the future doesn't exist. This moment is a gift; that's why we call it the *present*.

Exercise for Principle Two

1. Sit comfortably, close your eyes, and relax each part of your body.
2. Take two deep belly breaths. As you inhale repeat, "slow," and as you exhale repeat, "down."

Principle Three
EMPOWER

⸎

*The best leader remains obscure, leading but drawing no
personal attention. As long as the collective has direction,
the leader is satisfied. Credit is not to be taken, it will be
awarded when the people realize that it was the subtle
influence of the leader that brought them success.*

— Deng Ming-Dao, *365 Tao Daily Meditations*

The subject of power is a huge one, worth looking at both within and outside the context of Tai Chi and Taoism. It is vitally important for parents to understand power, because the way we use or misuse it in our own lives is the way we teach our children about their power, our power, and other people's power and that is probably the most significant lesson we teach. The proper use of power results in self-respect, respect for others, confidence, fearlessness, and balance.

The Tao or the Way is where all true power resides. In Tai Chi, the exercises learned with the body teach you something about *chi* or the life force, the power of the Tao that comes through the individual. In the Indian system of yoga, issues of power reside in the second and third chakras, located roughly in the navel area. In Tai Chi, our center of power is called the *tan t'ien* (in Chinese) or *hara* (in Japanese), and is located in essentially the same place. It is from there we get and transfer power, which is rooted in the earth, and comes up through the feet and legs.

Controlled belly breathing not only relaxes and centers you, it increases the power available to you from the *tan t'ien*. In Tai Chi there are many other breathing exercises that work on this area, and on your awareness and use of the *chi*, which is increased by these exercises.

What Is the "Opponent?"

Tai Chi is a martial art as well as a spiritual practice — and certainly raising your child should not involve fighting or power struggles, and it should definitely not require punching or striking of any kind. When we look at Tai Chi practices, it is within the metaphoric context of using our power correctly, knowing how to change the energy in a situation of potential frustration, anger, or power struggle, and knowing how to help our children learn to get in touch with and utilize their own internal power.

When I speak of your "opponent" in this context, I don't mean your child should be perceived as an enemy, to be overpowered or controlled. Again, it is a metaphor: the "opponent" is any energy that is causing disempowerment, separation, or frustration between you and your child. Combative situations will always arise, either in your personal life that spill over into your parenting, or in your relationship with your child. As Tai Chi teacher Ron Sieh says, "To be calm in the midst of chaos cannot be accomplished by avoiding chaos. I have a choice concerning aggression and combat and I can choose from my heart, not out of fear."

In Tai Chi, one of the first exercises practiced with an opponent is called "attaching steps." The student paces the partner, trying to perfectly match his moves and intentions, as if he is attached to her. This requires learning how to get inside the other person's shoes, so to speak, to be so at one with him or attuned to him that one automatically moves with the other, not a moment after.

With the aid of breathing and meditation practice, the student can then move on to what is called "listening power" — building a connection and communication with the opponent so one can then precisely detect the opponent's level of strength, center of gravity, motivation, speed, and so on. This gives one tremendous power, as one can then anticipate an opponent's moves and use the opponent's own force to defeat the aggressive energy coming from him.

Another important practice for parents, which I alluded to in my description of the Tai Chi master who could not be moved by five strong men, is called "sinking power." The student learns to "sink," through his *chi* and his *hara,* and use his connection with the earth in response to his partner's attempt to uproot him.

To "empower," in Tai Chi, involves a technique called "transferring power." It can be used for harm, that is, to transfer your power through a punch or kick, without losing your own power. It can also be used for good by helping another become aware of his or her own power, without giving or loaning them yours.

Empowerment also means overcoming human frailties that can block progress. Dr. Stephen T. Chang, author of *The Integral Management of Tao,* has wonderful insight into this:

> Most people do not realize that they have done their best in the time that has been given, and they neglect to move ahead onto other missions. If excuses are used to hold onto present conditions, the ways of others are blocked. A leader must understand the limits time places on the accomplishments of missions and move himself and others ahead, so that upon accomplishment no one will block the path of others. Otherwise, a possessive attitude toward a position will block all progress, the greatest crime from the standpoint of Taoism.

So Principle Three, empowerment, is linked intrinsically to Principle Seven, flow and let go. We will see how as we go along.

The *t'ui sho circle* exercise (as mentioned on page 40) represents the Tao in that it *seems* empty and transparent. But when you utilize its power, you find it is inexhaustible. As the Taoist sage Lao Tzu said, "When you follow Tao it will round off the sharp edges, untangle confusing threads, dim all glaring light. It molds and smooths the dust."

The kind of power we seek to cultivate as parents is the power of the Tao. Like water, it is smooth, flowing, yielding, penetrable, yet strong enough to "round off the sharp edges" of things.

Wong Chung-Ya, an ancient Taoist master, emphasized the importance of avoiding "double weightedness" — that is, reacting the same way every time, getting stuck on one way of responding, being always on one side of the *yin/yang* balance. He had his students practice constantly moving so when they were up, they became aware of down; when they were right, they were aware of left. They learned that not responding to the "opponent" appropriately for *that specific moment* and *that specific person* and *that specific interaction* results in difficulty and awkwardness, which leads to defeat.

We are so accustomed to "taking a stand" that we forget the universe is constantly moving, shifting, and changing — even rock changes, over a period of time. So in our approach to our children in this ever-changing phenomenon we call the world, we must be flexible enough to remember that each child, each situation, each time, each incident, and each interaction is different from any other. Though we connect ourselves to principles that don't change, such as unconditional love, respect, and empowerment, the way we respond within those principles must be very flexible according to time, place, and person.

THE OPPOSITE

To empower does not mean to overpower or disempower. We need to learn to separate ourselves from our children in order to empower them correctly. *Enmeshment* — too much identification with our children — can lead to tightening and anxiety as they move away and begin to be who they are.

There are many examples of situations that could be perceived as "failures" but, because of internal empowerment, are actually successes. For example, it took Thomas Edison more than twenty years and *thousands* of failed experiments before he invented the electric light. Many famous authors were rejected numerous times before being published. Most successful people had many failures along the way. Helpless people who are not internally empowered cannot respond to rejection and adversity in their proper context. Life may not be fair, but our response to obstacles and adversities is learned.

If you are overly concerned about what others think of you as a parent or what they think of your children, you cannot be genuine and flexible — two important aspects of empowerment. If your own sense of success and happiness is dependent upon your children behaving a certain way, making certain choices, or living up to certain standards and expectations that are predetermined and rigid, you can't empower your children to be healthy, powerful adults who make good choices for themselves. If you feel like a failure when your children make mistakes, get bad grades, or don't make the team — if you feel constant pressure to make them a certain way so that you feel good about *yourself* — you will have difficulty with this principle.

Teaching and Modeling Respect

Using force, physical punishment, lectures, and tirades does not empower; it means you are stuck in the *yang* side of the *yin/yang* balance. Your children will then inherently try to balance you by either yielding too passively and losing their own power, or by resisting you to maintain their own power. The predominant style of our grandparents' generation — "You had better ... or else!" — is outmoded. It will not only block you from using this principle, it will disempower you, for eventually your children will laugh at you, knowing they were born with more internal power than you will probably ever have in your lifetime.

This is the secret to raising children in the new millennium: understanding that these kids are coming in with more knowledge, greater power, more intensity, and more ability to keep pace with the speed of the new age than you have. They will be dependent on you to walk your talk — to *model*, not just *tell* them, what to do. They depend on you to be honest, for they have even better radar for hypocrisy than we did when we were their age. If and when you must take a stand, you must do so with great deliberation, grounding yourself in principles (using "sinking power"), so that the result is respect for you as an elder. As your relationship becomes more healthy, interdependent (able to need others and respond to others needing you, appropriately), and respectful, the need for you to motivate and/or discipline your child decreases.

These days, respect goes both ways. When I teach infant massage, one of the first things I teach parents, or help them to remember, is that infants are human beings and deserve respect. We have specific techniques we use to show infants that respect; we touch them respectfully and allow them the power to communicate what they want and don't want, so they see right away that they have power and are not just playthings with which their parents (or anyone else) can do whatever they wish.

Discipline conducted with respect does not disempower or overpower. The concept of obedience tied to ultimatums is not empowerment. It may get short-term results, but will end in long-term losses. Making too many choices for your children leads to a loss of empowerment, too. They become overly dependent on others — authority figures — to tell them what to do, and why and when to do it. They lose the capacity to think deeply for themselves and to go against the "norm" when they need to.

In Tai Chi, power is often thought of in terms of aggression versus non-aggression. But non-aggression does not mean passivity. It means you do not constantly *oppose* your children, their ideas, wants, or needs. You follow them, with "listening power," listening closely to them and mirroring back what they say from *their point of view.* When you do this, they learn to think more deeply. You respect their ability to come to sound conclusions and learn from their mistakes, and you communicate that respect through your words and actions.

Abandoning your children to their own devices, their peers, and the world does not help them learn the right use of power. In fact, it pushes them into learning the wrong use of power, as we can see in the headlines every day. Many parents do not understand the difference between healthy separation and abandonment. Often, parents are so disempowered themselves that when faced with a rebellious or challenging child they go into what I call the "Wizard of Oz

Syndrome." They act as if they are big, all-knowing, all-powerful, scary, and so on. This works temporarily. But eventually the child gets curious and pulls back the curtain to discover the parents' show of power is all pulleys and levers, smoke and mirrors. Respect disappears, and you've lost your leverage with your child. So don't even try it. Get yourself straight first in terms of dealing with your own childhood, and continually work on your own use of power as you go along, showing and sharing with your child how you work on it, so when he or she becomes a parent, they will know what to do and will not resort to techniques that don't work.

YOUR PERSONAL POWER

To help your children learn how to use their own personal power, you must be able to access yours and use it on a daily basis. Principles One and Two, relaxing and slowing down, help you begin to get in touch with the infinite power available to you, power that comes through the earth and is in the *prana* all around you. As my spiritual teacher P.R. Sarkar said, "The Force that guides the stars guides you, too." That's a powerful force.

Showing your children the right use of power is simple. Set goals for yourself and take small steps toward them every day until you reach them. Share the process with your children — it makes great dinner-table conversation. During the writing of my books, for example, I always talked about the process with my kids. I didn't lead them to believe it was effortless. I shared how sometimes it was really hard just to make myself write a paragraph that day, and that sometimes I knew that paragraph would end up in the wastebasket! I emphasized persistence, and said that sometimes we have to go backward in order to go forward, or re-route around an obstacle in order to achieve what we want. It wasn't easy to remain patient and self-motivated, but it was worth it to me for the long-range satisfaction of having completed a book that might help others. Sometimes I'd read small parts to them and ask what they thought, and that would open up a whole new area of conversation.

I tried to show my kids that, even though we often didn't have a great deal of money, it was important to be contented and try to do the things we wanted to do. Going to India to see my spiritual teacher every couple of years was important to me. So I would save and borrow and do whatever was necessary to achieve that goal. I explained to my kids that those trips fed my soul, and were therefore important to my long-term feelings of connectedness to the world, to God, and service to those in need (in India, service was part of what I did). When we were in financial crisis, my kids saw me take on an extra job to bring in more money so they could continue going to an elementary school that was important to them and to me, too. It was important for my own personal power and self-respect that I provide what I knew my children needed.

Many challenging things happened to me during their childhood — I had serious illnesses and surgeries, and spent almost two years in bed, due to virulent forms of diseases I contracted in India. I lost my second-hand car (that I had saved up for a year to buy) the day after I bought it, when someone without insurance borrowed it and totaled it. I knew how I handled these things would be an important example for my children in the future, when unforeseen crises may come into their lives. I didn't always do a great job of responding powerfully, but I tried. When I didn't — when I behaved in a powerless way — I would find some way to laugh at myself, and to point out to my kids what I'd done and discuss other, better ways I could have responded.

I fought my feelings of despair, anger, and helplessness, and tried to emphasize what I was learning: that things can be replaced, starting all over is part of life, and just because you are disabled you are not unworthy of love and life. These things were not always clear and obvious to them, but I do believe from talking to them now that they got these messages. I gradually got better and began to be able to meditate and do my yoga and Tai Chi again. And eventually I even found the car of my dreams.

I think my children and perhaps others, too, were able to see that there is no one way to act powerfully. Sometimes power comes from a very quiet, compassionate, seemingly "weak" looking place.

To find your own sense of power it is important to learn to listen to your inner voice and to follow it, regardless of what others tell you. You may seek out the input and advice of others with more experience, but ultimately the only way to increase your access to your own power is by relying on it and respecting it, regardless of how it looks in your life. For some people, it looks like a big, muscular, fighting spirit. For others, it looks like a small, serene, compassionate, redemptive heart. Look at Mother Teresa — look at the power she had! When your power comes from the infinite source of power, the Tao, it is right, good, clean, and clear. Do whatever it takes to stay connected with this aspect of your being. You will need it over and over again, throughout your entire life.

PARENTING WITH PRINCIPLE THREE

Tom Markham, in *Joyful Child Journal,* says, "Children born since the early 1980s are especially aligned with the rapidly increasing vibratory rate of earth. By focusing on this accelerated — or superconscious — level of awareness, we will grasp the essential nature of our children." I might place that date back about five years, but I think he is right. Children today are coming in with more awareness of the "superconscious" or higher and deeper levels of being than we did — and this may be true of each successive generation. The trouble our parents got into was holding onto the styles and values of their own parents. But some of those values and styles don't work any more. The acceleration of awareness has increased exponentially because the media has exposed "The Wizard" — the figures of power and authority — as being fallible, *not* all-powerful. In fact, we have all seen their flaws, their struggles, their hypocrisy, and their vulnerable humanity.

While I have always been able to relate to and have been interested in the time of my parents' youth (the 1930s and 1940s), my kids have little interest in the era of my youth, the 1950s and 1960s. In fact, as my daughter told me last night, these times seem like a "fairy tale from another planet." Maybe later she will develop an interest, but it is apparent that most kids today are future oriented in a more realistic way than my generation was.

Our kids are more open, in a sense, to what *is*. They know in their cells how rapidly things are changing. For those who don't have a solid spiritual grounding, this makes them feel lost, hopeless, and meaningless. For others, who want the wealth their parents generated in the wild 1980s, money seems to be the key to life and they pursue it with a single-minded zeal that may or may not include integrity. And for those that are poor, with neither spiritual grounding nor the experience of wealth (either in the sense of money, security, or love), the hopelessness is even more deeply ingrained. A sense of purpose is not even part of their picture, much less the goal of a meaningful life. They can be so disempowered by their experience, their parents' example, and their parents' style of discipline, that personal power and the concept of integrity are beyond their reach.

It's certainly clear to me that it is important for us to try to live a life based on spiritual and/or ethical principles, and model for our children healthy alternatives to a disempowered, frustrated life.

Principle Three in Pregnancy

Working with Principle Three begins as soon as you get pregnant. You will need constant access to your own power to make the hundreds of choices you must make. In an ideal world, people wouldn't have children until they have solidly connected with their own power. It's difficult enough even then! Imagine a teenager, who is barely coming into awareness of this aspect of her being, suddenly having to be a role model for a child, having to know the right use of power as a parent. It's nearly impossible. How can we expect these young people to be good parents, to properly empower their kids to lead healthy, meaningful lives? It is a lifelong challenge, an endless spiritual path.

I encourage you to use your pregnancy, whether it is your first or fifth, as an exciting opportunity to exercise the right use of power. Notice all the decisions you need to make, connect them with your parenting mission statement, and make them on the basis of what your inner sense tells you is right. Do not allow the so-called experts to run your life. Consider their advice, but consider yourself the ultimate authority. Doctors and researchers are not gods. Be willing to surrender the results to the universal forces, God, the Tao, or whatever you choose to call that which guides you. Trust that force, and trust yourself. Let your inner sense tell you what is right and back it up with power from your very root. If you don't know what to do, get all the information you can on all sides of the issue, let it sit for a while, ask for guidance, and then go with what feels right.

Principle Three with Babies

When my son was born, the prevailing norm, even among my spiritual group at the time, was that circumcision was a must, a given. It didn't feel right to me. So I did a lot of research about the reasons for it and its history, and found different points of view. Finally, my husband and I made our own decision: we would not, as vegetarians, inflict pain on animals, so why would we want to do that to our newborn baby? We would teach him cleanliness, and when he was old enough to make that decision for himself, he was welcome to have it done, without disapproval from us.

When we made the decision, it was an act of empowerment for us and for our infant: your body is not mine, it is yours. You get to decide if it is changed in this way, when you are old enough to do the research yourself. So far it has not been an issue for him at all, and he is now in his twenties.

So often, we project our own "what-ifs" on our babies and, to spare them the possible embarrassment of being different, we make a decision like this for them, even though circumcision teaches the newborn child he is not the owner of his body and that, at any moment, his power over his own body can be painfully taken away by strangers without his permission, his understanding, or any preparation. New research proves that circumcision has no medical value or health benefits for babies, and the American Academy of Pediatrics has said it is an unnecessary procedure from a medical standpoint.

I'm using this as an example only — I realize many of you have your own good reasons for choosing the ritual of circumcision. I ask you only to try to engage, in whatever way you can, the child's own power — his permission, his self-hood — in the process. If it must be done, I'd be much more in favor of a spiritual ritual at the hands of a wise and kind practitioner, surrounded by love and celebration, than the stark, painful, lonely circumcisions that go on in hospitals.

Principle Three with Young Children

Practicing Principle Three gives us the ability to recognize that each child is entirely unique, with his own personality, needs, and thresholds. So parenting has to be tailored to the individual. This means there are very few "rules" that *everyone* must follow, and the few rules there are will be subject to change from time to time, with the child's involvement. New rules may be put in place and old ones deactivated. Because there is open communication, the children understand that a rule for a toddler may not apply to a seven-year-old. Things are explained, not just declared. When a child feels he has been respected enough to be a part of the rule making process, he has a stake in the household and is more likely to follow the rules.

Martial arts expert Dawn Callan, in *Awakening the Warrior Within,* talks about empowerment in our culture:

> Our entire education, beginning with our parents (even those with the best intentions), and including our schools and religious systems, has taught us who we ought to be, so that we fit the accepted mold, rather than supporting us to break the mold and be ourselves. We have been taught to be controlled rather than to have our own power.

We want to try, as much as possible, to encourage and allow our children to express and use their power appropriately, without over-powering or disempowering others in the process. We want to work in partnership with our children, and teach our children to be in partnership with others. If we are to do this, we have to learn to do it ourselves.

Babies and toddlers rely on their parents' and caregivers' reactions to learn how to respond to uncertain situations. They observe their caregivers, and learn about their environment through indirect experience. If a child leaves toddlerhood without trust in his caregivers and a healthy sense of his individuality and his personal power, problems can arise later on in adjusting to social situations.

Privacy

Privacy is an important part of Principle Three. Each child needs things of his or her own that no one else, not even Mom or Dad, is allowed access to without permission. Knocking on doors and requesting permission to enter respects privacy. Manners such as "please" and "thank you," "may I," "good morning," etc., practiced consistently by parents and taught with love from infancy, help reinforce dignity and respect for oneself and for others, an important part of empowerment.

Making Choices

In the previous chapters we discussed choice making, another crucial aspect of empowerment. Use every opportunity you can to help teach your children (1) that there are many choices in any situation; (2) which choices lead to health and happiness, feelings of self-respect and dignity, and which don't; (3) that they do not have the right to make choices for others; and (4) the consequences of choices can be far-reaching.

There are endless opportunities for discussion of these topics. Television shows and/or news stories are filled with them. Point out what came before an act of violence or self-destruction, and ask kids what other choices that person may have had. Underscore the idea that we always have choices and can make nonviolent, life-enhancing choices in every situation.

Dealing with food gives us plenty of opportunities to learn about choice. When my kids were little, I would let them have a sugary treat, and then later, when they got grouchy and mean, I'd point out the connection. Then I would give them a protein snack, and their dispositions would radically improve. I'd point out that it was the protein making them feel better.

Eventually, they were able to be aware that one of their options when feeling grouchy was to have some cottage cheese, nut butter, or other protein, and they would feel better. They also knew they might feel jittery and bad if they chose the sweets. My son, of his own volition, stopped eating chocolate altogether because he hated the "hyper" way it made him feel. He knew this wasn't the case for everybody; it wasn't a value judgment. The choice was purely his, from his own experience.

Be sure to share your own choice-making dilemmas with your kids. As they get older, ask for their opinion. Let them know clearly you are making your own decision, but you are interested in what they think — that way they won't feel responsible for your decisions. Then tell them what you decided and how you came to it. Show them how you get more information when you feel you don't have enough to make a good decision. Always maintain your dignity in the role of parent, and your own personal power. It is a huge mistake to turn that power over to your kids. They want you to have already figured out some of this! They *need* a strong model to show them how to make appropriate choices and to point out the consequences to them.

Empower your children to care for others by having the older children help take care of the younger ones. I'll never forget how common it was in India to see a nine-year-old with a baby sister, brother, or cousin on his hip, and how rare it is in Westernized cultures for siblings to "mother" one another. This can be taught in many ways, and changed as the children grow older. An older child can massage a baby. It helps them bond, and helps the older child realize this new being is a real person, his or her sibling, to be loved and protected. They can imitate your technique, but keep it simple, with easy rubbing motions. They love getting massage oil on their hands and feeling grown-up in the way they care for the baby.

Older children can push the baby in a stroller, pull a wagon with a toddler in it (with careful supervision, of course), help pick out baby items at the supermarket, or help feed the little ones. As a baby grows, the sibling bond becomes stronger, the baby is more fun to play with, and they become both friends and rivals.

I suggest having fairly strict rules in place about hitting, such as "in our family we *never* hit each other." This statement of rules should always be given with "sinking power" — first ground yourself, relax, get powerful from your very core, and deliver the directive, eye to eye, in a way that says it is non-negotiable. This can be a powerful message that sets the stage for nonviolent conflict resolution later on.

Teaching children to respond with empathy to a younger child's distress helps them learn to behave more selflessly later on. You can extend this outside the home, and have children help in charitable activities that have a direct and positive impact on those in need, such as visiting the elderly, making deliveries for a food bank, and raising money for charitable causes. Research has shown that children who learn to care about others and are involved, even in small ways, in helping others in need, are at a lower risk of developing depression later.

Children who learn to be empathic (to feel another's pain and want to help them) and learn to stand up for what they believe in perform better in adult life in their work and social lives. On the other hand, kids who are raised being disciplined by physical violence, force, humiliation, embarrassment, or withdrawal of love grow up having great difficulty feeling compassion for others. Every man who batters his wife has a skewed view of his actions; he usually believes she deserves it and it is "for her own good." It is minimized in his mind because when he saw it done as a child, or when he was a victim of violence, he was told it was not abuse, it was discipline — or else he was lied to — "Mommy fell and broke her arm." Most abusers don't even realize their behavior is antisocial or wrong, because overpowering control was so normal in the homes of their childhood.

Discipline

This leads us to a tough question for every parent: How do we discipline our kids? There are plenty of violent prisoners in penitentiaries who were disciplined as children with spankings and beatings. Though I had my children take "time out" sometimes, now I even question the popular use of that as a disciplinary technique because it links quiet time alone with punishment.

When children, even young ones, are given explanations for rules, allowed to voice an opinion, and even to disagree, they become more skilled at exercising their power, their social "muscles," when they relate to others and learn to cope with problems by reasoning out the right responses. It may take more time to talk than to hit, but in the long run the lessons you are teaching will be more far-reaching and will develop a broader range of social skills in your child. Use reasoning to help your child understand the concepts of restitution and making amends, to understand that apologies don't automatically excuse them from out-of-control behavior, and that words can hurt as much as punches. Many research studies have concluded that the use of reasoning and discussion as disciplinary tools is one of the most effective ways to foster a child's positive moral development.

One inventive mother went to a nature store and purchased several small rocks with words carved on them such as: sisters, brothers, family, love, kindness, peace, truth, forgive, gentle, cooperation, and so on. When one of her children misbehaved, she chose one of the rocks and gave it to the child. If the child wasn't old enough to read or didn't know how to read the word, she repeated the word for him several times, having him repeat it back, and explained its definition. Then the child was led to his room or his "safe place," and asked to think about what that word meant to him for fifteen minutes. Then his mother would retrieve him and they would discuss the word. In this way, the child was not punished, but an "intervention" took place, which allowed the child to learn values and connect those values to his behavior.

Learned Powerlessness

In addition, there are many ways we unknowingly teach our children to be helpless rather than empowered. Helplessness is taught by:

- Doing things *for* children instead of teaching them, in steps, how to do it themselves.

- Explaining poor performance in school in terms of intelligence or inability instead of effort or motivation.
- Explaining the cause of difficulty as internal ("You're not good at that") rather than external ("You can try harder next time and do better").

Girls are socialized to be more vulnerable to criticism and tend to interpret it as permanent and pervasive rather than temporary and external. They are more likely to explain difficulty as their fault, due to their character defects, whereas boys are socialized to attribute difficulty more to outside circumstances or temporary lapses. So with your girls be especially conscious of explaining, when disciplining, that when they've done something wrong it does not mean there is something wrong with them. Explain to them that wrong behavior is something that is temporary, related only to the subject at hand, and is something that can be changed. Remember also that we all need to feel we have some control over a situation and/or our feelings about it in order to develop resilience and resistance to adversity. Helplessness robs us of resilience.

Reasoning

Tai Chi's "listening power" can be used to reason with your kids at any age. In this practice, you stay with them and feed back to them in your own words what you hear them saying about something they have just done, *from their point of view*. Stay with them long enough to be able to act like a mirror, and help them reason their way to the conclusion that delineates right from wrong. You can help them "be their own boss," and evaluate their own performance. You can help them see how consequences are tied to actions, and how, if they have done something wrong, they can make amends with dignity. At first you may sometimes have to take the role of teacher and guide them firmly through this process. When you do this, try to refrain from filling in silent spaces with lectures. When your feedback is wrong, they will let you know. Be patient and ask them with sincerity to explain again what they mean.

Dr. Suzette Hadin Elgin says that "Talking to a child, especially after the age of five or six, is essentially the same thing as talking to an adult you outrank." They understand much more than they are given credit for. She also says, "You have to let a child choose and introduce the conversational topic. You have to support that topic through a few conversational turns, instead of switching to a topic more of your own choice. You have to give the floor back to the child every few sentences. And — hardest of all — you have to *listen* while the child talks, with your head and with full, courteous attention."

When you ask your child to do a chore, be sure you include all the information he needs. For example, instead of saying, "Jack, take out the trash," you could say, "Jack, please take out the trash now because the garbage truck is coming at noon." Tone is important. Try as hard as you can to use a respectful, relaxed tone that assumes your child wants to help. Along with your tone, smiling eye contact or a touch can help communicate your positive intention. If you mess up, apologize. Say, "I didn't mean to sound harsh (angry, impatient, and so on). I'm sorry. I'm kind of stressed out right now and could really use the help." And be sure to thank the child when the task has been completed. At dinnertime, you could say, with an eye-contact smile, "Jack, it was a great help to have the garbage taken out on time. Thanks a lot."

Try to be alert to whether your child is hearing what you are saying the way you want him to. If you feel a negative reaction, you can say, "I'm not sure I said that right. Let me try again." Or, "Did I say that in a way that didn't feel good to you?" Again, communicating respectfully with your kids helps them learn respectful communication, and empowers them to take responsibility for themselves and the way they communicate. You are laying a solid foundation for their future relationships, so it is definitely worth the time. We'll explore this issue more deeply later on.

Empower Your Children to Care for Animals

Taking care of pets is another way to empower your children. Teach them how much responsibility they have toward their fellow creatures and show them that responsibility can feel good. Try not to overwhelm them with tasks, but find age appropriate, fun things they can do for their pets' well-being such as:

- Feed the fish or help change the water in the tank.
- Clean the birdcage and fill its bowls with food and water.
- Help walk the dog, and later, walk the dog themselves (not every day).
- Help feed the cat, opening the can, putting the food in the bowl, or giving a treat.
- Accompany you to the pet groomer or vet, and help in whatever way they can.
- Play with the pet, reminding them pets need love, too. You can use the concept of the "love bucket" my friend Julie came up with. She'd say, "Oh, I think Fluffy's love bucket is getting low. We better fill it up! How can we do that?"

Principle Three with Teens

A good way to empower your teenager is to begin preparing him or her for adulthood. Open a checking account for her and teach her how to use it, read the monthly statements, and balance a checkbook. Many banks won't even charge a monthly fee for teens, and the balance can be kept very low. Teach her basic car maintenance, with practice sessions: how to change a tire, how to check the oil and/or change it, how to check the radiator, fill the fluids, and how to keep the car clean. Have her accompany you to the mechanic or quick-lube shop, and then, when she has her license, have her take the car for you. Have her fill the gas tank sometimes.

When you need to do a simple job around the house such as changing a light bulb, ask your teen to do it. When you need to do a little more complicated job like fixing the toilet, painting a room, or trimming the hedges, have him do it with you, showing him how to do it, what tools work best, and so on. Eventually, some of these jobs can be delegated to teens.

I recommend against paying kids to do jobs that are a normal part of household functioning. Your goal is to empower them as team members, responsible in their own ways for the smooth running of the household. For example, if a teenager is responsible for cleaning dishes after supper and doesn't do it, don't do it for him. Using "I" talk instead of accusations, the next day you might say, "When I get up in the morning and there is a big mess in the kitchen, I feel grumpy and angry. I can't make breakfast. If the dishes aren't done at night the food sticks to them and they are even harder to clean later. It starts the day off badly for everybody. Is there some reason you weren't able to do the dishes last night?" Then listen to them *without interruption,* and sincerely try to understand your teen's point of view. Feed back what you hear. You can then ask, in a cooperative tone, "Well, how do you think we can get this done so we can make supper tonight?" Again, do not do it for him, even if it means not having supper, or having something odd that nobody really likes.

Modeling Empowerment with Authority

When my daughter was in high school, she had a best friend who came from a very difficult home. She had been abused early in life, and her mother took hard drugs. This girl, I'll call her Josey, spent a lot of time at our house, and I tried to mother her as best I could. Her envy of my child's good parents and apparently wealthy lifestyle eventually became obsessive, and when my daughter expanded her circle of friends, Josey became enraged and turned on her. At the same time, Josey began taking drugs and got into dark music that my daughter didn't like much. Josey became obsessed with the serial killer, Charles Manson. Her room became almost a shrine to him. Because of her jealousy, her entire junior year of high school became focused on torturing and ostracizing my daughter, who would come home from school in tears from being tripped, slammed, and insulted by Josey.

Josey had a loud mouth and aggressive demeanor, and no one at this small-town, rural high school could stand up to her. My daughter — already a little different because she was from somewhere else, small and quiet, and a vegetarian — had no chance against this girl's onslaughts. I watched her self-esteem plummet as the year went on. We talked a lot, and I tried to help her keep her head up, to ignore Josey, and to concentrate on her own life. But in such a fishbowl environment, it was a hard test for her.

Just before spring break, Josey trapped my daughter in the girls' bathroom at school and beat her up. She came home with a black eye and scratches all over her body, and with a note she had found in her locker containing a disgusting poem, basically threatening her life.

Naturally, the lioness in me wanted to go and beat some sense into that girl and her no-good mother to boot. I called the school officials, who had had to pull Josey off my daughter, and their reply was that it was "just one of those girl fights, it happens all the time." I told them no, it had been part of a months-long systematic harassment of my daughter and if something wasn't done I would get the law involved.

I photocopied the nasty poem and wrote several carefully worded letters, which were not excessively angry, but clear and to the point about the fact that I would go as far as necessary, under the law, to protect my daughter. I enclosed photocopied portions of the school board policy on violence and the poem, and sent these letters to the girl's mother, the school officials, and the county prosecutor. I made it clear to the girl's mother that if her daughter should even touch my daughter again, I would take her to court for stalking, harassment, assault, and whatever else I could think of.

In the meantime, I contacted the county prosecutor and informed him of the situation. I got a clear understanding of what our rights were.

All along, I told my daughter everything. She didn't really want me to get involved at first (at that age, it is embarrassing for parents to step in) but I told her, "I'm really sorry, I'd like to go by your wishes, but since I'm an adult I can see the bigger picture. We've tried ignoring it, going to school officials, and going to her family. Now the situation is dangerous, and it's my job as your mother to step in and set limits if no one else will. We aren't bullies, but we don't let bullies get their way with us either. And I need to teach you how to deal with these situations now."

I enlisted her agreement and support. I knew that the most powerful way to act in a situation like this is with calm perseverance, knowing your rights, and following through on your warnings. Emotionally, I'd have liked to do any number of vengeful things. But we couldn't let ourselves be ruled by emotion or we would have become just like the bullies.

The girl's mother was mortified; she called me and begged me not to go to the authorities. I sympathized, saying it must be very embarrassing for her and I couldn't imagine as a mother she would ever approve of such behavior. I didn't mention what I knew of her own drug use. I let her know that if the behavior did not stop, I would have no choice but to have her daughter put in jail.

Then Josey called, crying, and apologized to me. I calmly explained how disappointed I was in her after I had taken her into my heart and home. I recommended that she get counseling and find out if any "medication" she may be taking could be affecting her personality so badly. Then I said I was sorry, but I could not allow her in our home again. Finally, in my lowest, most powerful voice — with "sinking power" rooted in the earth — I said, "Josey, if you even so much as look at my daughter again, I will have you put in jail faster than you can take a breath. I have spoken to the county prosecutor, and he is ready. Do you understand me?"

She sniffled, "Yes . . . " I said, "Please try to straighten yourself out. You are a good girl with a lot of potential and a lot of life to live. But you have to do it yourself, nobody will do it for you."

My daughter never had any trouble from her again. She was able to see how adults can work through difficult situations without resorting to violence or childishness. It was a great lesson in empowerment for us all.

A Paradigm Shift

An experience I had with my son has always stayed with me, because it so beautifully illustrated Principles One, Two, and Three.

When my son was sixteen, he got his driver's license. We lived in the rural Ozarks, about four hours from St. Louis, Missouri. We were driving home from the store one day, and he said, "Mom, I have a friend who is visiting his parents in St. Louis and I want to go up there and see him. Can I borrow your car?" I immediately reacted, "Absolutely not! No way am I comfortable with that. You just got your license!" His face fell, and he became very quiet. A heavy silence fell over the car, and I felt bad about disappointing him, but I felt I had reacted the way any mother would.

Later that afternoon, he came to my office and said, "Mom, would you please sit down? I need you to hear something." He handed me this letter (printed here with his permission):

Issue: Mom has written books on parenting, motherhood, etc., so why the problems with me? Idea: Everything has basically turned out great, except for a few things, i.e., responsibility, defiance, and laziness. My idea is that a lot of this stems from a lack of trust. In other cultures such as the old time Native American ones, there was a point, usually at puberty, when a boy was initiated into manhood. This was done in many ways, sometimes painful rituals or taking him out on his first hunt or whatever.

These ideas were brought to me by a TV program I was watching where a father was having trouble with his kid, and his way of trusting the kid was to let him use the welder's torch for the first time. I think that by showing this trust it motivates the kid to show responsibility to the parent, thus starting this value within the kid. I know you trust in God to guide me. But I'm not sure you have any faith or trust in me personally.

One incident that supports my idea is, surprisingly, from my stepfather. When he asked me to change his car tires, I realized he was really trusting me with this, and I agreed and eagerly helped him, which is unusual for me. What's more, however worried he was, he never displayed it to me. He didn't even say, "Be careful," which meant a lot to me, and I drove as carefully as I ever have. My point is, well, I don't know really, but it's just an idea, and I hope you will consider it.

As I read this letter, my eyes filled with tears, for so many reasons. To me it was a culmination of my entire life as a mother, to have him sit down and be able to work out his thoughts this way. Then to be able to communicate them so clearly, to stand for something he believed in and to back it up, to evaluate his own behavior, and to tell me how he was feeling and why he was feeling that way.

I had an instant "paradigm shift." This was a way for me to double-check how my principles were guiding my life. I was out there empowering everybody else, but was I really empowering my son? He was right. And that's what I told him. I looked him in the eye and said, "Honey, you are right. I'm wrong. You can take my car to St. Louis. I trust your judgment that you can do this. Let's just work out some ways you could check in to keep my fears at bay."

He burst into tears, threw his arms around me, and said, "You're the best mom in the whole world." He cried from his heart. He came back to me later that night and said, "Mom, you know what? I don't need to go to St. Louis."

That was a great turning point in our lives. It made the rest of his teenage years so much more smooth, and all of my daughter's, who was coming up two years behind him. From then on, I was usually able to remember Principles One, Two, and Three — to relax, slow down, and empower — to release my fear, trust them, and watch them come up to that trust. I tried to empower them, to help them get the skills to do what they wanted to do with their lives, not what I wanted for them. Sometimes, happily, these were one and the same. But sometimes they have been very different, and I never allow our differences of opinion or our different lifestyle choices to come between us. I try not to let my fear run my reaction to whatever they think or do at the moment. Even if their choices are vastly different from mine or from what I wish they would choose, I try to empower them to go as deep as they can, to operate from principles, and fully explore and believe in whatever path they have chosen. In this way, we are all constantly learning from one another and staying close and bonded, no matter what the external circumstances of our lives look like.

I had a similar opportunity with my daughter, but because my son had prepared me well and I was grounded in these principles, I handled it with more ease. One day when she was sixteen, she came in and said those frightening words: "Mom, sit down, I have to tell you something."

After quickly moving through Principles One and Two, I sat down and said, "Okay, shoot."

"I have a boyfriend."

"Oh, that's great, sweetie," I said, "You've been wanting a relationship for a while."

"He's twenty-one."

"Oh."

If you had asked me during her childhood if I would ever allow my sixteen-year-old daughter to go out with a twenty-one-year-old young man I would have said *never in a million years*. But here it was. Principle Three required me to see my daughter for who she was at that moment, and not to take her power from her, or abandon her either. I knew my daughter to be grounded, mature, and sensible. Her description of her new boyfriend didn't set off any alarms. After quite a silence (in which I was thinking, breathing, and relaxing, and she was terrified of my potential reaction) I asked her to tell me why she thought she was old enough to go out with him. I listened carefully as she presented her case, feeding back to her what she said, so she knew I understood, from her point of view, why she should be allowed this.

Finally, I took a deep breath and said, "I trust your judgment. I know I've raised you to make good decisions. But I would like to meet him."

"Sure!" she said, so relieved I hadn't reacted negatively. "I'll bring him to dinner tomorrow, okay?"

The young man came over, was delightful, and was obviously very much a good friend to my daughter. They were together for eight months, split up amicably, and today they are still good friends. Predetermined, hard-set rules never work, because each person, each family, is an ever-changing, ever-growing, ever-learning entity. Look for the opportunities to grow with your kids, to widen your views, and to help them feel they have accomplished their growth themselves. You will never regret it.

Empower Your Teens to Take Healthy Risks

Dr. Lynn Ponton, a veteran University of California child psychiatrist, thinks that parents should rethink their conclusions about adolescence as a hormone-driven, continual state of rebellion. The teen years are a natural time for taking risks as children begin to exercise their choices, test their abilities, and discover their identities. Western cultures have come to believe that adolescence is a time of upheaval. Dr. Ponton says that this has "blurred the lines between normal, exploratory behavior and behavior that is dangerous. . . . When we assume that all risk taking is bad, we fail to recognize both the very real dangers some risks pose, and the tremendous benefits that others can be."

Research shows that 80 percent of adolescents — including urban youth — negotiate the teen years with few problems. Dr. Ponton counsels parents to discuss healthy risk taking with their kids, and teach them how to weigh the dangers and benefits of a particular activity and how to know their own strengths and weaknesses. She says she often sees parents of teens being extreme (see Principle Six) — either too controlling or abandoning their kids to negative risk taking.

Teens need and want adults in their lives to help them evaluate risk and to help direct their behavior in positive ways. Parents can help by providing information about difficult subjects like sex, drugs, and alcohol, and by modeling positive risk-taking behavior, such as speaking in front of an audience, learning to ski even though you may be afraid you'll fall, or participating in other medium-risk sports. You need to educate yourself and your teen, in a safe manner, how to protect yourself, and then take a risk.

Exercise for Principle Three

1. Sit comfortably, close your eyes, and relax each part of your body.
2. Take three deep belly breaths. Inhale silently and, as you exhale repeat, "empower." Feel your feet rooted to the earth, and feel the power of the Tao, the power of creation, flow through your body.

Principle Four
BE YOURSELF

———— ⚜ ————

*I do not need to pretend that I am anyone other than
myself. I do not need to feel insecure about my perceptions.
The self-cultivation that I undertake is to perfect who I am,
not to become someone other than who I am. I pursue the
spiritual because it gives me tremendous satisfaction.*

— Deng Ming-Dao, *365 Tao Daily Meditations*

"**B**eing yourself" sounds so simple. But in order to understand
this principle from a Taoist perspective, we have to try to
understand what makes us who we are, and how much of that is our
personal, conscious choice and how much of it is our cultural,
social, economic, familial, and educational conditioning.

In Tai Chi, you strive to find harmony and oneness with your
own *chi*, or vital energy, through physical movement, breathing, and
meditation. There is a particular flow to it, a pattern that arises
spontaneously from your own internal energy, linked with the
Universal Mind or the Tao. A great many practices can help you get
in touch with who you really are, beyond your ideas, philosophies,
appearance, moods, or stages.

For some, sitting meditation is the best way to do this. Before I
had my children, I did several hours of sitting meditation a day for
about four years. I was lucky to be working for a spiritual-social service mission that allowed me to do this, and to have the right diet

and yoga postures to keep me in balance. I am so grateful for that time. I realize very few people these days have the luxury to take that much time to "find themselves," to get rooted in their spiritual being before becoming a parent — yet an important part of the reason for this book is to show that much of what I learned and practice in my everyday life I learned directly *from my children.* They have been my best teachers.

My previous meditation experience taught me about Principles One and Two, and allowed me to see, beforehand, the potential of these two new child-teachers that came into my life. I saw that if I approached parenthood with this attitude, I wouldn't be "losing myself" in the mundane world, rather, I would continue to find myself with my children's help. They would be a mirror for me, and if I could be humble enough to accept what I saw there even when it was not what I wished it to be, there would be a tremendous amount I could learn. I could see where various kinds of conditioning — even my spiritual teachings — created prejudices and preconceived notions. I could see the places where my walk didn't match my talk, where my own childhood and familial patterning ran my behavior, and I could find other, more productive choices. My children gleefully blew apart my self-absorption, ego, and attachments. They were masters at deconstructing the walls around my true Self, if I would only let them.

Especially in their early lives, children are masters of being wholly themselves, and they relate to their parents in a way that embodies the completely natural relationship between the individual soul and God. My spiritual teacher in India, P.R. Sarkar, often pointed this out. He would say (my paraphrasing), "When a child wants his mother to hold him, she can give him toy after toy, but he throws them aside, for he is one-pointed in his goal — to have his mother's love and attention. In the same way, a spiritual aspirant accepts no substitute for oneness with the Creator."

I learned from my children what true devotion is. I had the opportunity to learn all about attachment and nonattachment, and how radically different the true meaning of these concepts is from what I had thought about them in the quiet of my single-minded meditation. For with children comes great attachment, and you can see how important that is: countless studies have proven that it is virtually essential for life. Without attachment, infants can and often do die. I discovered as a parent that the aim of spirituality was not to continually detach from everything, but rather to expand your circle of attachment so that it gradually becomes so wide it encompasses all of the universe. This is what leads to true devotion to God — not giving up or pushing away the things and people we love.

And then, just when this idea takes root, you have to learn to let your children go on to their own lives and destinies. You have to let loved ones go to their death. If during this process you are not aware of your true self — a unique individual, and yet connected to the far greater whole of creation — you get caught up in the drama of the process, attached to the results rather than the core, and you lose track of who you are.

Being yourself means being genuinely what and who you are at this moment. As I said before, children have a finely tuned radar for hypocrisy. You can try to say one thing and be another, but eventually you won't get away with it. You can try to make your children be what you are not, but the result can be disastrous. You can try to pretend you are incapable of being wrong, you have no faults, and are always in charge, but in the end you will be exposed.

So the best thing is just to be who you are, and move toward who you want to be every day with integrity and honesty. In Taoism, being yourself means to be who you truly are, the way a tree is a tree and does not strive to be anything else. Our true nature can be described by the metaphor of "the uncarved block" — the being that is truly you, not enhanced, toned down, carved into something more "acceptable" or normal.

The Simplicity of the Uncarved Block

Tai Chi teacher Chungliang Al Huang, in his book *Embrace Tiger, Return to Mountain,* gives us good words to ponder:

> There are many basic concepts in Tao that emerge in Tai Chi when you practice. One is the word *pu,* which means the original material, before it is trimmed and modified, fixed and polished. Sometimes we translate it as "uncarved

block." It's the raw material before it is carved into artistic form, the essence that exists before you change it. Learn the grain of the wood before you carve it. *Pu* is the basic substance of the real you, before it's manicured or painted over. Expose your own basic essence before you clutter it up. Don't let all the external things blind you so that you lose the uncarved block within.

A wonderful book that explores this subject with humor and whimsy is *The Tao of Pooh* by Benjamin Hoff.

The simplest person, if he or she lives in that simplicity comfortably, without guile or apology, is respected by all. You don't need complicated teachings or practices. If you can find who you are and be yourself, your children will naturally love and respect you regardless of your education, your job, your "standing" on the illusory scale of wealth, or your race and class. If you are truly yourself with dignity, you will be respected, whether you are rich, poor, or in between.

Being yourself also means you allow others to be themselves. As it says in *Embrace Tiger, Return to Mountain,*

> When you look at nature, everything has its own motion: the tree and the rock and the running water — they somehow tie together without making a point to fit. When you watch the waves coming over the rocks, you see that the wave has wave-nature, the rock has rock-nature. They do not violate each other's nature.

You learn to allow your children to be who they are — not mere reflections of you or who you wish you were. You are not afraid to share yourself and your history with your children, and show them what you have learned and what you still want to learn. You are not afraid to be wrong and apologize and to talk about the times when you have veered off course. Inside, you have a determination to constantly learn and grow, and you know you learn a great deal from adversity and mistakes. When you can truly be yourself all the time, you allow your children to learn right along with you.

THE OPPOSITE

In my parents' day, anything that might have exposed a parent as vulnerable or not perfect was hidden away. So there was a duplicitous quality to their parenting. For example, many of them were closet alcoholics who were appalled when their children experimented with drugs.

The rebellion, when it came, was great. The hypocrisy of our parents' lifestyle was suddenly repugnant to a whole generation of teenagers, who stood up together and said, "No!" — in effect, as the children's story goes, "The Emperor has no clothes!" All we really wanted was for our parents to be themselves. But we didn't realize that was nearly impossible for most of them, for they had been conditioned — their minds had been scripted — in an entirely different world, where there was only one definition of "normal." With the explosion of worldwide communications media, we discovered that there were many definitions, and that some of them were much healthier and more integrated than what we had been brought up with, and some came from age-old cultures that were about to be wiped off the earth forever by the materialism of our culture. We felt an urgency to learn how to find and be our true selves, and to apply that knowledge to our western cultures, which seemed riddled with fake values, with false faces, and no substance.

What Is "Normal" Anyway?

Not long ago, in most communities, there was only one way to be "normal," to fit in and conform. There is a Chinese story about a woman who always cut off the end of a ham, before she cooked it in her oven. Her daughter asked her why she did it, and she replied, "I don't know. My mother always did it that way." When they asked the grandmother, she said, "I don't know. My mother always did it that way." Finally, they asked Great-Grandmother. "I did it that way," she said, "because otherwise it wouldn't fit in my little pot."

When I was a young housewife, I folded the sheets precisely the way my mother had taught me, and got upset when my husband didn't fold them "right." Finally I realized how silly it was; there was no real reason for folding them that way, but my mother, and probably her mother, made it seem as if it had to be done in just this way. To this day, when I fold my sheets however they happen to fold in that moment and stuff them in the closet so I can go do something else, something more interesting, I smile to myself, and I see my ancestors in my mind, shaking their collective heads, arms folded in consternation.

There is no such thing as some kind of "normal" behavior for any group of people that doesn't change over the years. It's futile to try to be normal. It's much more fun and fulfilling to be ourselves.

Share Your Journey

Being oneself is, obviously, not being a clone of one's parents, friends, teachers, television personalities, or anyone else. It's not conforming to anything. It isn't requiring your children to fit into some preconceived notion of what children "at that age," or in your neighborhood — or of your race or family history — should be.

Have the courage to find and be who you truly are, and to share yourself and your journey with your children. That doesn't mean you don't protect them from some parts of the adult world that may frighten or harmfully influence them. For example, it is not wise for parents to fight with each other in front of their children. The children don't understand the complicated dynamics of marital relationships, and if you find yourselves yelling at one another, you should work with each other (or go to therapy if necessary) to find other, healthier ways to communicate — certainly for yourselves, but also to model for your children how to work through problems and differences in a healthy way. So don't fight in front of the kids — but don't, also, pretend that all is well if it isn't.

If you are having difficulty communicating, you can explain to your children that there are some things that are just between Mom and Dad. You can reassure them of their safety and of your love for them. That is enough to keep it real without lying to them, scaring them, or involving them in problems and responsibilities that are not theirs. And, for goodness sake, make sure they understand that your problems are not their fault.

BEING YOURSELF

All too often when we become parents, we think we need to play a role, and often the role we try to fulfill isn't synchronized with our own values and principles, and isn't updated to the culture we live in now.

Being yourself means being available to your loved ones in whatever condition you happen to be — not hiding away when you are hurting or imperfect, and then showing yourself only at your best, pretending you never have those "human" moments of vulnerability, mistakes, wrongdoing, and regret. It entails working to make your inner and outer life fully integrated with each other, so your life is a relatively "open book." This requires a commitment to honesty, which is sometimes very difficult. Temptations to lie, either overtly or by withholding, are constant these days. My teacher once said, "In ancient India, when you found someone lying, you were surprised and shocked. These days, when you find someone who is really honest you are surprised and shocked." But you can't expect honesty and integrity from your kids if you aren't that way yourself.

Sometimes we get into a bind because we have a lot of "shoulds" controlling our lives that may not match our deepest needs and wants at all. So we spend important moments of our lives doing things we think we *should* do or acting the way we think we *should* act, or judging ourselves against someone else's standards. We forego our deepest needs; we silence ourselves through these judgments and thus convey to our children that it's not okay to be who you are and, far worse, that you will *never* meet the standards set for you.

Personal Mission Statements

A good way to start checking in with yourself about how integrated you are is to craft a "personal mission statement." I recommend reading Steven Covey's book, *The Seven Habits of Highly*

Effective People, if you want to explore it further. I also recommend Marc Allen's book *A Visionary Life,* which has a very easy, under-standable set of "keys" to use in defining and creating the life you want. I have also included here some good exercises to help you get started if you so desire.

In order to identify your personal mission, you need to find out what it is you really want your life to be about — not just what you want to accomplish, but who you want to be, and what you want to leave as a legacy, and, if you are not already expressing those qual-ities as much as you want to, how to begin finding ways to do so. Sometimes this means big shifts in lifestyle: going back to school, changing jobs, simplifying your life, studying the teachings of the great people you admire, or changing the kind of people you asso-ciate with, the look of your home, your financial plan, and so on.

Principles, Practices, and Paradigms

Three concepts influence our effectiveness in our families. The first is the most important, and that's the concept of *principles.* Principles should and actually *do* guide everything in the universe. Principles are true to all human beings all over the world. They are unchanging, unarguable, and self-evident. They are those things that all of us know in our hearts are true. Principles are not inter-nal as we may think; they are actually external to us. We can fail to live up to our principles, but the principles themselves remain, for-ever unchangeable.

Principles may be in harmony with our values, but they may not be the same as our values. Values change — they are what we like from time to time. But principles are true and unchanging. Gravity is a good example: You may not believe in gravity, you may not understand gravity, you may not like gravity, but if you jump off a building, you will experience gravity. There is no way you can change that. We have to go to great lengths to escape its pull, but when doing so we don't change the principle of gravity. Principles are natural laws that involve cause and effect. They are long term. What you do today because of your principles influences you and your family and the people around you for generations to come.

Principles are true for all religions. We think that principles would be different in two very different sets of philosophical views, but they're not. There is a basic agreement in every culture about principles such as integrity, kindness, and honesty — we all know they are essential for a healthy society.

Practices, on the other hand, change. Practices are the things we do that change with changing times. We may do something differently because of new knowledge. For example, a long time ago they gave babies opium when they cried. Now that would be considered child abuse. Obviously that is not a principle, it's a practice. In the midst of complexity we always seek security in practices, so it is very easy to teach practices. A nurse mechanically rubbing a baby in a nursery is an example of practice without principle. You may get short-term value from practices; you may get limited benefits. Principles, however, give you long-term benefits — on every level — that never end. President Thomas Jefferson's words are worth reflecting upon:

> In matters of style, swim with the current. In matters of principle, stand like a rock.

A *paradigm* is a way of seeing things; it's the picture we have in our minds of how our universe works. It's our best guess at how things are, our best assumptions about how things work, where people are coming from, and what is true.

Paradigms, though, may be based on inaccurate information. Let's say I invite you to my house in Colorado, and I mistakenly give you a map with a misprint — it says "Colorado" at the top, but it's actually a map of Illinois. You get in your car and you get lost because you do not have an accurate map. That's what a paradigm is: it is our map of the territory. But *the map is not the territory.* So our paradigms are subject to updating. This is where we try to cultivate teachability or humility, the frame of mind where you *think* you know what's right, but you're always open to new information.

For the longest time, we thought that babies couldn't see at all when they were born, much less see in utero, so we behaved accordingly. Then suddenly — seemingly overnight — we discovered they *can* see and actually they can see quite clearly. It shifted our paradigm of what the infant's reality is — and that shift continues to happen over and over again.

As soon as we think we know all about an infant's experience — what the world looks and feels like to them — we discover they know and experience more than we thought. At one point we also thought babies couldn't feel until a certain age — that they didn't feel pain! That paradigm was very convenient for adults, but it wasn't true.

We correct our paradigms by listening — to other people and to information that comes to us when we think deeply about what our paradigms are — and by trying to adjust them to what is real. We use our principles as a guide for doing that.

A Mission in Life

One of the most useful projects I have undertaken is to write a personal mission statement for my life — something broader than the parenting mission statement we looked at in the beginning of this book. I wrote a personal mission statement several years ago, and every year on the first of January, I review my statement and make changes to bring it into alignment with what I understand to be my chief purposes. I also review the past year, and evaluate what I did and how I expressed my stated mission in my everyday life. If there is an area that is being neglected, I try to understand why and figure out how I might address that aspect in the coming year.

My personal mission statement comprises my guiding principles. It is a statement, in my own words, about how I wish to be in every area of my life. Throughout the year, as I plan all my activities and goals, I review this statement and ask myself, "Does this project, plan, or goal resonate with my mission in life?"

You probably already have an overall sense of purpose about being a good person, serving humanity, maybe even realizing God, and so on. Breaking that general purpose down into specific behaviors can be very helpful — you will find yourself doing more thinking, less reacting. We are often pressured, cajoled, manipulated, and maneuvered into doing countless things that do not necessarily move us any closer to our goals, and that may, in fact, pull us away from our fundamental principles. Stating these principles can be the first step toward gaining the inner strength and courage to be what we really, truly want to be, deep down in our souls.

Your "Flight Plan"

I read Michael Crichton's techno-thriller *Airframe*, and it made me think about my favorite analogy about mission statements: the flight plan. Most of the time a commercial aircraft is off course, but using feedback systems it corrects its course and reaches its destination, usually on time. In much the same way, a personal mission statement serves as a flight plan. It tells you where you want to go. It can provide the system through which you can receive feedback to keep you on purpose in spite of the many events and decisions that may cause you to veer off your original plotted route.

In thinking about the analogy of a flight plan, I wondered what would happen if two pilots with different flight plans tried to fly the same plane? The plane would probably get off the ground easily, but as the pilots settled in for the trip, power struggles would erupt as each tried to steer the plane according to his or her own flight plan. Unless some kind of synergy could develop, there would be a crash.

In addition to writing a personal mission statement, many people find creating a mission statement with their partner is an exciting and fulfilling thing to do. Questions you never thought of before will come to you as you clarify what is deeply important to you both. In most partnerships, a shared mission can be arrived at joyfully.

CREATING YOUR PERSONAL MISSION STATEMENT

If you would like to get started with this and not take too much time, I suggest you do the short version of the following exercise.

When you have finished, write a paragraph, a sentence, or even a few key words that will comprise your personal mission statement. As you continue to read, you may come up with new ideas.

If you prefer to skip these exercises, move on through the rest of the book, starting with "Parenting with Principle Four," and come back to these exercises later if you feel they would be helpful.

A suggestion: Answer the questions in the present tense, stating your answer as if you had already attained your mission. Say, for example, "I am a reliable and trustworthy friend," rather than, "I would like to be reliable and trustworthy in my friendships."

Short Version

Make a list of all the roles you play in life. For example: spouse, parent, employee, friend, co-worker, teacher, student, family member, and so on. For each of these roles write one short sentence, starting with "I am ...", that describes your ideal self in that role. You will then have several sentences you can combine into a single paragraph for your personal mission statement.

When you have finished your statement, you may want to frame it and put it where you can read it for inspiration. Whenever you plan your year, your month, your week, or your day, review your statement first to be sure all your activities contribute to your personal mission in life. When you have stated concretely what is most important to you, it is a lot easier to say "no" to things that are extraneous to your mission.

It is important, when doing these exercises, to be completely honest with yourself. You may have a list of qualities in your head that someone else put there — what you are "supposed to" feel, think, and do. But this mission statement will be of no value to you if you do not write it in your own words, from your own heart, reflecting who you are and what you want. If "selfless service to humanity" is a life purpose for you, how can you express that in words that make sense to you right now? What are you doing right now that reflects this purpose? In what specific ways can you express this purpose in your behavior toward those who are closest to you? If you are not expressing this purpose, why not? In some cases, you may discover that you have been given a purpose by someone else and you have never really made it your own. This is a time to re-evaluate those preprogrammed ideas and discard what doesn't resonate deeply with you right now.

Longer Version

To work a little more deeply with this exercise, first complete the short version, so you have a list of statements for each role you play in your life. Next, choose ten words that you feel represent meaningful guidelines and values in your life; make them ten words you can't live without. Look over the list of words that follows — it might help when searching for the right word to express your values:

to accept	to enjoy	serenity
to energize	to design	peace
to support	to participate	clarity
to enhance	to achieve	love
to challenge	to listen	humor
to create	to empower	joy
to understand	to help	trust
to heal	to relate	respect
to share	to enlighten	regard
to love	to communicate	empathy
to master	understanding	surrender
to inspire	inspiration	acceptance
to enable	compassion	friendliness
to seek	unity	unselfishness
to synthesize	responsibility	kindness
to produce	humility	honesty
to serve	spirituality	integrity
to liberate	creativity	

Now write a statement for each word that is active, present tense, specific, and reflects how you wish to be. For example: "I use my creative talents to inspire others by teaching painting classes."

Revise and rework these statements until they resonate with your spirit. This process may take a long time. You may go back to it again and again over a long period of time before it feels just right to you.

An Example of a Personal Mission Statement

I'll share my own mission statement exercise with you to show you what I came up with. Remember, yours may look very different. Allow yourself plenty of creative freedom.

My Life Roles

Spiritual Being:

I am at all times connected to my Creator and surrendered to God's plan for me. I align myself as perfectly as possible with my spiritual being and express God's love in my thoughts, words, and actions.

Mother:

I offer my children unconditional love and help them realize their dreams in every way I can.

Friend:

I am there for my friends when they need me. I keep their confidences. I encourage them to be all they can and wish to be. I treat them with kindness and respect. I remember their birthdays.

Artist / Writer:

My art brings beauty and spirituality into the lives of those who see it. Through my art and writing, I blend and unify seeming opposites to express universal truths and help people find and be who they want to be.

Family Member:

I experience being a member of my family, both of origin and chosen, as a contributive, honest, caring, loving, and supportive person. Whenever a member of my family needs me, I try as hard as I can to provide or be whatever they need, from a place of limitless love, acceptance, and understanding.

From these statements of my life roles, and with a list of other values that are important to me, I was able to come up with my own statement:

My Personal Mission Statement

My mission in life is to create a loving, healthy, interdependent extended family that celebrates, encourages, supports, and uplifts everyone within and surrounding it, and to share the joy it brings me with others through my work.

PARENTING WITH PRINCIPLE FOUR

Using this principle of being yourself in your everyday parenting comes naturally when you have worked on yourself. Tai Chi teacher Chungliang Al Huang summed up nicely the message we want to get across to our kids:

What you need is an acceptance of yourself as you are. You are like a seed. You don't know what you're going to be when spring comes — maybe a chrysanthemum, or an orchid, or maybe just a plain dandelion. . . . *Be* with the process and *enjoy* it.

When we look at the analogy of flowering, we remember that flowers don't bloom until near the end of the plant's life cycle. This is especially pertinent these days, when we live so much longer than our ancestors did, when people have several careers and maybe even several marriages. Blooming, going dormant, and blooming again is a realistic paradigm for how our children's lives and our lives are likely to be. It is our job to assure our children that they have many choices and that they never have to settle on just one thing forever. Rather than pushing them into what we want for them, we help and support them as they try out many things and go with what brings them joy.

Principle Four in Pregnancy

Pregnancy, birth, and infancy are periods when you are required to make many decisions; sometimes it can be overwhelming. You get so much advice and input from relatives, friends, books, and experts that you can lose track of what your inner guidance is trying to tell you. Using Principles One and Two can help you relax and slow down, and firmly rooting yourself in Principle Three can empower you with the "sinking power" you need to communicate with others. Principle Four requires that you act in accordance with your own deeply held values.

Only you can decide, according to what feels best to you, whether you give birth at home or in the hospital, choose to immunize or not, breast-feed or not, whether your children wear natural fibers or not, whether or not you choose day care, how to discipline and communicate with an older child, and so on. Make your decisions from a deep inner place that makes you feel like a good parent, instead of simply going with the current cultural flow.

Over and over again, it has been shown that the current cultural flow is often *wrong*. At one time it was common and accepted to give babies opium to keep them quiet. At one time, mothers were told to wear masks and not to breathe on their babies or breast-feed them for fear of "contaminating" them. At one time, parents were told not to respond to infants' cries for fear of "spoiling" them. At one time, it was widely believed that babies didn't feel pain and that they could not see or hear in the womb or for the first weeks of life after birth. Take the experts with a grain of salt, and listen to your own heart about what is right for you and your family. Refrain from judging other parents and their decisions for the same reasons; you are not in their shoes.

Principle Four with Young Children

Constant praise unconnected to behavior can inflate children's egos so that they get a distorted picture of themselves and become devastated by mistakes, flaws, and being just "one of the team." A child who is praised too much in a superficial way cannot handle being "a simple dandelion," even if that is what he is meant to be. Self-esteem boosters are more effective when connected with behavior. For example:

- "I love the colors you chose for that drawing. They're so vibrant, just like you!"
- "Thanks for doing the dishes without being asked. You really know how to be a team player."
- "Good grades on your report card! You must have really worked for those. Congratulations. I knew you had it in you."
- "The teacher told me know nicely you shared the toys today. That makes me feel so happy. You're very considerate." (You may have to define "considerate" — a great opportunity to continue the conversation and teach a new word.)

In this way, you show your children that good values and character traits are demonstrated by behavior and must be consciously worked at. In the same way, incorporating reasoning into the discipline process can also get the point across. For example:

- "I felt disappointed when you hit Jason. I know inside you are a kind person, and hitting isn't kind. What other ways do you think you could use to express your angry feelings?"
- "I'm so happy you got a B in math; I know that subject has been hard for you. What about this C in history? What do you think is the problem?"
- "Doing chores around the house is part of us being a close family. What do you need to help you do your share more often?"

When a child misbehaves it is usually because he or she has a need that isn't being met, and often the child can't articulate that need. We need to become very astute detectives and observe them for a while to see if we can figure out what the need might be. We could then ask them something like this: "Have you been feeling as close to the family as you would like lately?" or, "Is your love bucket getting low? Need a hug?"

If your child answers with denial, continue feeding back what you *think* it may be:

- "You haven't been doing your chores, so I just thought maybe you didn't feel as close to everybody as you want."
- "Your grades have dropped, so I thought maybe you have some stress you'd like to talk about."
- "You've been acting very unhappy, so I thought maybe some extra attention might help."

Usually the child will then open up and try to tell you what is going on. Offering a massage, putting your arm around your child, or holding his or her hand can help sometimes. Again, you need to stay focused on the child's need, and feed back what you think you're hearing without judgment. Don't force the child to talk; give him time to come to you when he feels safe and *wants* to. You can say, "If you want to talk about *anything*, I am here to listen."

Sometimes sharing your history, in small doses, can help. Let your child know you had similar experiences and feelings at his or her age, if it is true. It can be a relief for your child, as long as you don't go on and on or suggest that you know exactly how they feel, because you do not. Show a genuine curiosity about your children's feelings and experiences. If they don't expect a lecture or judgment, they will open up to you. Never interrupt them! Sometimes kids need to talk for a long time. You don't need to solve their problems. Let them solve their own. You could give a couple of suggestions, emphasizing they're only suggestions, and always end with, "I have faith in your good judgment and ability to solve problems. If you need any help or just want to talk it through, I'm here."

This is not an easy lesson for parents to learn. You'll find yourself blowing it again and again. But you can always go back to your child and say, "When we talked I really blew it. I jumped in with a boring lecture about my own life instead of listening to you. I hope you'll give me another chance."

It may not be at that moment, but usually your child will give you another chance to just listen, skillfully, without telling her your autobiography or trying to solve her problems unless she asks you to. Even then, use questions to try to get her to come to the solution or possible solutions herself, so she feels empowered. When it works, you can say, "Great job! I knew you could do it!" instead of, "I told you so."

To help your child find herself, listen and observe. Give her feedback about what you see in terms of what she is good at, what seems to make her feel happy, what traits seem to come naturally. In this way, you help her build a solid sense of self from the beginning, so that she is not afraid to follow her own drummer, and rarely falls into the self-esteem destroying trap of comparing herself with others. Opportunities for building self-esteem abound. For example, when your child expresses admiration for someone, you can ask her, curiously, "What is it about her you admire the most?" Questions like these help the child clarify in her own mind what her opinions, desires, goals, and wishes may be.

Principle Four with Teens

An important part of growing up is to try on different personas, and often parents react to these experiments with great dismay or ultimatums, or by clamping down with rules and regulations, which only draws out the process and creates distance between you and your child. He wants to know that no matter what his choices are, you will love and support him. Try to remember that external phases always pass, and don't react too strongly to choices you may not like. My son went through what we all now jokingly call his "head-banger" phase, when he listened to heavy metal music, wore ghastly T-shirts, and expressed admiration for rock groups that I considered very close to evil. I let him know candidly what my opinions and preferences were, but I didn't stop him from exploring this side of himself. Part of what made this easy for me was that I remembered blasting Cream and Janis Joplin in my mother's house when I was that age! I bought him headphones so we wouldn't all be subjected to the music he chose.

In light moments, I'd lie on his bed, let him play the music, and ask him about the lyrics:

Me: "Did he just say 'kill the bitch your mother'?"
My son (sheepishly): "Yeah. It's just a song, Mom."
Me: "You don't really believe in that do you?"
My son: "*Mom!* It's just a song! Jeez."
Me (smiling): "Okay. What*ever!* Just wondered if I should hide the garden tools."

Making light of it without ridiculing his choices helped him move through these phases. Knowing he'd get no big reaction from his parents meant there was no fuel for the fire, so to speak. Sometimes, I would take an opportunity to go deeper, and give an opinion:

"It's just my opinion, but it seems to me that if we feed our bodies healthy food, and they grow strong, that the same thing would apply to our minds. I wonder what constantly hearing stuff like 'kill the bitch your mother' does to your spirit." I'd leave it at that. Food for thought, but no ultimatums. Again, you want to reinforce your belief in your children, and let them know you respect them and believe in their ability to judge and discriminate for themselves. Whether they outwardly show it or not, they will try to live up to your high opinion of them and your belief in them. When you constantly censor and make choices for your children, you send the message that you don't believe in them, you don't think they have been raised with good judgment. What does that say about you?

My son basically blew off his first two years at college. He partied and became a rather nefarious character in his dorm. I was paying for his education, so it took a great deal of patience and tongue holding to get through these years without ultimatums and other distancing tactics. Though I let him know that his choices could affect his future, I didn't step in with threats. I let him make his own mistakes and learn. Later, when he had to spend almost two extra years in college and pay for them himself, and when he was refused admission to the journalism department because of his low grade-point average, he realized what he had done. He dug in, continued to apply to the journalism school, brought up his grades, learned good study skills, and ended up with two degrees and a love for learning.

Throughout this period, I encouraged him to keep going, to have faith he was being guided by a higher power, to take risks to get where he wanted to be, and not to take "no" for an answer. I kept giving him the big picture and reminded him that life is long, and he would want to have access to many choices along the way. I shared examples of people who had combined writing, teaching, traveling, and other things in their careers.

Encouraging Innate Talents

My kids sometimes wished they knew what they wanted to do from childhood, like some of their peers. But ultimately they are happy that they have a lot of options, and some inborn talents they can use in any occupation they choose. As they were growing up, I always looked for opportunities to point these out and show them that not everyone had their talents.

My daughter showed a proclivity for art from the time she could crawl, so I fed that by giving her art supplies, displaying her work, and telling her about several of our ancestors who were artists. As she got older, I'd tell her stories about things she didn't remember, such as when, at the age of two, she made an amazing sculpture out of torn up paper. I carefully saved her artwork and treated it with respect. Pieces I particularly liked were mounted, framed, and hung on the wall. I would ask her to critique my art pieces, to help me solve problems I encountered, and we would talk about color, design, balance, and so on.

My son taught himself to read at age two, and loved stories. I provided him with lots of children's books and blank books for him to write his own stories in. In the beginning, before he was old enough to write, he dictated them to me. When he wrote a story or a homework piece, I pointed out where it was very good from a writer's standpoint, and why.

I always tried to give both my children a lot of good feedback and adult-level respect for what they produced. I showed them how these talents came fairly easily to them, and so might be clues as to what they might do and be as grown-ups, even if it was outside their "regular" careers. Again, I showed them a range of options, choices, possibilities.

This doesn't mean I didn't encourage and display my son's artwork or give my daughter good feedback about her writing. But I noticed that the feedback "took" when it was on target with each child's natural talent.

Physical appearance and physical ability are other make-or-break self-worth issues for kids of all ages. My daughter has always been very petite, and it's been an issue she has had to deal with. Using questions, I tried to help her see that being different did not make her "less than" anybody. I told her she was beautiful, always adding "inside and out," and emphasized that beauty comes in all shapes and sizes. The most beautiful people we knew personally were beautiful inside and it radiated from them and made them beautiful outside, too.

During her teen years, we talked about the way advertisers try to make you feel less than others so you will buy their product to feel better about yourself. She wrote a paper once about the beauty industry, discovering through her research how it capitalizes on people's lack of self-esteem and helps create problems like anorexia and bulimia as well as drug and sexual addiction. She fought back in these ways, building her own sense of self-worth by using her mind rather than concentrating solely on her body.

With her attitude and spirit, she *is* a beautiful young woman. When she was eighteen, I shared with her that my illness really made me feel anything but beautiful. Her feedback was something I'll never forget. She said, "Mom, you are so beautiful. Even when you feel very sick, your courage shines out and makes you really attractive." I knew at that point I must have done something right in bringing her up.

This morning — after letting my twenty-two-year-old son borrow my car for an entire day and night — he called me from work. He thanked me and said that he drove very carefully because he knows how important it is to me.

"You know Mom," he said, "I think I got my generosity from you. That is such an important quality for me. I don't even like to be *around* people who aren't generous — you've taught me to be that way by how you are." It was my turn to soak it in!

Exercise for Principle Four

1. Sit comfortably, close your eyes, and relax each part of your body.
2. Take four deep belly breaths. As you inhale repeat, "be" and as you exhale repeat, "yourself."

Principle Five
BE RESPONSIVE

❧

*In adulthood we often see responsibility as something
dreadful. Why should we dig the ground when the
weather is disagreeable? We see activities only as
obligations, and we strain against our fate. But there is a
joy to working in harmony with the proper time. When
we do things at just the right occasion and those efforts
bear fruit later, the gratification is tremendous.*

— Deng Ming-Dao, *365 Tao Daily Meditations*

This principle follows closely on the heels of Principle Four. It
deepens our awareness of how to respond rather than react
to our children. It helps us learn how to accept and deal with our
responsibility to them throughout our lives, for being responsive
also includes responsibility.

In Tai Chi, being responsive is the practice of learning to
become sensitive to others without becoming enmeshed with them.
It cultivates a balanced awareness of our surroundings and of the
people we interact with. We are often so loaded with preconceived
notions, family scripting, and societal conditioning from the popular media or our social circle that it is difficult to approach anything
new without filtering the new through the old.

The Tai Chi student's most important work is to learn to be
aware of the flow of *chi* and to work with it as he or she does the

exercises and movements of the martial art, including sparring with partners or "opponents." In the same way, we as parents are given endless opportunities to practice awareness about our children's energy, their own individual way of being — what comes *with* them — so that when we respond to them we are responding to them uniquely, not just as "my kid." As Tai Chi master Huai-Nan-Tzu says,

> When you master the outward by means of the inward, all affairs are unspoiled. If you can attain this within, your internal organs are peaceful and your thoughts are calm; your muscles are strong, your eyes and ears are alert and clear. You have accurate perceptions and understanding, you are firm and strong without snapping.

This principle also relates to how we teach our children to respond to circumstances and people, and how we model and teach responsibility.

THE OPPOSITE

A lack of responsiveness comes in many forms, mostly unintentional. When you see an irresponsible, disrespectful child, you can look to the parents and the home environment where the child is constantly modeled adult interactions. Often the child is mirroring something going on in the home that is not apparent to the outside world, or even spoken of in the home itself.

Sometimes a particularly sensitive child will unconsciously take on the parents' problems. Often, when a child goes from being friendly, inquisitive, radiant, and loving to closed down, irresponsible, and difficult, he may be acting out the parents' unspoken problems. That is why, when a child is taken in for therapy, many therapists want to see the whole family. The therapist knows the child is probably feeling the heavy weight of "something wrong" and is justifiably angry about having to bear the brunt of unspoken problems.

Some irresponsible parents may neglect their children, but it goes deeper than that. Setting up an environment of win-lose, wherein the parent is always right, and where blaming and help-lessness prevail prevents us from using this principle in any way. When there is no mutual respect, boundaries cannot be set and negotiated as a child grows older. There is confusion about who is the child and who is the parent. If anger and emotional and physi-cal reactions are the only feedback a child receives from his parents, the child grows up with little self-motivation and less and less respect for the parents. As a teenager, the tables may turn. The par-ents become afraid of their children's anger and cave in to his every demand. Eventually the child looks for other people with whom to have reactive relationships.

So often this child never really grows up; in his adult relation-ships he is either the controller or the one being controlled, by anger and reaction. The child never learns to be sensitive to other people — their feelings, their histories, or what they need. He becomes self-centered, and wants the world to revolve around him and his — by this time — endless need for validation from others.

Responsibility is self-management and sensitivity to the needs of others. So it follows that it requires empowerment (Principle Three). A person who is disempowered cannot think of others, and cannot even manage his own choices. His *chi* has been disrupted and siphoned off, so to speak, by the disempowering environment in which he grows. Building that back up as an adult is a difficult and usually lifelong process.

If you grew up in a home where you were either neglected or constantly on the losing end of a win-lose situation, you will be try-ing to build the responsiveness and responsibility of Principle Five in yourself at the same time that you try to maintain it in your house-hold — not an easy task by any means, but one you can handle.

CHOOSING TO BE RESPONSIVE

You can make the choice to turn your family dynamic toward health and spirituality. It's up to you. Look forward to it as a tremendous challenge and opportunity, as another important aspect of the path of parenting, if you choose to see it that way. The foundation you lay now, even though you may slip back sometimes, will only grow stronger in the future. And just think: By the time you are a grandparent, this will all come much more naturally to you, so you can help your kids even more, and your grandchildren's foundation in these principles will be taken for granted by them. When you leave this earth, it will be with the knowledge that through your struggle, you have changed *generations* of unhealthy, unskillful ways of being and have affected all the people that come within the circle of influence of your children, your grandchildren, and future progeny. That is quite a legacy.

The Key is Listening

The keystone of Principle Five is learning how to listen. As Steven Covey says, "Seek first to understand, then to be understood." This is difficult if, as many of us, you did not grow up with a model for effective listening. Most of the time, many of us just wait for the other person to finish talking so we can say what is on our own minds. The other person does the same, so conversations can be unsatisfying, and they may escalate into arguments because nobody is listening.

Listening involves all your senses, physical and spiritual. It means attending to the other person with your whole being, and responding to what she says genuinely and curiously. In order to feel heard, people need gentle eye contact (not glaring or staring). Turn off the television or other distractions; perhaps go into a room where just the two of you can talk. Pay close attention to the other person's cues — whether it's your spouse, a friend, a parent, an employee, or your child. Notice their body language; downcast eyes or nervous gestures or a posture of defense often indicate shame, anger, or distrust. Don't expect children to meet your eye contact; it is too charged with power for them, and often they must look away. I remember all too well the parental chant of the fifties and sixties: "Look at me when I'm talking to you!" It was only said when the parent was lecturing or yelling at the child, so naturally eye contact became connected with fear, disempowerment, and shame.

Go back to Principles One and Two: relax and slow down. It's okay if the person talking to you is angry or distressed — it doesn't mean you have to feel that way too. Remember Principle Three, as well. When you're empowered, you want to understand how they feel and why, even if you or your words or actions may be the source of their distress.

This doesn't only apply to distressing situations. Cues will tell you the person really wants to be heard. Perhaps they had a great achievement or good news to share. Still, the need to be listened to is deep, and attending to that need is one of the greatest gifts you can give to another person.

Learning how to listen also involves learning how to feed back what you are hearing. The wrong way to do this is by parroting exactly what the person says. Everyone knows when a "technique" is being used on them, and almost everyone resents it. Your aim is to genuinely understand what that person is telling you, so you say things like, "So it sounds like what you're saying is . . ." and finish the sentence in your own words. They may say, "No! Not at all . . . " and go on to try to make themselves clear.

One of the worst things you can do is go on the defensive and correct or argue with them at this point. You can apologize for not understanding or for misunderstanding, and assure the person you really want to understand from *their point of view,* and that's why you are trying to repeat back what you think you are hearing. When you learn how to do this you'll find you've taken a giant step toward becoming a better parent, and a more empowered, grounded person.

Listening also involves your response to what you hear. Most of the time you want to keep your judgments and opinions out of your responses, unless they are asked for — and even then, temper them with, "This may not be true for you, but . . . " or, "It's only my judgment off the top of my head but I think . . . " Most of the time you want to respond by saying things like:

- "That must have been painful."
- "Wow. That must be really hard to figure out."

• "I can see how excited you are about that! What an opportunity!"

You can also ask clarifying questions. This tells the person you really heard what they said and are genuinely interested in their thought process. You don't want to disempower them by making your own pronouncements. For example:

• "What did you mean when you said . . . ?"
• "What choices do you think you have about this?"
• "What makes you feel confused about this?"
• "When I was a kid, 'going out' meant dressing up and going out to the movies with a date. Is that what you mean when you say you want to 'go out' with Josh?"

If you discover that the person's need is to communicate something *you* did or said that hurt them in some way, you need to use Principles One and Two to relax and release your defensiveness. If necessary, pretend in your mind that it is someone else they are talking about, so you can really be there, to hear their pain and understand *from their point of view* what happened.

If you are the "culprit," your response has to be more than merely empathizing with how they feel — if you do that, they will walk away feeling patronized or worse. You need to go deep within yourself to genuinely understand that, intentionally or not, you have broken trust with this person, and they need a genuine, eye-to-eye apology. In addition, you need to ask what you can do to make amends. And hugs don't hurt.

It doesn't matter if you believe they are right or wrong. If someone is hurt by what you say or do, that is a fact, and to practice this principle, you must express your remorse at the fact that they felt hurt. If you need to explain why you said or did what you did, how the hurt was unintentional or a misunderstanding, save it for later, or for when you are *certain* the other person has felt heard and understood, and that they are *certain* you are very sorry for hurting them. Begin with something like, "I'm not trying to excuse or justify hurting you, I'm still very sorry. But I want to make sure you understand where I was coming from when I did (or said) that."

If necessary, ask the person to feed back to you what they are hearing, so you are sure they aren't getting hurt all over again. If the end result of your listening session is not reunion, with everyone feeling better, with nothing hanging in the air, you need to go back, at another time, and try again. It takes time, especially if you have not seen them modeled, to develop the outward skills that demonstrate your innate, inward sensitivity toward others.

Responding vs. Reacting

The moment between stimulus and response is the precious moment when trust is built or broken. We need to train ourselves to pause in that moment, reflect, and respond rather than react to what is being done or said. Sometimes this means we need to take a time out for ourselves, to calm down, relax, remember our principles, and choose our response consciously, rather than reacting like we would to a bee sting or snake bite.

Chungliang Al Huang states, "One principle in the practice of Tai Chi is understanding that your energy will rebound naturally unless you interrupt." This principle, perhaps more than all the others, requires us to be grown-ups, to intentionally re-script ourselves to respond in a deep thinking, empathic way to the people around us — even if we seem to be the only "grown-up" present in a room full of adults.

The great psychologist Carl Rogers said that the true communicator enables the other person to explore feelings and to mature. He was the first to describe the core conditions necessary for a positive, helping relationship. These include unconditional positive regard (respect), genuineness, and empathy (true understanding, from the *other person's point of view*).

Respect means you accept the other person as she is and you care about how she feels. She does not need to change in order to earn your respect.

Genuineness means you come across as a real, authentic person, not a "role." You are straightforward and sincere. You let people know who you are and what you stand for in ways that are kind and compassionate rather than judgmental or argumentative.

Empathy is the ability to feel what others feel and to accept others' experiences as valid. You can trust an empathic person with your feelings. An empathic person doesn't judge how you feel, tell you how you feel or should feel, analyze you, or gossip to others about your feelings told in confidence.

When you learn how to practice being responsive, you will also get a good handle on Principle Three, and become far more empowered. As adults we have the choice to move from childlike joy, wonder, and fun to adult reasoning, sensitivity, and the ability to set boundaries. Principle Five, being fully responsive, includes learning to easily and naturally move between these poles — of our own volition, not because outside forces trigger it in us.

Being responsive is more than the ability to respond sensitively to your environment. It is the ability to take *responsibility* for your life, to refrain from blaming circumstances and other people for everything that happens in your life. This is also a "grown-up" principle to practice, because often it certainly appears that circumstances and other people are responsible for a lot of what happens to you. But you are responsible as well. The challenge is to take responsibility for your part in whatever happens, and to see the part of you that must change in order for the externals to change.

If you have been subjected to a lot of shame and blame in childhood, this principle may be difficult to master. There may be unconscious processes going on that you don't even understand that help create problems for you — still, putting the responsibility for them squarely on your own shoulders is the first step. The beauty of it is that you also get to release the things you are *not* responsible for to those who are. We are not responsible for the words and actions of our parents. Yet, we can only blame our parents for so long if we cannot control our temper. At some point, we have to take the responsibility to learn how to do it, and then to teach it to our children if it was not taught to us. The same principle applies in many other areas of life, physical, emotional, and spiritual.

PARENTING WITH PRINCIPLE FIVE

One time when my child was four, he was waxing philosophical in the bathtub — something about the bath brought out his spiritual nature — and he asked me,

"Mommy, do you know you have an inner ear?"

"Yes . . . " I thought maybe he had learned about the structure of the ear from a book or from *Sesame Street*.

"Where is it?" he asked. The way he eye-balled me and expected the correct answer reminded me of my spiritual teacher. I quietly said, "In your head?"

He looked at me with great compassion and wisdom, and a tinge of amusement, just like my teacher would have.

"No, silly, it's in your heart."

He went on to play with his rubber ducky like any other four-year-old as I sat in speechless wonder, taking in this ancient wisdom from my greatest teacher.

To listen to our children from our hearts, we have to let go, for the time being, of our roles of parent and mentor, and just be — one being listening to the needs, opinions, or wisdom of another. Sometimes the greatest response is respectful silence, or to give the child feedback such as, "Sometimes you are so wise, it just blows me away."

Principle Five in Pregnancy

You can begin to practice responsiveness when you are pregnant by taking time every day to tune in and communicate with your baby. It may be during your "controlled belly breathing" meditation, which is so good for you, and also good for the baby, for it freshly oxygenates your blood with life-giving *prana*. Sit in a comfortable position, rub your belly (or have your partner rub it) with massage cream, and close your eyes and imagine waves of love going to your baby. I am visually oriented, so I used to picture a figure eight of golden light moving from my baby's heart to mine, binding us in a beautiful, endless light of love.

You might listen to some calming music or focus on your

breathing and the rhythmic massage of your hands over your baby's body. Listen, with your intuitive sense, to what your baby may have to tell you. Studies have shown that parents and their children are naturally inclined to be telepathic, and if nurtured, this sense can grow. Very early on, it gets you in the habit of taking the time to listen to your child wholeheartedly, giving him or her all of your attention.

Numerous studies have also shown that massage during pregnancy has a direct impact on mothering skills. Mothers who are massaged regularly are more nurturing, can more easily read their baby's cues, and can tolerate the fussiness of infants more easily than those that aren't. So it doesn't hurt to have your partner give you a massage and/or schedule one with a prenatal massage therapist occasionally throughout your pregnancy.

Principle Five with Babies and Young Children

Continuing daily massage with your baby (or at least every other day) after birth until at least the crawling stage is the best way to keep "in touch" with your baby, to learn what your baby's body is like when it is tense or relaxed, to help his or her internal organs function properly, and to increase the emotional and spiritual bond between you. Mom and Dad might want to take turns massaging (only one parent should give the massage during any given session, though). Regular massage increases healthy weight gain and helps develop the nerves in the baby's brain, thus readying your baby for the intense learning and growing that happens in the first two years. Human babies are not fully developed at birth, so massage is a natural activity (one which we as humans have for the most part forgotten) that helps stimulate the development and healthy functioning of internal organs.

Colicky babies benefit from massage because it tones the digestive tract and helps their bodies eliminate more easily and not trap painful gas bubbles in the lower intestine. I created a routine for this specific purpose, and for massage in general, in my book *Infant Massage: A Handbook for Loving Parents,* because I believe so strongly, from massaging my own babies and from over twenty years of teaching infant massage, that there is no better way to continue the bonding process, which is so important to your connection with your child later in life.

Why Babies Cry

Babies cry for many reasons, and it is important to learn your baby's personality and his or her different cries so that you can respond to them. There are cries that mean, "I need affection," "I'm hungry," "I'm in pain," "I'm tired and cranky and don't know how to get to sleep," and still others that are simply "venting" for all the stress the baby takes in, adjusting to the world of non-stop stimulation. Each of these different cries can and should be responded to appropriately. Each baby will differ in his or her need for physical affection. Some need to be held nearly all the time for the first few months, others are curious and independent almost immediately. To force an infant one way or another is to disempower her and disrupt the flow of *chi* she needs to become strong, healthy, and independent.

Some folks think that babies who cry always need to be calmed and shushed, or, conversely, should be left alone to cry it out. This is not true. Infants should never be left alone to cry, unheeded, but sometimes they need to cry in the safety of a parent's arms, without being shushed, to discharge stress. After a certain period, when they sense they are being attended to, they calm themselves, and usually sleep much more deeply.

This is one of the most important reasons to massage your pregnant belly and to massage your infant regularly after birth. You learn, as nothing else can teach you, what your baby needs, and her cries and fusses don't distress you so much as inform you of what you need to do to respond appropriately and thus allow your child to grow and blossom like a well-tended flower in your garden. If you respond in these ways, you needn't worry about when to wean, when to potty train, and all the other advice people want to give you. You will become an expert on your child, and you will naturally know and understand what she is ready to do and when. This gives you the confidence to listen to the so-called experts and then go by your inner sense of what is right.

If you want to create a transition environment for your baby that imitates aspects of the in utero experience, you may want to get a baby pack that keeps your infant close to your body so she can hear your heartbeat. Some pastel organza material, draped over the cradle, can soften the light. Putting a nice, warm cap on her head when going outdoors will prevent heat from escaping from her head. A baby monitor can help alert you to your baby's sounds if she is sleeping and you are in another room. Other aids include a heartbeat simulator for the baby's cradle and setting the volume low on your stereo or television.

Some parents want to try family co-sleeping, which is a much debated practice in Westernized countries. We practiced family co-sleeping until my youngest was around five years old. The tales of accidental suffocation by "overlying" are just that: tales. Dr. James J. McKenna, Director of the Center for Behavioral Studies of Mother-Infant Sleep at Notre Dame University says, "It is a curious fact that in Western societies the practice of mothers, fathers, and infants sleeping together came to be thought of as strange, unhealthy, and dangerous. Western parents are taught that 'co-sleeping' will make the infant too dependent on them, or risk accidental suffocation. Such views are not supported by human experience worldwide."

This arrangement, in my experience, allowed me to breast-feed my babies without having to fully awaken. The warmth of my body was just the right temperature for them. We could respond quickly to cries, chokes, or other needs. The babies could nurse frequently, giving them more antibodies to fight disease.

Dr. McKenna goes on to say, "Human infants need constant attention and contact with other human beings because they are unable to look after themselves. Unlike other mammals, they cannot keep themselves warm, move about, or feed themselves until relatively late in life. It is their extreme neurological immaturity at birth and slow maturation that makes the mother-infant relationship so important."

One of my fondest memories is when we were sleeping with our little ones in a "family bed." Once, in the middle of the night, my eighteen-month-old daughter awakened to nurse. She looked up into my face and patted my cheek. "I like you, Mommy, I like you," she said, then closed her eyes to sleep with a sweet smile on her face. Every time I remember that moment, my heart fills with love, joy, and gratitude that this child has come into my life.

Dr. McKenna agrees that this type of interaction is beneficial for both parents and infants. He says, "Studies have shown that separation of the mother and infant has adverse consequences. Anthropological considerations also suggest that separation between the mother and infant should be minimal. Western societies must consider carefully how far and under what circumstances they want to push infants away from the loving and protective co-sleeping environment. Infants' nutritional, emotional, and social needs as well as maternal responses to them have evolved in this environment for millennia."

Some parents reject co-sleeping because they are concerned about its impact on their sex lives. We found other rooms in the house suited nicely when the children were asleep. This may not be an option everyone chooses, but I encourage you to read up on it before deciding. It can contribute immensely to implementing Principle Five with your baby. My favorite book on the subject is *The Family Bed* by Tine Thevenin.

Boundaries and Consequences

A parent's need to control and protect will always conflict with a child's need for freedom and growth. So from the time your child can move around independently, you will constantly monitor and negotiate boundaries.

As in Tai Chi, you need to cultivate "listening power," to help you attune to your child's phases and needs without imposing your expectations upon them. Someone once said, "Pick your fights carefully." In good parenting, there should be some, but very few, non-negotiable rules, and these should be for the child's well-being and safety, not the parent's need for total control. "You may never talk back to me" is not a good one. "You may not cross the street without an adult" is a much better rule. "Don't talk to me in that tone of voice!" is unskillful. A better way to say it is, "I will listen to you when you speak to me in a normal tone of voice."

These kinds of boundaries must be set with "sinking power," so that the child knows you mean what you say. Then, of course, even the non-negotiable rules must change as a child grows. They won't be the same for a three year old as a ten year old, and families that talk and communicate understand this. To keep life simple, keep the non-negotiable rules simple and few. That way, you do not forever extend invitations for rebellion. Set these boundaries using all your principles. Relax, get centered, sink your power into the earth, and state the boundaries in a setting that allows the child to hear what you say, digest it, ask questions, and clearly understand that this particular rule is not negotiable.

You must also be able to explain what the consequences will be if the rule is broken, and have the internal power to follow through. Remember, your child will see, hear, and feel your true resolve. For example, instead of saying, "Clean your room right now, or you'll be in trouble!" a better way to inform your child of consequences is to say (in a normal tone of voice), "You are welcome to join us for dessert as soon as your room is clean."

Some children stay within the boundaries you set for them very well; they like the safety of those invisible fences. Others are what I call "boundary testers." They constantly push at the boundaries as if, because the boundaries are invisible, they aren't sure the boundaries really exist. These children used to be called bad or difficult. Now they are called "spirited," a much better way to see them. They are usually people with a lot of power, energy, and curiosity who, if not broken by harsh punishment and shame in childhood, will use that energy for great things and will probably be leaders and even visionaries in their adult lives.

If your child is a boundary tester, you can expect to have to pay much more attention to what he does. These are the kids that have an overpowering curiosity to see what happens if they try to cross the street without an adult or strike a match in a closet. They need to experience the consequences that follow when they test a boundary. Sometimes an explanation of why the boundary is there will do: you could get hit by a car and hurt very badly; you could start a fire, burn down the house, and be seriously hurt. Sometimes, along with an explanation, a consequence such as the removal of a favorite toy for a week, not being allowed out of the house for a day or two, and so on, needs to be put in place so the child knows the boundary is firm.

Try to anticipate and set boundaries ahead of time, so that the boundary is not set because of something the child does first. For example, the child goes into the street and gets yanked back and given consequences when he never knew that was a boundary in the first place. This is reactive, not responsive, parenting. This kind of boundary setting only encourages unsafe exploration, because the child has no idea what he can or cannot do without consequences.

With young children you must explain again and again why a certain consequence is being given to them. Take them through the whole story so they can link cause and effect, for their memories are short. Do not expect small children to remember rules and boundaries. Constant repetition and imitation will teach them. Without anger, simply remove the child from the situation, or show the child what to do by doing it yourself and then leading his body through the correct action as you speak. This way, the body-centered child learns to connect actions with words, and later the words will connect to right action.

For example, if the child inappropriately handles the cat, you can say, "We pet the kitty gently," and do it yourself. Then take the child's hand and repeat. Then let the child show you how she can do it by herself. If she is verbal, she will repeat the words; if not, you can repeat the words as she does the action. Again, do not expect her to remember this and never handle the cat inappropriately again. The whole sequence may have to be repeated many times to become a learned pattern of "how we love our kitty."

Martial arts expert Dawn Callan defines boundary making beautifully: "If you know how to set boundaries, you don't have to build emotional walls." Setting boundaries for your children helps show them how to set boundaries for themselves. Teach and model boundary-setting skills to empower your children to be free of fear and help them "danger proof" themselves.

If you need to give a consequence when a child persists with inappropriate behavior, explain that if you let nature give her the consequence, she could get hurt (in the example above, the kitty might feel scared and scratch or bite), so you need to teach her by giving her a consequence that helps her learn and remember. Empathize responsively with her pain while holding firm with the consequence. Use your listening skills to let her know you understand it's hard to stay inside when everybody else is playing outside. You can be sorry for having to impose consequences while still letting the child know it is her own actions that brought about the situation.

Don't ever withhold love and affection from a child as punishment for a misdeed. This reinforces the notion that it is the child himself who is bad, not the action he took or the words he spoke. When a child feels rejected in this way, he no longer links behavior with consequences — instead, he starts to believe that he is bad and he will begin to act like a "bad" kid would act. You do have the power to define your child in this way, so use it carefully. Try to avoid labels; if you must use them, use good ones that have the energy of love within them, and pride in who your child is *inside*.

Use the concept of "listening power" to attune yourself to which consequences will work for each child under each circumstance. Remember, this is your path, too, so take the time to do it consciously as your spiritual practice, not just a thankless job you must perform because you are a parent. Don't make the consequence overly harsh, and link it as closely as possible to the behavior. For example, if a child knows it is a family rule to put dirty clothes in the laundry basket and he does not, he may have to wear something other than what he wants and then later, with your help (depending on the age), do a load of laundry himself. You are not trying to inflict pain or shame, you are teaching him how life works: behavior has consequences, and each individual must take responsibility for their behavior.

Principle Five with Teens

Teens need to be midwifed into adulthood, not treated like children. By the time your child is a teenager, you will have, hopefully, a relationship of openness, trust, affection, and few conflicts. Both of you can set boundaries together — this allows your teen to participate in win-win negotiations, so that both she and you get most of what you need. For example, when you set curfews, don't arbitrarily set a curfew that you had as a teen or that is a reaction to what you did as a teen. Do some homework. Find out what is "normal" among teens these days. Then sit down with your teen and honestly share your concerns, and ask her for her help in addressing your fears while meeting her needs, too.

This type of discussion helps your teen begin to learn adult ways of negotiating, and to respect other peoples' boundaries and feelings. She will be motivated not by fear of consequences so much as by his love for you and by not wanting you to feel afraid for his safety or well being, or disappointed in her. It helps her gradually feel more independent without losing the feeling of safety she had as your child.

I don't agree with people who say you cannot be friends with your teenagers. I believe, if you have been a steady parent with plenty of "sinking power," you can remain a respected elder and gradually loosen the reigns of parenthood as you ease into the role of friend and mentor. For the rest of your life, these two things will go hand in hand, if you want to maintain close relationships with your kids. If you choose only to be a parent, your child will distance himself from you as he gains independence. If you relinquish your parental authority, your child will lose respect for you and find other role models. So there must be a gradual, shifting quality to your role during these years, similar to the movements of Tai Chi: Sink, move forward, fall back, all in response to your child's growth and needs, not in reaction to her words or actions.

These are the messages your children need to receive from you as you learn to be a responsive and responsible parent, and teach them to be responsive and responsible people:

- All feelings are okay. I will help you learn how to express them appropriately.
- I will help you learn how to calm yourself when you are out of control (see Principle Six) without judging you as a bad person.
- I will not give in to your demands when you are out of control.
- I will respond to you and listen when you talk to me in a normal tone of voice.
- When you have intentionally or unintentionally hurt someone, I will teach you how to apologize and make amends without losing your self-respect.

The next principle further explores the issues of anger, rebellion, and boundary setting so we can help our children learn the "middle path," so emphasized in Taoist teachings, and so we can allow our children to help remind us to remain firmly grounded in the center of our being.

Exercise for Principle Five

1. Sit comfortably, close your eyes, and relax each part of your body.
2. Take five deep belly breaths. As you inhale repeat, "be," and as you exhale repeat, "responsive."

Principle Six

AVOID EXTREMES

No matter how extreme a situation is, it will change. It
cannot continue forever.... Natural events balance
themselves out by seeking their opposites, and this
process is at the heart of all healing.

— Deng Ming-Dao, *365 Tao Daily Meditations*

One of the best things about Taoism and the practice of Tai Chi is its connection with nature and the way it shows us how to be in balance. Everything happens in nature in order to maintain a balanced ecology. Sometimes, because of our ignorant or unconscious intervention, we court disaster by forcing nature's hand. When we clear-cut the rain forest, for example, we compel nature to balance the loss of *prana* or *chi* and other important elements and initiate a process that may result in more natural disasters, global warming, and so on. Nature is constantly doing the *yin/yang* balancing act.

Observe how this phenomenon of middle-path balancing happens naturally, everywhere, including in your everyday life:

- A pot of water boils over on the stove. What do you do? You grab a pot holder and take the pot off the heat completely. Then you turn down the heat to a medium point where the water won't boil over.
- You don't want the television or stereo too loud or too soft. So you find a middle volume that is comfortable.

- Most people like the air temperature to be at a steady, middle level, and so we have heating and air conditioning. In countries without these luxuries, blance is achieved in other ways, such as midday siestas, wet fans, suitable clothing, and climate-sensitive architecture.
- There is a customary middle-range volume we are used to in our conversations; whispers and shouts carry different meanings than everyday conversation.
- When driving our cars, we always find a middle range of speed, and become uncomfortable with those who drive too slow or too fast for a particular area.
- Our bodies, when not interfered with by our minds, usually find a middle-range weight that is appropriate for our age, heredity, and condition. Emotional and cultural factors, yo-yo dieting, and eating disorders contribute to an imbalance, one way or the other.
- When you observe our most serious social problems carefully, you find extremes in behavior and in views about appropriate behavior. You can be sure that those with extreme behavior and views were brought up by parents with extreme views.

In Taoism, we strive to walk the middle path, which seems almost innocuous in its simplicity but in reality is the most difficult — physically, mentally, and emotionally — because it requires a constant and conscious awareness. We try to find a perfect, grounded balance with the body in Tai Chi or yoga. We try to see all sides of a question and find the middle ground that is most sensible. Sometimes we want to go to one extreme or another. Sometimes we *want* to do something outrageous and spontaneous. But for our lives to work, we must always return to center. If you observe closely, you will find that at some point, after such an excursion into extremity, you will strive for total calm, rest, or solitude. You'll want the opposite end of the extreme.

THE OPPOSITE

People with extreme views are usually unconsciously compensating for extreme circumstances in their lives. A child born into and suffering in poverty may grow up believing that being extremely wealthy is what he wants, and that this will solve all his problems. At the same time, he may believe that wealthy people have money only because they are selfish and greedy. In his own effort to escape poverty, he creates a self-defeating conflict of beliefs that causes him to swing constantly between extremes in his own being. This prevents any real progress because it consumes the energy that could be put into learning how to build the security he needs in slow and easy steps.

A person of great wealth, however, may believe that those in poverty are lazy and shiftless, and may attribute character defects to them in an unconscious effort to balance, in his own psyche, the vast gap between him and "them." Rather than living a middle-path life and using the excess for the betterment of others, he may insulate himself from the extreme of poverty. The way the Tao works in this situation is that often, by insulating himself, such a person also isolates himself from life and true spirituality, so his poverty comes in another form, balancing — again — what nature cannot tolerate for long: the extreme.

In *Vitality, Energy, Spirit: A Taoist Sourcebook,* master Lu Yen is quoted, "If you do not care about your vitality and waste it arbitrarily, that is like putting water into a leaking cup; it will not fill the cup, but will gradually leak away." Often the tenets of Taoism, when not taught by example in youth, come only with hard experience and age. The abundant energy and health of youth can be easily squandered if a person is not grounded in this principle.

Extremes are easy to slip into. They provide the comfort of certainty; if you have extreme beliefs, if you think win/lose, if you accept all or nothing, not much thinking has to take place. You won't wrestle with decisions, your conscience only operates from an extreme position, so it is not really operational. The discomfort of thinking and feeling your way through choices does not have to be endured: life is mapped out for you. Whatever extreme position you have taken allows you to easily dismiss all other ideas, positions, input, and choices. This is the lure of religious cults, gangs, and other types of more subtle insulation such as gated communities and extremist political parties. But the Tao does not tolerate extremes for long, and eventually you will either find yourself on the other extreme or you will feel the discomfort of being isolated and out of touch, and you will want to move toward the center.

A recent example of extremism in parenting is provided by a California-based group led by a charismatic preacher and his wife. The core of their teachings and their books is essentially, "Baby is not the boss." They advise against feeding on demand, carrying a baby in a sling, or rocking an infant to sleep at night, citing biblical verses to back up their ideas.

The American College of Pediatrics repudiated the program, and its breast-feeding task force sent a letter to Christian leaders in the area, telling them about the program's potential harm. In fact, the county in which the group is based recorded an increase in the number of babies who failed to gain adequate weight for optimal growth. The physicians cautioned that rigid schedules of "parent-directed feeding" are likely to contribute to dehydration and poor weight gain, and lead to malnutrition, learning impairments, and a host of other problems.

The program advocates rigid sleeping schedules, allowing babies to cry alone in their cribs, and spanking them at as early as five or six months of age when they drop things from a high chair. The program discounts maternal instinct and mother-infant bonding. Their books portray a parent as being like the CEO of a corporation, using terms such as "infant management strategy." This is a clear example of extremism in parenting that can damage children for life. Research has shown us that such practices, while producing "model" children in the early years, can contribute to the behaviors exhibited by serial killers and other sociopaths. The bottled-up rage of having been "managed" instead of heard finds release when the parents are no longer there to exert such extreme control over their children.

AVOIDING EXTREMES IN YOUR LIFE

Take a look at your own life and behavior. Do you tend to fall into extreme positions because of your upbringing — either unconsciously repeating your parents' extremes or rebelling against them? For example, are you a bulldozer ("I always get my way") or a doormat ("I never get my way")? Do you tend to be self-centered or self-abandoning (other-centered)? Do you consistently find yourself being defiant and rebellious or conforming and obedient, or swinging between the two? Are you angry most of the time and aggressive in your demeanor, or always nice, perfect, and passive? When bad things happen, do you always blame others, or always blame yourself?

In college I had a professor (a professor of psychology, no less) who said, "I used to get ulcers from other people. Now I *give* ulcers to other people, and I think I'll live longer!" Maybe. But he certainly wasn't someone I wanted to be around for long. It seemed to me that he had gone from one extreme to the other: To avoid the pain his previous "nice" passivity had brought him, he had turned extremely aggressive, and he was heading toward being a lonely, mean old man.

If you find that you do fall into these extremes, it would be helpful for you, before you become a parent if possible, to work on some of these aspects of your values, beliefs, and behavior, either through self-analysis, in a group, and/or with the help of a good therapist. It's never too late. Even if you already have kids, you can begin to work on these issues, and your work will be an excellent role model for your children. While extreme beliefs and behavior may not seem hurtful now, they can leak into your parenting style and really affect your children. Taking a Tai Chi or yoga class can help you find your own center, and will automatically help you move toward its peace.

Any extreme eventually brings discomfort, and that pain will begin to move you toward balance. But it is not a healthy way to go about it, and it is risky to wait for natural consequences to move you there. For example, if you are always angry and uncomfortable to be around, you will drive people out of your life. The loneliness of that position will finally cause you to either become ill and/or seek out help. This can be just as true of the extreme of passivity. But if you can consciously begin to seek balance in every area of your life, you will find that eventually more and more peace will also seep into your being, and you will become strong, not like the hard, dead tree that breaks under pressure, but like the life-filled bamboo, that can bend and come back to center when extreme conditions cause chaos in the outer environment.

PARENTING WITH PRINCIPLE SIX

Children bring a certain amount of chaos with them. You never know what is going to happen, and what will be required of you as a parent. Your child could develop a life-threatening illness that requires enduring courage, strength, and a steady center in order for you to get through it and make appropriate choices along the way. And then, the children inevitably leave. You retain your position as role model and mentor while being required to return to independence as an adult. Each stage of each child's life requires different skills of you, and throughout it all you must also develop and maintain the skills of self-love and independence so that when your children leave, you still have a life.

Principle Six in Pregnancy

One of the easiest ways to fall into the trap of extremes when you are pregnant is to become attached to a certain plan for your pregnancy and birth. It is so easy for parents-to-be to think they are in control! Even if it is your second or third child, you can still experience this desire to be in control, and allow your attachments and expectations to become rigid. Flexibility is the keynote of Principle Six. The idea is not to go through life without attachments, plans, or goals, but to be flexible enough in your thinking to factor in Plan B, the karmic-unfoldment plan. In this way, you attach yourself more to the spirit of things than to the letter of the law, and when external events call for change, you are able to change creatively, without losing the spirit of what you want.

My first child's birth is a good example. He was born in 1976, during the heyday of natural childbirth. Dr. Frederick Leboyer, an obstetrician from France, had just revolutionized the medical birthing establishment by creating a more "natural" transition environment in his hospital birthing room: dimming the lights, quieting the noise, warming the room, and, immediately after birth, immersing the baby in warm water to simulate the environment of the uterus. He invited the father to be present to help birth his baby, cut the cord, and bond with his child and spouse privately in peace and semi-darkness.

The home birth movement soon followed, as my generation began to rebel against the institutional model of birth, which reduced pregnancy to a disease and birth to a life-threatening event that could only be managed — "delivered" — by a medical specialist. Under that model, newborn babies had been routinely whisked away from their parents, cleaned up, and put in warming isolettes (perhaps a better name would be "isolaters") before being presented to the mother, almost as a *fait accompli*, by the medical staff. By this time the mother was rousing from the coma-like state induced by drugs that prevented her from experiencing and remembering the birth of her baby. Fathers paced outside, even further distanced from the critical bonding period that would help them feel involved with and attached to their infants. Who knew fathers had hormones, too, that needed the birth experience and bonding period to be triggered into action?

By the time my first baby was born, much had changed. Only the year before, fathers were finally allowed to be present at their babies' births, Lamaze childbirth preparation classes had become a normal part of pregnancy, and mothers were taught relaxation and breathing methods, with spouses coaching, to get through the discomfort of labor without drugs. Even more recently, mothers needing cesarean section surgery have been able to choose to use epidural and spinal blocks to stop the pain, which allows the mother to be conscious and able to see and bond with her baby and begin nursing as soon as possible. In the late 1970s, the La Leche League, an organization for nursing mothers, was very active, and offered support groups and information for mothers who chose to nurse — a radical choice in those days.

Being who I am, I was uncomfortable with extremes. Though it went against the expectations of my peers, who were all vehemently for home births, I chose a hospital birth because my inner sense told me to. We prepared for natural childbirth with great enthusiasm, and after reading about all its benefits I chose to breast-feed. So, as usual in my life, I was not following a path mapped out by either my parents or my peers — I was somewhere in the middle, making everyone uncomfortable!

As it turned out, I was fortunate to have followed my instincts and planned for a hospital birth. My baby was perfectly comfortable where he was and labor never started. When the placenta began to deteriorate, we had to go for X-rays, and discovered the baby was far too large to fit through my pelvis, which, unknown to me, had been slightly malformed by a bout with rickets when I was a baby. My baby had not turned and was sitting in a lotus-like posture in my womb, seemingly content to stay where he was: "breech" in medical terms. So we had to schedule a cesarean delivery. I opted for a spinal block, but my husband was not allowed into the surgical suite.

Though I never had the chance to experience labor, the birth happened without any problems. I bonded deeply, eye to eye, with my baby right after his birth, and began breast-feeding as soon as I was back in my room. Three days later I went home, having had a wonderful birth in spite of all the dire expectations of my peers.

Their extremism initiated my activism. I helped form support groups for post-cesarean parents and lobbied for more cesarean-section education and preparation. Eventually, my group prevailed and within a year the hospital had built an entirely new area for cesarean births that was family friendly and made it possible for parents not to feel as if somehow they had failed when, through circumstances beyond their control, surgery was their only option. Fathers were finally allowed into the surgical suite, if they chose, and handed the newborn baby after delivery, just as in a "natural" birth.

Envision What You Want, Surrender to What Is

I am not saying you shouldn't envision the birth you want and do everything in your power to have it that way. Just remember the *principles* you are striving for and factor in other possible external scenarios and where you can maintain your principles even if the external circumstances change. When you do this, you will not feel in any way a failure regardless of how events unfold. Planning and living in this way requires a lot of communication and surrender — but so does every other aspect of family life.

Taoist master Liao's advice is excellent:

> Regardless of how rapidly the situation changes, you should remain calm and easy…. Even if a difficult situation builds into a seemingly uncontrollable situation, you should still control yourself in a peaceful and easy manner.

Principle Six with Young Children

Feelings are very powerful, and often our feelings cause us to move into extremes of thought and behavior. When we learn how to identify and express our feelings by thinking out loud, we can begin to model for our children how to identify and express their feelings. It is the first step toward doing something about our feelings that is constructive and non-violent. For example:

- "I feel angry because when I went into the kitchen to make dinner, the sink was full of dirty dishes. I need some time to calm down. I'll be back in fifteen minutes."
- "I feel frustrated because I had a hard day at work today. I need to go for a walk to help work off my stress. I'll be back in twenty minutes."
- "I feel sad because my friend is very sick. It's okay to be sad sometimes. I think I need to cry and then I'll feel better."
- "I feel ignored. It hurts my feelings when I say something and nobody listens. Can I have a hug?"
- "I feel so happy! Winning that award made me feel really good."

- "I feel so proud of my friend. She just got her degree, and I know it means a lot to her. I'm going to send her a special present."

When your children, even the pre-verbal ones, hear you and your spouse and the other kids in the house identifying their feelings and voicing solutions in this way, they learn how to do it for themselves. One of my son's first phrases was "I angry!" Though of course I didn't want him to be uncomfortable, I rejoiced that he already knew what he felt. I could begin mirroring for him right away:

"You feel really mad! When I interrupted your play to change your diaper you didn't like it at all. I'm sorry I had to do that. Next time, I'll tell you first, okay?"

He may not have understood everything I said, but he happily replied, "Okay!" Don't assume that because your child doesn't have verbal skills he doesn't understand you. When I learned the Bengali language, I was embarrassingly slow at speaking, so I rarely spoke. But I understood almost everything I heard. I often heard whole conversations that the Bengali-speaking people in the room assumed I didn't understand.

Young children, even babies, understand your tone, your expressions, the energy you put out, and even some of the words they've heard for the last couple of years. (Yes, they can hear in utero!) While "motherese," in other words "baby talk," is a perfectly acceptable and integral, playful communication style, you can also talk to your pre-verbal child with adult words and concepts. They may not understand all of the words, but they will take in more than you expect as well as the respect you show for them as separate beings deserving respectful communication.

You *Eat* with That Mouth?

You and your partner must decide what type of language is considered appropriate in your household, and make a commitment to uphold that standard yourself. If you don't want your three year old using swear words you had better eliminate them from your vocabulary, and watch your R-rated movies when the kids are gone or asleep. Even if you don't believe certain words to be bad for adults (and older teens who use them as a way to separate), you probably wouldn't want your small children using them, so you may want to make it a family rule not to use swear words. One of the worst things you can do is laugh when your child uses a swear word.

Explain what is considered unacceptable language in your home, and why. Ask what other word she could use. And if it happens again, follow with clearly defined consequences, which may include you leaving the room and not listening until appropriate language is used. Rules about language can be loosened a bit in the teenage years, but I recommend you put a lid on it for the duration of your children's childhood, not only for the sake of your family's reputation, but also because of the type of energy some language produces and encourages in impressionable children. Studies have shown that swearing in young children can be a precursor to violent behavior.

One way a family I know handled the issue was with a "fine jar." Anyone in the family, including Mom and Dad, who used certain words accidentally, out of anger, or for any reason, had to contribute money to the fine jar. If the children didn't have the requisite quarter or whatever the fine was, an IOU slip was put in the jar, and when allowance time came around, they'd have to pay up. The money was then donated to a worthy cause. Other fines could include certain household chores no one enjoyed, such as cleaning the kitty-litter box or birdcage, washing and detailing the car, or shoveling snow. These kinds of fines, of course, should be age-appropriate, supervised tasks.

Another family made a game out of finding outrageous substitutes for swear words that would break the tension and make everyone laugh. It became almost a family competition to coin expressions that fit the situation without breaking the family rule. Taoist master Liao said, "When one part feels heavy, make it feel light and disappear." Thus, the principle of *yin/yang* balance can be applied to the most mundane situations by seeking the opposite of whatever extreme is happening in a way that will move the energy back to center.

In Tai Chi, you strive not to do too much or too little. You use "listening power" to pace your opponent, so you know how to respond to his energy with the kind of opposition that will balance and thus end the conflict. You only move when it is absolutely necessary, and then you move with the idea of harmony and balance in mind, not with reactivity, which leads to extremes. Failure to respond consciously results in an awkwardness that throws you off balance and makes you vulnerable to being "uprooted." Master Wong Ching-Yua says the most important practice is to understand the importance of the flow of internal power from *yin* to *yang*. He says, "The Tai Chi principle is as simple as this: yield yourself and follow the external forces." When you "yield" to an opponent you control his energy; you are able to use his force as if it belongs to you. In regard to parenting, this practice helps you guide your child's energy back to center when it is necessary for you to take control.

Anger

The way you handle and express your anger is the most powerful teaching tool you have. Contrary to popular opinion, it is not a good idea to encourage your child to beat a pillow or other object to release his anger. It doesn't work, and worse, it reinforces the notion that it is okay to act out anger with violence. The only healthy way to express anger is verbally, exploring the cause of it and the fear that lies behind it, and then finding positive ways to use the energy and power it generates. Children need to know it is okay to be afraid and to express it to safe people (parents) and to explore what might be done about it. Often, just talking about anger diffuses its power, and having a parent listen with empathy, not interruption or interpretation, can make all the difference. The child can then solve his own problems appropriately, with a clear head.

For example, your young child comes home in tears, angry that a trusted friend hit him and took away his toy:

Parent: "That must have felt awful! You probably feel very angry."

Child: "Yeah! I'm gonna hit *him!*"

Parent: "It would feel better if you could take back what he took from you, wouldn't it? Hitting is one of your choices, but it might make things worse later, don't you think?"

Child: "No, I'd feel great!"

Parent: "What other choices do you think you might have?"

Child: "I dunno. But I'm not just gonna take it like a baby!"

Parent: "Hmm. This is a hard one to figure out, isn't it? If you hit him, he could just hit you back, and pretty soon everybody's hitting everybody, and you get in trouble with the teacher, and you get in trouble with us because we don't hit in this family. So you know it would lead to consequences at home. But you don't want to feel like you have no power at all."

Child: "Yeah."

Parent: "Let's see, what other choices do you have? Well, you could just let it go, choose another toy, and let him know he can't make you feel afraid or angry, even if he tries. Or, you could tell him what he did made you angry, and then walk away. You know, there's a song that was written by a young man who was very brave and respected for the non-violent ways he fought 'bad guys.' The song goes, 'He who fights and runs away lives to fight another day.' I think it means sometimes we walk away strong on the *inside,* with a different kind of courage, and find other ways to fight back. Anyway, I'm sure you'll figure out what to do. Let me know if you want to talk about it some more. And thanks for sharing your feelings with me."

A friend of mine in Taiwan told me that once when she was in the park with her baby and her five year old, they saw a mother nearby hitting and yelling at her young child. The five year old suddenly and fearlessly marched up to the woman and looked her right in the eye.

"If you beat your children, it's against the law," he said. "You should talk to her, not hit her." Then he turned around and walked back to his mother, as the woman stood, open mouthed, having just been scolded by a five year old. As Polly Berrends says so beautifully in her book *Gently Lead:*

> When we try to master parenthood or to master our children we just stay stuck and hurt each other. But when we let our children be our Zen masters and approach problems and failures as something to learn from, parenthood becomes a joyful, fruitful grope. . . . Your children will not always do what you tell them to do, but they will be — good and bad — as they see you being.

Once my sister and her daughter witnessed a man beating his three boys, all under age seven, in a large department store. He slapped them hard across the face and slammed them into walls — no gentle spanks. He was obviously out of control. My sister knew she had to do something about it, and at the same time model for her daughter how to intervene in such a situation without getting caught up in it. My sister was very angry and felt helpless, watching this strong man throw his babies around like rag dolls. God only knows what he allowed himself in private if that was the way he acted in public.

She found an onlooker nearby who was willing to go with her and follow the man to his car to take down his license plate number. They then called the police, and waited there to make statements. By that time, her willingness to step forward gave other onlookers the courage to give corroborating statements. When the man arrived home, there was a police car waiting for him, and people ready to inspect his children for signs of abuse and arrest him for assault.

My sister modeled for her daughter and other bystanders the appropriate and dignified, middle-path use of the energy generated by her anger; it was neither the extreme of total non-involvement and abandonment nor the extreme of reactivity — that is, hitting him over the head with a shovel, which is what she *felt* like doing.

Whining and Tantrums

Whining and tantrums are common extremes children resort to if they can't find ways to be heard when they want to get their needs met or control their energy. If your child has a habit of whining, a good, consistent response is, "I can't hear you when you talk that way. Say what you want in a normal voice."

If your child has tantrums, it is not because you are a bad parent. Your child just has energy spiraling out of control and needs your help to teach him how to control it and get his needs met in a productive, healthy way. Studies have shown that children whose tantrums are catered to are at risk for emotional problems later in life. If they learn that when they whine, scream, and sulk they can get others to do what they want *right now*, they become self-centered adults with no ability to enjoy delayed gratification or to negotiate win-win agreements.

If you have modeled appropriate communication and anger management, and if you have taught your child controlled belly breathing, you have already made a good start on helping your child control tantrums and choose alternative behaviors. Do not let your child pull you into the energy of the tantrum. Use your power to break from that energy and allow it to whirl around by itself. That will begin to take away whatever energy the child "borrows" from you to keep it going. Here are some ways to deal with a tantrum if it continues:

- Place limits on the tantrum. Tell your child he needs to calm down and speak to you in a normal voice or you can't respond to him at all. Give him a time limit, such as a count of ten, or a timer placed above his reach, or put some music on and tell him by the time it finishes, he must stop the tantrum. If possible, leave the room, go about your business, and ignore the tantrum. When the time limit is up, return to the child, and in a normal voice say, "It's time to stop now. If you don't stop, for every time I count to ten and you continue, there will be a consequence. You will have to do _____ or your privilege of _____ will be removed for one day." When the child stops, hug and praise him for learning how to calm himself down. Then ask him to talk to you in a normal voice about what he wants. If you have to say no, and the tantrum starts again, you must have the fortitude to begin the process all over again, and to follow through with the consequences.

• If your child is particularly prone to violent tantrums, you may set aside a place, such as a giant bean-bag chair in the corner of her room, where she is taken when she begins to have a tantrum. Then the above sequence would be carried out, as you say something like, "You must settle down now. You have to my count of ten to calm yourself. If you don't, _____." State the consequences clearly.

• If the tantrum happens in public, remove your child to an isolated place outdoors or in the car. If you use the car, make sure the windows are open if it's hot and the child is restrained in a car seat. Sit in the front for the time limit, ignore the child and do your controlled belly breathing. When the time limit is up, let him know he must stop and that consequences will follow for each time you have to count to ten. Follow up. Be sure to hug and praise your child when he settles down, and ask him to say what he needs or feels in a normal voice. If passersby question you, explain your child is having a temper tantrum and you are having a "time out," everything is okay, and thank them for their concern.

• When your child is calm, explain to her that before she can get what she wants, she must be positive in the way she expresses herself, she must talk in a normal voice and be polite. If so, you will listen with understanding and support, and try to help her get what she wants or needs in a way that is good for her. Explain that sometimes you have to say no for adult reasons, and though you don't want to disappoint her, having a tantrum will *never* change your mind.

You must use "sinking power," so that your child knows that in this instance, you are the teacher, she is the student, and the terms are not negotiable. Regardless of how frustrated and/or triggered into your own childhood powerlessness you feel inside, you must pull up strength from the earth to be what your child needs you to be at this moment: an unmovable force, without anger or tension. Consider it wonderful practice for yourself, and you will find your reactive emotions diffusing as your interest becomes engaged in what you are learning and how it can be applied in other areas of your life.

Make staying calm and in control your top priority. Demonstrate how you do this by "thinking out loud" — as we saw earlier — when dealing with your feelings:

- "I need to calm down because I'm beginning to feel very angry. I'm going to my room to lie down for ten minutes and relax. Then I'll come back and we can finish talking."
- "I'm beginning to feel too tense to continue. I need a break to get myself together. I'm going to do my breathing for five minutes in the other room. Then I'll come back and we can finish talking."
- "I think I'm overwhelmed and may be over-reacting. I need to take a break. Then I'll be ready to listen better. Can we talk again in fifteen minutes?"

Rebellion

When children rebel, they are trying to communicate some-thing to you. Is there something in your behavior or attitude that isn't congruent with your principles and values? Take some time to consider these questions:

- Are you stressed out, "all work and no play," and not pay-ing attention to your kids?
- Are you over-controlling, and not recognizing your child has gone through a period of growth and you need to shift gears?

- Are you over-involved, and smothering your child, who is trying to push you away to gain some independence?
- Has your child entered adolescence? Can you accept the natural storminess of this period without getting hooked into the energy? Can you let some of it pass without reacting to it?
- Is your child picking up on something you are going through? Or something you and a family member or partner are going through? Does she need reassurance or questions answered?

When you are able to sit down with your child, with a relaxed, open demeanor, honestly wanting to know, from the *child's point of view*, what is going on, your child will usually tell you what is bothering her. If you use your listening skills and don't react or try to analyze your child, often the tension can be diffused. Explore what motivates your child's behavior. Listen — don't interrupt, lecture, or judge.

Sometimes, talking about dilemmas in the third person is more comfortable for a teen, especially boys. By using a movie, an example from what you've heard about or seen, or something from your own experience, you can often get your teen to open up and talk without the threat of coming too close to his own private feelings or experiences.

When your kids know their feelings are important to you, and you are willing to respectfully listen to their point of view, the need to rebel is lessened or removed. My kids often smilingly complained to me, "Mom, you're no fun! There's nothing to rebel against!" They also often said, "All my friends envy me. You're the coolest mom. They all wish their parents listened to them like you do." Some of my children's friends would come visit me, even without my children present, just to talk. I listened respectfully and always suggested ways for them to try to talk to their parents or teachers about what was bothering them. Being a mentor can thus extend beyond your own small family.

Principle Six with Teens

Feeling anger is normal during developmental shifts; it is a response to the fear those changes generate. This is one reason teens so often swing from helplessness to anger and rebellion; the inevitable separation from their parents is frightening, and the easiest way to express fear is through anger. Like the blowfish who puffs up into a spiny ball when afraid, your child may act angry when the underlying feeling is fear. Often fear is the last straw that pushes kids into gangs or other borderline peer groups. Their constant fear can be reduced by joining a group, and the anger, which they act out toward symbols of power or toward weaker, more vulnerable people, feels better than fear and helplessness. In this way the child is trying to avoid depression, even though it is self-defeating. He doesn't see its self-destructive nature; he sees empowerment, which is often what anger makes us feel, and an antidote to the powerlessness of constant fear.

When I have explored, through conversation, the reason for a change in their behavior with my own kids I have usually ended the conversation with something like, "Wow, I've been so caught up in my own stuff I haven't noticed you may need some new ways of doing things. Thank you so much for opening up to me. Let's both think about it and see if we can come up with a new way to deal with . . . (your curfew, your allowance, and so on). We'll talk again tomorrow."

I have also used letter writing with my older kids to help us express and explore our feelings without resorting to arguments. If I have very strong feelings, I'll put them in a letter, using "I" statements, and taking responsibility for my own feelings and reactions. ("When you said _____, I felt _____.") My kids, too, have written me letters expressing their strong feelings and asking for changes in my behavior. Then we get together and negotiate a solution in which both of us get what we need and both of us make some concessions to the other out of love and respect.

My kids may not always make exactly the choices I'd want, but they are empowered, centered, and very much in control of their lives. The other day when we were having a discussion about lone-liness, my twenty-two-year-old son said to me, "I don't feel needy very often. I feel like I have an abundance of love to share with other people, and being alone doesn't scare me. I enjoy solitude, but I love being with a lot of people too. I don't feel a hole inside that I need someone else or some group to fill. When I'm sad, I know it is just my heart wanting to be nearer to its Godness. It's just part of being human. I think I got so much love growing up, that's why I feel secure inside myself."

During the teen years, kids discover a whole new part of them-selves: their philosophical, reasoning ability. If you use "listening power" with your child you will be attuned to this shift and aware of your child's growth. You will know when it's time to use "trans-ferring power" — to concentrate your own wisdom and transfer power to your child in small doses, allowing her to experience adult reasoning and responsibility while she still has the safety net of home and parents.

Teens need to try on all kinds of personas and try out many dif-ferent ways of perceiving how the universe works. They need to explore the universe and their relationship to it — their own spiri-tuality. Take time with them to discuss the deeper questions of life. Share what you think, from your own reading and experience, and allow your teen to question your values and assumptions without getting defensive. Allow them to question your beliefs and to try dif-ferent ones.

Relinquish your domination over their spiritual or religious beliefs for a while. Let them have the last word sometimes, leaving some questions open for more thinking on both sides, and be willing to sometimes admit, "I just don't know." Leave books around for your teen to notice and look through. Let movies stimulate discus-sions about spiritual matters, and explore them without attachment to having your teen believe what you believe. You can use the multi-tude of opportunities afforded by the media to point out where extremes differ from the more difficult but integral middle path.

When we parent our children emphasizing the balanced rhythms of nature, avoiding extremes whenever possible, parenting becomes a meditative art that not only gives us beautiful, whole, and healthy children, but improves our own understanding of ourselves and the universe.

Exercise for Principle Six

1. Sit comfortably, close your eyes, and relax each part of your body.
2. Take six deep belly breaths. As you inhale repeat, "avoid," and as you exhale repeat, "extremes."

Principle Seven
FLOW AND LET GO

———— ⚜ ————

All our efforts are temporary. They borrow from
pre-existing forces, ride the current of natural events,
and disappear according to the dictates of the situation.
It is best to realize the transitory nature of things and
work with it. Understanding the world's ephemeral
nature can be the biggest advantage of all.

— Deng Ming-Dao, *365 Tao Daily Meditations*

Taoism recognizes the fluidity of life. Nothing is permanent, everything constantly changes and transforms. Tai Chi uses this principle with its flowing motions of the body. As Tai Chi teacher Douglas Lee writes, "From motion you obtain serenity and stability by the release of tension through continuously shifting weight from one foot to the other. It is through this shifting that one side of the body becomes soft (muscles relaxed) and the other side hard (muscles contracted). As a result . . . circulation is improved and the person feels relaxed and not fatigued." Yoga works on the same principle.

Principle Seven works for us when we are able to flow, not fight, with the changes life brings. This seems a natural thing to do. All of nature and most animals operate upon this principle and are in harmony with it. But because as humans we have free will we have the constant challenge of mastering the mind. Our minds are analytical, planning, problem-solving tools. They are great servants and terrible masters.

Meditation, Tai Chi, yoga, prayer, and other spiritual practices help us learn to work with the mind and its constant craving. The mind, in order to maintain its existence, must always be engaged. That is why when you sit to meditate, you must give it an object to work with such as the breath, a *mantra*, or a visualization. It is impossible to completely suspend the mind without years of practice. As Indian mystic Ramakrishna said, "The mind is like a mad monkey, stung by a scorpion." It constantly works, obsesses, plans, rehashes, worries, remembers, and desires. It is its nature to want control. But it is only a small part of our being; it is not who we are. If we get caught up in the mind's reactivity and allow it to control us, we find ourselves spinning in an endless wheel of thought, and we cannot merge our souls with the universal flow and find peace.

Floating in Faith

During a critical period in my life, everything seemed to have blown apart. All I thought I wanted, all I was supposed to have to be happy, all I was supposed to have achieved by that point in my life, was gone. It was as if the earth had been abruptly pulled out from under my feet. I was confused. I felt alone, ill, depressed, and full of anxiety.

My mind obsessed about all the bad "what ifs" it could come up with. After all, if so many bad things had happened, and I was a good person who did not hurt others, lie, cheat, steal, or in any way deserve what was happening, my mind told me, anything could and would happen. I began to feel the worst terror I have ever experienced, all a production of my own mind. I was being tested — testing myself is perhaps a better way of putting it — as to how much I truly believed in my inner spiritual reality, with which my mind constantly wrestled. My mind, given free reign and power to interpret the situation, judged me in its own logical way: if bad things happen, you must have done something wrong. I became more and more confused as I listened to its endless loop of chattering and judging.

With some support from some compassionate people who could help me see through all this, I was finally able to begin find-

ing myself again, to stop the self-judging critic of my mind, to kind-
ly turn a deaf ear to the judgmental criticism of others, and to trust
again in the eternal Tao. I had a recurring visualization at the time
that was very helpful.

When I allowed my mind or emotions to control me instead of
my deep inner soul, it was like standing on the shoreline, looking at
the ocean. I could see its vastness, I knew its depth, but I was connected only by the moistness at my feet. Every big wave that came
in — every "bad" thing that happened — knocked me down. As I
drew up the courage to step out farther into the water, the waves
had less and less affect on me. When I was able to have the courage
to move out to the place where my feet no longer touched bottom,
where I just floated on the water, each wave moved me up and
down gently as I continued to float, and gently move out to the
greater peace of being one with the flow of that ocean.

In *365 Daily Meditations*, Deng Ming-Dao says,

> Winter storms may destroy some things, but they also pre-
> pare the way for life. If things are swept away, it is appro-
> priate. There must be an opportunity for new living things
> to emerge and begin their own cycle. All growth comes
> with a shock.

Sometimes getting the courage to go out there where our feet
don't touch the bottom, to float in the faith that we are part of the
eternal flow of creation, is difficult. And I believe at different stages
of life, regardless of our beliefs or plans, each of us is called to this
test. Some respond by holding even more tightly to the familiar, and
are pulled under by life's riptides.

Mental Craving

Whatever we give the mind to try to satisfy its cravings, it will
want more. Therefore, we must find ways to suspend the mind and
link ourselves to a deeper state of being through that part of us we
can call the "observer" self. There is a part of us that can stand
apart and observe ourselves. When we say, "I am," who is it that

can say this? It is the part of us that is connected to the greater whole, to the universal, macrocosmic "I" — the mind of God. If we can achieve connection with that greater "I," even in a limited way, we can flow with the natural Way (Tao) and let go of small, individual mental attachments to plans, desires, and cravings.

This doesn't mean we no longer think or feel, we no longer grieve or rejoice. But our deeper self can observe this grieving and rejoicing with the awareness that all things pass and there is no limit to our connection with each other, the earth, the universe, or God. The Tao is infinite, and we are an integral part of the whole. A cup dipped into the ocean contains the ocean, and when the container is broken, the water again merges with the ocean and cannot be separated out. Our bodies and minds are like the container. They provide us with boundaries and a sense of ourselves as individuals with limits. But if our awareness encompasses the ocean, we know our true being is the ocean, not the container.

Another analogy is often given in yoga teachings: When a clear pool reflects the moon at night, that image is perfect; it reflects the moon, but is not the moon. When the water is disturbed, the image breaks into a thousand images, but the moon itself remains untouched. That is also true when our minds are in turmoil and our connection to Spirit is fragmented and doubtful. When we still our minds, it is like stilling the water so that the moon's reflection can be seen in its entirety, and then our God-self, the Tao, can be perceived in its entirety through our spiritual senses.

We are all, in our individuality, like those thousand images, reflections of the one great Tao, Supreme Consciousness. The more we are able to still the turbulent waters, the clearer the reflection becomes. Eventually, realization goes beyond even this, and we know we are the moon — our deepest self or soul *is* the Tao or God, and the mind is merely a temporary reflecting plate.

The Big Picture

To be aware of this "big picture" is the experience we strive for, and is the reason we have evolved mind in the first place. Meditation cleans the pool, the mirror, the reflecting plate, so that we more readily and easily reflect our true being while still maintaining our individuality, our bodies, our emotions, and our loving connections with others.

Principle Seven is about letting go of the small things in lieu of the larger relationships in our families. It is more effective to work on the long-term view than on short-term goals. The urgency of short-term goals makes us feel they are important. But if we remember the long-term goals and take time to work on them, which sometimes requires letting go of short-term goals, the "small stuff" will work out on its own. Our focus must remain on our positive, trusting relationship with our children. Dr. Jane Bluestein, author of *Parents, Teens and Boundaries*, says, "It's not that taking out the trash, doing homework, or staying clean and sober aren't important. It's just that focusing on these goals instead of the relationship can be shortsighted."

Believe me, when your children are grown the age at which they were weaned or potty trained, the number of times they took out the trash, and how clean their rooms were pale in comparison to the connectedness and trust you feel between you.

THE OPPOSITE

Most of us live the opposite of Principle Seven much of the time. Even those who live "spiritual" lives often slip into mental craving, because of the difficulty of controlling the mind. People who live strictly in reactivity are embodiments of this principle's opposite, and it is easy to find them all around us. When we try to control everything, when we expect things to always go in the way we desire or plan, when we become overly attached to the outcome of our endeavors, we fall into this trap.

Tai Chi teacher and writer Ron Sieh's advice to students fits perfectly here:

> Rather than taking a shape even if it does not feel right, change the shape so it feels more powerful. Do not adopt the idea that if one does a powerless but correctly mimicked shape for ten years one will become powerful.

Often artists, because of their creative work, find it easier to understand the nature of these pitfalls. They discover that until you are able to release your attachment to exactly duplicating what you see in your mind, and at some point allow a different part of yourself — the deeper, more right-brain, spontaneous, integrated part — to take over, you will never be satisfied with the outcome of your work, for it will reflect the mechanical nature of your mind, not the more spiritual, ephemeral nature of your soul.

Holding onto your plans as if they are carved in stone is another way to be in opposition to Principle Seven. Parents who have planned their children's lives out, even if only in their own minds, are risking the downward pull of this energy. This type of thinking leads to frustration, disappointment, and stagnation. The result is the same as in Principle Six: When we hold extreme positions, it blocks the natural flow of progress in thought, nature, and spirit and leads to limitation, judgment, and failure.

It is easy, in a busy life full of things to accomplish, to get caught up in the mind's way of thinking: empty the "in" box at all costs. But only the spirit, not the mind, knows the "in" box is never empty and never will be empty. The busy mind fills it to overflowing as a survival mechanism. Knowing this, we can accept it and allow it to be, and we can relax and do things as we can, accept the limits of time and space, and realize that most of those things are transitory, having nothing much to do with the real stuff of life anyway.

The Fable of the Magic Genie

I was told a story when I first began to meditate that has always stayed with me. Once a man was so busy he could not possibly get everything done. He prayed for a genie to appear, and the gods granted him his prayer. The only condition was that the man had to keep the genie busy at all times or it would turn on him and kill him.

"No problem!" he said, "I could never get everything I want or everything done that needs to be done." So he gave the genie all his tasks and wishes, and the genie went to work. For a long time the situation worked out nicely. But eventually the man started to run out of things for the genie to do. "Help!" he cried, "Oh no, what shall I do! I am no longer interested enough in the things of the world to provide this genie with never-ending work! I am doomed!"

A wise old woman appeared before him. "I have a solution for you," she said. "It is very simple. Give the genie a dog with a curly tail. Tell him he must gently straighten the tail of the dog."

So the man followed her advice, and the genie spent the rest of the man's life straightening the tail of the dog, only to have it curl again. The man was then free and, for the rest of his days, he meditated on the eternal. This story was told to me in connection with a mantra or chant that is often given in meditation. It is like giving the genie-mind the tail of the dog, to keep it occupied so that the soul can find union with the Creator.

If we allow our minds to run our lives, they become like insatiable genies, never allowing us to unify ourselves with the eternal flow of the Tao. As a result, we cannot, as parents, intuitively sense our children's growth and let them go without abandoning them. This is one of the most difficult tasks of the spiritual aspirant, and, not surprisingly, one of the most difficult tasks of conscious parenting; letting go without detaching from the eternal love that keeps us connected.

LEARNING HOW TO LET GO

In *Vitality, Energy, Spirit: A Taoist Sourcebook*, master Lu Yen is quoted,

Human life in the world is no more than that of a dayfly. This is true not only of ordinary people but also of wizards and buddhas of all times as well. However, though a lifetime is limited, the spirit is unlimited. If we look on the universe from the point of view of our lifetime, our lifetimes are those of dayflies. But if we look on the universe from the point of view of our spirit, the universe, too, is like a dayfly.

Taoism gives us a way of looking at all life in the context of the big picture. When we can begin to evaluate things through this bigger lens, what is important and unimportant becomes more and more clear. The best way to begin is by imagining our single lifetime, picturing our own death in our minds, and reviewing our life. In this context, how much weight does a particular matter have for us? If we do this every day for a while, we come closer and closer to our true purpose for being on this earth. Seemingly big matters become small, seemingly insignificant interactions become more important.

If we can go beyond even this, if we can imagine a view that encompasses an eternity of lifetimes, we can step into a flow of energy in which everything is part of one, eternal flow. It becomes easier to relax because we feel no pressure to get things done; we have all eternity to get it done, if indeed it needs doing. *Being* assumes more importance than doing.

It is said, "It is better to be a human *being* than a human *doing.*" It becomes easier to choose to be good, because none of us wishes to have to spend time paying for our wrongdoing with interest. It becomes more important to complete our relationships fully, with love and forgiveness, so we don't have to repeat painful situations. It becomes easier to let go, because we know no one is ever truly "gone." When we spend our lives in goodness and love, we can look forward to death and new life, knowing it can only get better, as we come closer to the bliss of oneness with the Creator and thus with all things.

Taking time every day for silent meditation or prayer is one of the best ways to still the mind enough to glimpse this level of consciousness. If you are in the midst of making a family, this time may be difficult or impossible to come by, and in that case, awareness and conscious attention are your greatest tools. Read the teachings of great masters and philosophers. Practice yoga, Tai Chi, or other activities that are spiritual in nature that help you contemplate your life and mission from a bigger perspective. Anything that helps you look at your life through the "big picture" lens will be helpful to you in parenting with this principle. In addition, practicing Principle Nine (being present) with your family can get your mind into the present and help you *experience* the big picture rather than thinking about it.

Synchronicity

Actively look for synchronicity: those "small miracles" that the mind may discount as coincidence, while the soul, which knows better, whispers, "See! It all fits."

When I was twenty-one years old, I went to India to become a nun. I renounced my marriage — not really knowing why, just following my inner guidance. It was painful for both me and my husband but we talked it through, and though I felt a great deal of pain and guilt, I knew this was something I had to do.

I went to India and got all the way through a difficult training. Toward the end I began to have dreams, every night, of two beautiful children playing in a meadow. I would awake in great mental pain, with a driving inner sense, just as strong as that which had gotten me there in the first place, that I needed to go home. Talk about confusion! I was angry with myself and thought I was being weak, and that I should rid myself of such attachments and follow through on my decision to renounce "worldly" life in order to serve all of humanity. I fasted, meditated, prayed, and tried to rid myself of this overpowering desire to go home.

Finally, the pain was too great to overcome and I knew I had to follow my heart back to the United States regardless of the consequences. I didn't know if my husband would take me back, or if I would be banned from my spiritual community, which at that time was very strict and judgmental about people who left training. I kept my decision to myself, waiting for the right time to approach the head trainer of the order. One day one of the monks who regularly taught us classes and was the head of this particular training center, called for me. When I arrived in his office, he nervously paced.

"I don't know how to tell you . . . " he said. "I went to see our teacher this morning and he was very upset. 'Why is Vimala here?' he asked me. 'Vimala should not be in the training center. She is a family person.'" The monk said he was so sorry; that he would try to change my teacher's mind.

"No," I said solemnly, "My teacher's words are my guide. I must do what he says." In my heart, I was jumping up and down, laughing like a child. I returned home to the United States, not in shame but in amazement at the synchronicity that led to my homecoming. I subsequently had two children, and one day, as we picnicked in a mountain meadow, I realized these were the children in my dreams. I also realized that I had made the decision for myself before receiving the guidance of my spiritual teacher, and thus was empowered by his observation rather than obedient to it.

It is so easy, in any culture, even those whose principles include intense individuality, to be so influenced by the cultural norms and your own conditioning that you carve a path for yourself that is rigid and inflexible, that leads to intolerance and exclusion, and that doesn't allow your soul room to expand and grow, to risk and receive. It will do you good, both as a person and a parent, to examine your inner "script" and how it plays out in your life; to examine how much of it is unconscious, and how much of it is your choice and why. It is my hope that these principles will help you raise your children with the values of inclusiveness, non-judgment, tolerance, and forgiveness; with the strength of knowing how to set boundaries; with the knowledge of true right and wrong; and with the ability to think and to change their minds when their heart suggests a better way.

PARENTING WITH PRINCIPLE SEVEN

Though it is perhaps the most difficult to maintain consistently, Principle Seven, flow and let go, is also the most powerful inner tool we have in our individual lives and our journey with our children. It is a force of nature, like gravity. If you fight it, you will only experience more pain and frustration. If you can learn how to go with it, your life will be an ever-expanding, inclusive, loving, and natural way of being.

The habit of living according to "supposed to" has to go. In *Embrace Tiger, Return to Mountain,* Chungliang Al Huang advises:

> When leaves fall from the tree, they follow the wind, and if they happen to drop on the water they just follow the currents. A leaf does not fight and say, 'I want to go back on the branch,' or 'There's a dry spot; I don't want to land there.' Your movement and your life can also become an easy happening that follows the winds and currents.

Animals do this naturally, as do most small children.

Principle Seven in Pregnancy

As adults, the first experience we may have of this universal principle may be when we become pregnant. Most pregnant women have a moment toward the end of their pregnancy when the inexorable nature of giving birth finally, really hits them, and their minds rebel at the lack of control. "Yikes!" we think, "Never mind! I don't want to do this after all." Perhaps the keyword here is *mind.* When the realization sinks into our heart, we know we cannot turn back, we must flow with what nature has set in motion.

It may be the first time in our lives we really experience, deep within ourselves, being part of a larger flow that is so much more powerful than our individual thoughts that it blows our mind. We realize an entirely different person is going to come into the world through our body, in a process we cannot control, and that person will then be our responsibility to love, protect, nourish, and attend to twenty-four hours a day for probably very nearly twenty years, and who will be with us in one way or another for life. It is our chance to truly experience Principle Seven in all its power.

If we can hold onto that experience, it can help guide us as parents for the rest of our days, for it gives us the ability to feel our connection with the great, flowing whole of creation and follow it naturally, sinking and floating by the power of the heart, not the mind.

Principle Seven with Young Children

There will be times in your children's lives when it will be very helpful for you to practice this principle. Of course, all along the way you experience the unstoppable flow of nature as you watch your children grow, wean, potty train, go to school, lose their baby teeth, develop as adolescents, express their sexuality, and make more and more choices for themselves. But there are a few big events that will really affect you personally and change your life.

It is important all along the way to keep your observation skills sharp so that you can attune yourself to each stage of development your child is in, and to the individual needs of each child. You need to picture yourselves as mentors, constantly using your power as parents not to put the child where you think she should be, like some sort of living toy, but to help facilitate the child in her effort to become who she is, independent of you, yet maintaining that close and loving bond between you.

Consequences

Sometimes practicing Principle Seven includes allowing natural consequences to guide the child. To show my children the dangers of the kitchen stove, I held them in my arms (at around the age when they began to walk), turned on one of the burners, and showed them how I did that, saying, "The burner is on." Usually the child would have the vocabulary to repeat, "On."

I would continue in a serious tone and with a frown, saying, "It is very *hot*. Oweee! It can *hurt!*" while holding my hand above the burner where it would not burn but where I could feel the heat.

"Hot! Oweee!" my child would repeat, mimicking my frown and, in the safety of my arms, waving his or her hand above the burner.

"Not for playing!" I would say, "Only for Mommy and Daddy! No, no, no!" in my most formidable tone, with "sinking power," frowning and shaking my head. That was all that was needed.

"Not for playing" was an often-repeated slogan in our house, as we pointed out to the children what was and was not intended for their use. Sometimes it would be necessary to repeat such a sequence two or three times to secure the child's knowledge and memory of

the lesson. It was a way to safely show the child the natural consequences of dangerous actions without allowing them to be hurt. Of
course, we also child-proofed the house as much as possible and kept
a very close eye on them, as all good parents must.

The same type of communication can be used to teach your
kids right from wrong, using stories, examples from the media, and
natural phenomena. You can point out to them why you are careful with electrical outlets, appliances, and so on. Explain how things
work. Tell them what is only for adults and why.

Principle Seven with Teens

When my daughter was a young teen, I often spoke with her
about the importance of being aware of her surroundings, protect-
ing herself as much as possible, getting self-defense skills, and so on.
I went so far as to buy her a personal alarm. She scoffed at me, saying, "Mom, you watch too many talk shows." I thought, maybe
she's right, but better to err on the side of safety. When a show was
on television that demonstrated effective self-protection techniques
for women, I asked her to watch it with me and talk about it. Of
course, she didn't want to talk about it. Not only was the thought
scary, but she, like most teens, thought those things only happened
to other people.

When we were on our way to a vacation in Florida, we stopped
at a hotel in Mississippi. We got separate rooms for our two teens
and ourselves. That evening, there was suddenly a loud banging on
our door, my daughter stood screaming outside. I opened the door
and she ran into our room, shaking all over, crying hysterically, saying that a man had just grabbed her while she was outside getting a
soft drink. I held her, listened to her story, told my son to stay with
her, and charged out of there on pure adrenaline. The mother in
me was in full-out protection mode. I ran down to where the incident had occurred and frantically scanned the parking lot. Then my
rational sense kicked in. "What are you going to do, Vimala," it said
to me, "beat him up?"

I re-routed myself to the front desk and told the hotel's security staff what had just happened. They called the police, searched

for the man, and sent security people up to our room to record my daughter's story. I was amazed as I listened to her. She described the man in detail. She said the minute she sensed something wrong she turned; he grabbed her and she whirled away from him, screaming obscenities at the top of her lungs with all the power she could muster, and then he ran away. My daughter is very petite; any man could pick her up with one arm. But her attacker was surprised by her power and her refusal to be victimized or act afraid, and it scared him off.

She was traumatized by this incident for quite a while. I continued to talk to her about all the things she did that were right — she had listened to her inner voice and acted powerfully. She berated herself, saying that, before she even went outside, her inner voice told her to ask her brother to go with her, but she felt she'd be a wimp if she did, so she ignored it. "I will never ignore that voice again, Mom," she told me.

Later, she said that incident changed her life. In some ways it saddened her; she no longer felt safe walking around by herself in the world. She had joined the world of women, in which one out of three women are assaulted at some point in their lives. But she had learned a valuable lesson. Now, she pays attention to her surroundings, she carries protective devices, she took a self-protection course, and she is confident that she will never ignore her intuitive guidance again.

From Manager to Mentor

A big change comes for you as a parent when your child enters adolescence. It is a critical turning point, when what you say and do can have a profound affect on the next ten years of your relationship with your child. It is important to listen closely to your child and respect her requests for you to stop treating her like a baby, not kiss her in public, and so on. It helps secure her power over her own life, and learn to exercise that power in safety. It helps her to start setting her own boundaries, learn how to express them appropriately, and learn what constitutes a healthy response. If you ignore, for example, your child's request that you knock on her door before entering, you are telling her she cannot set her own boundaries — it is okay for others to override her requests. That is not a good message for her.

When these requests begin coming from your child it is a good indication for you to shift gears into a mentoring mode; one person called it going from "manager" to "consultant." This is often difficult for parents whose own adolescence was painful, smothered, or abandoned, and/or who don't want their children repeating their own painful mistakes. You must remember your child is not you and separate your issues from his.

If you need some temporary therapy to do this, consider it a gift to your child. You will be a much better parent, with a much healthier, happier relationship with your children. So often, we go overboard in either trying to duplicate and live out our fantasy adolescence with our children or do just the opposite of what our parents did in an effort to heal *ourselves* of a painful adolescence. You need to get clear about what is yours and what is your child's, and begin letting your child fulfill his or her own destiny and mission in life.

In Principle Three, empower, we discussed some ways to do this, such as teaching our kids how cars work and how to fix them or get them fixed, how to use a checking account, and so on. Other ways we can help them include showing them that when they have trouble dealing with something emotionally, it is perfectly okay and very healthy — not "crazy" — to go to a good therapist, just as you would go to a doctor for a broken arm. We can also begin to allow our teens to schedule their own dental and doctor appointments while explaining how, when, and why to do so, how to choose a good health care professional, and why to have insurance and how it works. Again, slowly, within the safety of home, our children can experience being an adult without too much risk. At first, we walk them through the process. Slowly, they take over. The same process is used when teaching a teen how to drive a car.

When Things Don't Go as Expected

I've learned from my experience, and that of many people I have interviewed, that many families have unexpected circumstances that throw off their natural way of doing and being. They end up feeling they have failed because they cannot conform to the kinds of spiritual standards I am talking about, in the exact way I am presenting them. I will address this topic in subsequent chapters where I discuss how to negotiate traumatic situations, crises, and so on. Here I want to talk about how the conflict between the needs of parents and children can become a near crisis when, for example, a family member becomes ill, there is a divorce, there is a big loss of some kind, or the children are asked to "grow up" and help the family sooner than their peers.

Even when trauma is not present, there is generally a conflict of needs during the teen and young adult years that can create confusion in the parent-child relationship and sometimes lead to hurt feelings, unnatural separation, and anxiety:

Conflicting Needs

Kids

Parents

• Need to detach, become independent. Life has usually not given them much experience of loss, therefore they have little empathy with a parent's feelings of loss.

• Need to experience a deep attachment to family and to realize that some sort of "family" is there even though the kids are growing up and out, or a loss has occurred. The need to become interdependent sometimes conflicts with the reality of dependency when something such as an illness occurs.

• Need to establish their own identity but still depend on parents for approval, help, support, and so on.

• Need to establish a new identity beyond being a parent; can feel confusion about when to help or not, when to say yes or no, when to push the child out of the nest, when to give the comfort of the nest.

- Desire to be approved of, but rebel against anything perceived as control.

- Need to release control, but fear for the child's safety and vulnerability sometimes leads to inadvertent controlling statements or behavior.

- Have little understanding of their parents' waning energy because of their own overabundance of youthful energy. Want to be perceived as adults without being abandoned by parents.

- Have little tolerance for kids' youthful off-the-wall energy, want to be respected as elders without being perceived as expendable and/or old.

Because of these conflicting needs, we may find ourselves saying things to one another in the heat of the moment that we later regret. As a parent, try hard not to hold your children, even your grown-up kids, to their past behavior or their words. You can and probably should let them know when something they say hurts you, but be willing to forgive and forget.

As we discussed before, be willing to apologize and make amends when you slip into reactive behavior with your child. Thus, respect is restored and a foundation can be laid upon which trust can be rebuilt. The underlying agreement is that the relationship is more important than the passing events that sometimes cause us to act in ways unbecoming to our true selves. As family members, our most important job is to reflect the truest, highest, most beautiful inner self of each of our family members, and even when they are going through weak or difficult periods, we can hold up that mirror for them.

Of all the principles in this book, the spirit of flowing and letting go has been the most challenging to carry out in my own life, partially because I have a chronic illness and am a single parent. I am still unsure what it means to "master" this principle, or if such a thing is even possible for a bonded parent. It may be that later, as a much older, wiser elder, I will understand it more completely, but the elders with whom I have discussed it, whose wisdom I respect, say essentially the same thing. It may get a little easier at times, but then it becomes more difficult again, and it seems your hard-won sense of serenity about going with the flow and releasing your children can be blown away as easily as dandelion fluff.

Learning to recognize even *this* ebb and flow is part of Principle Seven. I remember a friend of mine joking, "Oh dear, there it goes again! I let go and then when I least expect it, something happens and I find myself clamping down like a pit bull dog before I'm even aware of it!"

Chungliang Al Huang, as well as many other Eastern teachers, talks about insecurity and uncertainty as part of the flow into which we must learn to let go:

> Insecurity and uncertainty are everywhere. If you don't let them become a part of your flow, you will always be resisting and fighting. If the ground here suddenly shakes and trembles, can you *give* with it and still maintain your center?... If you can become fluid and open even when you are standing still, then this fluidness and openness makes you able to respond to changes. You will then be able to play with the changes and enjoy them.

Maintaining an awareness of the importance of Principle Seven, and of the need to work at it, is vital to your progress on the path of parenting. The way you practice flowing and letting go will differ from parent to parent, child to child, and relationship to relationship. Certainly the way I practice it with my son is utterly different than the way I practice it with my daughter. Age, personality, birth order, and parenting experience all come into play. But the spirit of this principle remains the same: Each child is his or her own being, with his or her own path to follow. A crucial aspect of our mission as parents is to help them find their paths and to develop the inner strength it takes to walk alone.

Exercise for Principle Seven

1. Sit comfortably, close your eyes, and relax each part of your body.
2. Take seven deep belly breaths. As you inhale repeat, "flow," and as you exhale repeat, "let go."

Principle Eight
MAINTAIN CONTINUITY

⋯⋰⋱⋯

No matter how much is going on outside of oneself, one
still reaffirms what is in one's heart, taking comfort in the
regular pulse. What works in the shelter of home or
temple works everywhere. Only when we know such
consistency will we know that our quest is succeeding.

— Deng Ming-Dao, *365 Tao Daily Meditations*

I n Tai Chi, the student learns movements that are all connected together. At the same time, she learns to experience her *chi* in connection with the flow of the eternal consciousness. Every day, as she practices, it gradually all comes together into one continuous, flowing, powerful motion, and when she finishes, coming full circle to the original position, she is relaxed, strengthened, energized, connected, and grounded.

If you look at Taoism's *yin/yang* symbol, it shows this continuous circular flow of opposites. It can represent the circle of creation: consciousness into mind into matter into mind into consciousness again. All Eastern traditions, many Western philosophies, and some of the latest scientific theories explain cosmology in basically this way. As the Quakers sing in their simple hymn, "We all come from God, and unto God do we return."

There is already a law of continuity operating in the universe. With limited lifetimes, seemingly limited resources, and sometimes limited energy, it is easy to doubt this law. Exposed to a materialistic culture that constantly gives you limiting ideas such as "you only go around once" and "survival of the fittest," and perpetuates the notion that only huge amounts of wealth can create security, the Western mind doubts the law of continuity even more. Somewhere inside you, there may be a gnawing fear, a feeling of "walking on thin ice." I don't know how many times I've heard it repeated that many Americans are "two paychecks away from homelessness."

Insecurity, uncertainty, and change are a regular part of life. The harder we fight and resist them, the harder we are hit when they come our way. A very good practice for the Tai Chi student who wishes to learn about this principle is to imagine or pretend she is on thin ice. Once accomplished in her movements and connected with her *hara* and her *chi*, she grounds herself to the earth with "sinking power," and begins to imagine she is on a very thin sheet of ice, and it is beginning to crack. She becomes acutely aware, shifts her weight, attention, and energy according to the subtle cues she receives from the environment. She becomes adept at walking on thin ice, and moving through every delicate situation with balance and ease.

Another analogy, given by Tai Chi teacher Chungliang Al Huang, is that of a bird hopping from branch to branch. You move from one place to another as if you are landing on a resilient twig that bends and bounces with your weight as you gently and slowly sink your weight into your new position. But at the same time, as he says, ". . . you are not rooted to that twig." If you sense the twig is not strong enough to support you, it is an easy matter to hop to another, while you listen for cues from the limited base (the twig) and use the unlimited base (the Tao) to tell you when and how to move with the changes. Then you can move ahead, rather than clinging tenaciously and rigidly to your chosen twig as the wind blows, and the twig cracks and falls to the ground.

The eternal base constantly moves, like shifting ice, or a branch in the wind, and the art is to learn to move with it. You learn to accept insecurity as normal. You develop the internal resilience to move with the flow of the universal within you rather than trying to use your mind to overpower your inner sense and lead you to the illusion that creates that needy, grabbing feeling in the pit of your stomach.

Change may be considered *yang* and constant as *yin*. Every day we have internal and external conflicts between coping with change and being contented with the constant. We often get bored with the constant but distraught and anxious with change. Our best approach is to accept both and learn how to be resilient and responsive to our lives.

A Deep Seat

A therapist friend who enjoys riding horses uses another analogy. She talks about riding a horse that spooks easily; the only way to ride it without getting thrown is to take a "deep seat." You sink into the horse's body and become one with the horse, and you learn to sense those milliseconds before the horse gets spooked and may jump or buck. You adjust your energy, using both "listening power" (following and anticipating the horse's movements) and "sinking power" (rooting your base into the earth). You sink into the horse rather than reacting by jumping up, and quite possibly getting thrown to the ground. It takes practice because the body may be conditioned to react to fear and insecurity by jumping upward, holding the breath, and, in other ways, moving off center.

When you are able to take a deep seat, to breathe deeply and remain one with the horse's energy, you can ride through the jump or buck and return to a lighter seat when the horse's cues indicate it is safe. Some of us have lives that resemble not so much a slightly spookable horse as a constantly bucking dragon. For us, learning to take a deep seat and read the cues is imperative if we are to continue to function at all. It may take a lot of practice, but once learned, our options in the world become limitless, for we are secure in the ever-shifting eternal base and are able to adjust to the constantly thrashing, changing, limited outer base of our chosen paths.

As Chungliang Al Huang so beautifully counsels,

> Wherever you are, whatever you do, you can always come back to this marvelous sense of stillness, the feeling of yourself, very, very much *here*. This is your reference point, this is your stability.

THE OPPOSITE

One great misconception is that continuity and consistency (as we define it in the West) are the same thing, when in fact they are opposites. Continuity speaks to principles, unchanging laws. Consistency is an invention of the human mind. It comes from faulty logic, something the brain has a great deal of expertise producing. You cannot be consistent in an ever-changing environment. But you can maintain continuity. This means that you cleave to universal principles, and change with the outer cues of your environment as you must.

Reacting with consistency can lead to an endless tug-of-war. But if you can respond with continuity, the energy you send back to the same person may be different each time, according to your information, your position, and your evaluation of time, place, and person, while the principles underlying your response remain the same.

In yoga philosophy this is called a subjective approach with an objective adjustment. That is, your spiritual values do not change, but the way you express them in the world *must* change according to all the shifting factors in each situation. Dr. Paul Stoltz, author of *Adversity Quotient*, makes a very good point:

> Those who embrace change tend to respond most constructively to adversity — using it to strengthen their resolve.

HOW TO MAINTAIN CONTINUITY

The way we maintain continuity for ourselves is, at a basic level, similar to the way we are drawn to moderation as opposed to extremes. Most days, most of us like to get up and get ourselves ready for the day in the same way; we have bedtime rituals, weekend rituals, things that give us a sense of continuity. We may change these as circumstances change, as we grow, and as we find healthier ways of being. But rarely does someone have an entirely different life every day. We also like the continuity of change, though that may seem to be a contradiction in terms. We like to be able to occasionally do things differently, take a break from habits, go on a vacation.

At a more spiritual level, continuity implies integrity. It means who you are on the inside is the same as who you are on the outside. You follow through. You keep your promises, you can be trusted with confidences and, in general, trusted to be there for the people you have pledged yourself to as a friend — including yourself! Taoist philosopher Wen-Tzu said in *Vitality, Energy, Spirit,* "When the vitality, spirit, will, and energy are calm, they fill you day by day and make you strong." The way to nurture yourself with Principle Eight is to calm these aspects of your being, in whatever ways you find that suit you, be it through your daily rituals, meditation, belly breathing, eating healthy foods, or perhaps learning a martial art or yoga to strengthen and center your will.

If you grew up in an environment of dysfunction, you probably have gaping holes in the sense of inner security usually obtained through the experience of continuity in childhood. So you will need to work at getting this back for yourself, either before or as you give it to your children.

A friend of mine recently told me she was well into menopause before she realized she had put off giving that sense of continuity to herself. She had come from an intensely dysfunctional family, and was determined that her children not suffer the constant upheavals, unpredictability, and insecurity she experienced in her childhood, so she made a heroic effort to provide continuity to her children. She stayed in a less-than-desirable marriage; her husband was a good father but he did not nurture or respect her, and he refused marriage counseling. She stayed with her husband in the same neighborhood, made sure her kids went to the same school year after year, created beautiful holiday rituals for them, and saw to it that they had connections with the family members who were the most "normal" and wouldn't let them down. She sacrificed her own energy and health to make enough money to keep her children in a school that nourished their spirits, and made sure they had what other kids had, didn't feel "poor" or inferior, and were involved, to the extent they wanted, in extracurricular activities and summer day camp.

In some ways, she told me, she felt she was giving these things to herself by giving them to her children. But when the children were grown, she had to start all over. The things that gave her children the continuity they needed did not work for her anymore. She was shocked to discover that there was still a gaping hole in herself, made even more painful by the feeling of loss she was experiencing as a mother and the non-supportive relationship she had with her husband. She finally divorced him, and found herself alone and terrified. Her life had been so much about others that she had neglected herself, and had forgotten — or never learned — how to nurture herself.

Slowly she began working on her own personal mission statement; she made lists of possible ways she could provide herself with a feeling of security and continuity, and she enlisted the help of a therapist and began a several-years-long journey to "re-parent" herself. For her, making a list of the ways she had provided continuity for her children was a starting point. She had learned how to create continuity by finding role models, reading voraciously, and attending to what she had missed as a child — all of which were parts of her inner compass that guided her as a parent. Now she needed similar skills to create continuity for herself. Some of the things she came up with were:

- To feed herself healthy foods and supplements.
- To create waking and sleeping rituals that felt good to her.
- To find out what it means to be a truly supportive person, and then slowly find friends who were supportive and who wouldn't let her down, and then slowly let go of unsupportive relationships.
- To do work that made her feel she was contributing and leaving a legacy, so that even if her full-time job of mother was over, she still had important work to do.
- To decorate her home in a way that pleased her and made her feel safe and comfortable.
- To create new holiday rituals that fit the new configuration of her family and that felt good to her.

- To find, within herself, the parent that would protect her and to whom she could turn when feeling lonely or fearful. She called this part of herself her "warrior self." She envisioned it as a strong presence guarding her heart, that would not, under any circumstances, allow her to be damaged — just as she, as a mother, had done for her own children.

In these and other ways, she was finally able to have for herself what she had given her children through tremendous personal sacrifice: the deep, secure feeling of continuity that allowed her to grow and change, respond to changes around her, and keep a "deep seat" when life got tough.

Chungliang Al Huang is very helpful in showing us how to find continuity in the midst of insecurity:

Most of the time we want not to change. We think we can find something nice and secure, and we want to hang onto it. We forget that the constant can only build upon change. The world keeps changing, so if you try to hang onto the moment, you're lost. But if you follow the changing moment, then you reach a constant moving. You go with what happens; you carry that sense of stability with your moving self. You experience both moving and stillness together. If you apply this idea to your daily thinking and your way of perceiving your existence, then it can help you.

PARENTING WITH PRINCIPLE EIGHT

In nature, continuity is maintained by an endless number of eternal rhythms. From the cycles of the moon to the beating of our hearts, everything around us pulses with a rhythm that is predictable, yet not entirely consistent. The sun doesn't rise at exactly the same time every day, but we know it will rise. The tides ebb and flow at their own rate, but we know their general pattern. Many of the habits we fall into or create in our own lives follow these natural rhythms.

Philosophers throughout the ages, and especially the Taoists, have emphasized the importance of rhythm in harmony with nature. Educational philosopher Rudolf Steiner, founder of the Waldorf Schools, embedded in his educational system the harmonious rhythms that help children grow in tune with nature and their own innermost being. The Waldorf classroom is carefully designed, as is the curriculum, to take greatest advantage of the calming, supportive qualities of natural rhythms, and to help children learn through repetition and imitation.

We all gain a sense of security through continuity, and thinking about this aspect of your home life and your child's life will be of great advantage to you as well; our ever-changing external cultural environment breeds insecurity and uncertainty enough to balance the scales.

Principle Eight in Pregnancy

Your pregnancy will have its own rhythms within the continuity of conception to birth. Each trimester brings with it different feelings and challenges, and prepares you gradually for parenthood. These days, attuning ourselves and our families to natural rhythms is a great challenge that requires conscious choices. Technology increasingly makes it possible for us to ignore natural rhythms. The circadian rhythms of our bodies, for example, are attuned to the sun and moon, but the invention of electric lights completely changed the way we work and play, allowing us to circumvent the natural slowing of our pace with sunset and to go shopping or exercise at midnight, if we want.

To allow Principle Eight to do its magic in your home life, begin to plan for it during your pregnancy. Talk and read about early childhood, and think about how you might create rituals (daily, weekly, monthly, seasonally, and yearly) for your children. Rituals provide them with a deep sense of being held in the warm security of the universal rhythm of life, even as their bodies grow and change, your family configuration changes, you move, and other big changes happen around them.

Start to keep a journal in which you write about each of your children. Videotapes are great, but the written word is more enduring and, because it is a private communication, it is more intimate and genuine. You won't remember many of the things your infant, toddler, and pre-schooler does and says, even though at the time you can't imagine forgetting. Write it down! And write down your feelings, too, and what is going on in the world, in your family, and with you as a person. I was so glad I did this. When my children were teenagers, I made a scrapbook for each of them, with photocopied excerpts from my journals and pictures of them at the ages they were when I wrote about them, along with some current commentary to give it context.

The journals follow each child from pregnancy to adolescence, and give them the immediacy of my own thoughts, feelings, and words at that time. I included information such as their first words, what they got for their birthdays, how we celebrated holidays, and the wise and wonderful things they said and did that, without that record, might be forgotten. They treasure their books as a record of their childhood, the happy times they had, their triumphs, and the times they grew up in, and as a peek into what their parents were like back then. Much of that record has been lost to their own memories, so their books keep their memories for them, and will be treasured through the coming generations, providing continuity for the entire family's "ancestral line."

Principle Eight with Young Children

Continuity, when maintained through rituals, prevents a lot of so-called disciplinary problems, because it gives the child a safe world to go home to, and things to count on and look forward to, and so it eliminates the fear of uncertainty, which can otherwise be acted out in unacceptable behaviors. Family rules and their consequences are part of this continuity. If daily life has a rhythm to it, much of the chaos and stress is removed for the parents as well as children. Everyone knows what to expect and how he or she fits into the whole.

Some ideas from my own life and from people I have interviewed may give you some ideas about how to make continuity an integral part of your path of parenting.

Rhythms of Massage and Rest

During pregnancy, try to set aside a certain time every day to massage your belly and talk intimately with your unborn child. That way when the baby is born, you will already be in the habit of making time for massage. Also during pregnancy, if you can create a rest or nap time during the day, it will help you maintain the energy you need, and after the baby is born, it can become a natural space for a rest or nap time for your child.

You can prepare your child for rest time by incorporating it into their play. For example, if your child is playing with a stick horse you can join in, ride around a bit, and then suggest that the horses are tired and need to be groomed and taken to the "stable" where everybody lies down for a rest. Each day at rest time put on the same soothing music, sing the same song, rock in a favorite chair, or take a little walk on the same route before lying down for the nap. This helps bring your child into the rest period without an abrupt cessation of play and the subsequent struggle that makes rest time feel like a punishment. Remember that young children are generally startled by abrupt changes, so try to find ways to lead them into the next part of their day in a natural way.

Bathing Rhythms

Bath time can happen at the same time every day, with special toys and soaps. Using a special bathing ritual such as first we wash our arms and legs, then we wash our tummies and chest, and so on, can be fun. If you can incorporate a fantasy or a song such as "The back bone's connected to the . . . " your child will engage in the fantasy play and look forward to the bath. Some people make time for massage either before or after the bath, which is then followed by rest time, so it is all one flowing sequence.

Rhythms for Meal Time

Meals can be ritualized with special foods, or with an emphasis on family togetherness at certain meals. For example, whether morning or evening is the easiest time for the entire family to eat together, the meal can be ritualized by lighting candles, or holding hands while giving thanks or saying grace. My children learned the poem "Grace" by Christian Morgenstern at their Waldorf School, and we used it in our house during their early years:

Earth, who gives to us this food,
Sun, who makes it ripe and good,
Dear Sun, dear Earth, by you we live,
Our loving thanks to you we give.

We would add our own thanks to God for special things, for bringing us together again, and so on. A house rule was to never have the television on during a family meal at the table. Just for fun, sometimes we'd have "TV dinners," where we all watched the Super Bowl together while we ate, but it was understood that these meals were a break from the routine and not an opportunity to allow the TV to creep into our everyday dinner time.

To reinforce the ritual process, each person can perform a specific task to pull it all together. One child can put out place mats, another spoons. One child can help stir the food or pour the drinks or serve.

One father set the table for breakfast the night before and, when possible, put fresh flowers on the table and a special "I love you" or "Have a great day!" message at each place. Then when his family sat down for breakfast the next morning he wasn't harried, and each family member felt nourished, physically and emotionally, before starting the day. Playing soft music in the background can help set a calming mood, while bouncy, upbeat tunes can create a happy start for the day.

Lunches can also be prepared the night before, either by parents or the whole family, and set out for easy retrieval in the morning. In fact, preparing lunch for the next day and setting out clothes to wear can become the beginning of a bedtime ritual, and can ease the process of getting everyone ready the next morning.

A short verse or song can be used to end the meal as well, rather than allowing everyone to drift away. Children appreciate beginnings and endings, though at times they may complain or rebel.

Bed Time Rhythms

Bed time rituals are important for deep, restful, restorative sleep for adults as well as children. In our home, Daddy was in charge of the bedtime routine. He got the children to brush their teeth, put on their pajamas, and get into bed. Then he read them a story, or made one up, and laid down with each child for a short period. The children called this a "lay with." At other times when they were stressed or needed attention, they would come to me or their father and say, "Can I have a 'lay with'?" This was their father's close time with them after he had been at work all day, and they all treasured it.

During this time, a candle or night-light can be lit, a story told with a back rub, or the child can say a prayer or verse before blowing out the candle or switching off the light. Singing a lullaby or playing soft, angelic background music can help the child relax and drift off to sleep. Having the ritual start and end the same time every night helps tune the child's circadian rhythms to sleep. There are even compact discs available that have scientifically programmed music that cues the brain to go into deeper and deeper levels of restorative sleep.

Some children resist bedtime fiercely. Easing a child's resistance may require some experimentation to find the right ritual, allowing the child to choose some of its elements ("Would you rather have a story or a song?"), and renegotiating the ritual as the child grows. Gradually, story time may be replaced by a simple kiss on the forehead and a special way of saying goodnight, always including "I love you." You can get a compact disc player for the child's room that plays gentle music as he is falling asleep and waking up.

Do not allow your children to get into a pattern of fighting the bedtime ritual. Solve the problem, no matter what it takes. You need time for your partner and yourself, and your child needs a lot of sleep to support his growth and to maintain energy for the day. Seven to seven-thirty p.m. is the best time to begin the bedtime ritual, with the goal of children being asleep by eight or eight-thirty. This may sound early, but it is perfectly natural for young preschool children and the time can be adjusted as they grow older. Even so, until their teen years, they need to be asleep about an hour or two before you think they do.

Picture everything slowing down in the evening. Talk more slowly, move more slowly, and lead your child slowly through the rituals of brushing teeth and hair, taking a bath, getting on pajamas, laying out clothes for the next day, and so on. Older children and teens can help the little ones with their rituals and thereby recapture some of the cozy feelings they remember from their time as the "baby" of the house.

Rituals for older children may include homework, tidying the room, and reading. Some parents find that pets can play a role in the bedtime ritual; playing with the cat or dog or watching the fish in the aquarium can be soothing. Teens may find it a good time for writing in a journal. A series of studies at Southern Methodist University showed that writing about feelings in a journal has a positive and enduring affect on the immune system; this is something your teen may not especially relate to, but it might help you to encourage the use of a journal as a tool for self-expression and venting feelings. Allow your teen to have a locked journal, and never *ever* violate its privacy.

Morning Rhythms

In the same way, mornings can be planned to begin with a slow waking pace that gradually increases in tempo. Reciting a verse or singing a song can be a wonderful way for you to wake up your child. One we learned from Waldorf friends was:

Good morning, dear earth,
Good morning, dear sun,
Good morning, dear stones,
And flowers, everyone!
Good morning, dear bees
And birds in the trees,
Good morning to you,
And good morning to me!

Try to move through the morning in an orderly way, with each task consistently following the next, such as wake, sing or pray, stretch, brush teeth, take vitamins, get dressed, fix hair, gather items for school, eat breakfast, get lunch, and kiss goodbye.

Very young children, just starting out at school, may need a special way to connect with their mother during their day. One mother puts a drop of her perfume on a hanky that can be tucked into her child's pocket and used to provide aromatherapy for naptime or when the child needs a calming reminder of her presence. When I had to go away on business trips during my daughter's preschool years, I gave her my nightgown to sleep with, so she could feel close to me and even smell my scent.

Weekly Rhythms

The weekly rhythm is reinforced by special activities done on specific days. At our house, we evolved a ritual for Sunday family dinners. A special meal was made, the table decorated, and either conversation, a video, or a board game followed the meal. Often, we would invite our teenaged children's friends. Everyone looked forward to it, and though several times we had to put the Sunday ritual on hold when I was ill, we always managed to revive it, and to adapt it to fit our changing lifestyles.

A weekly rhythm can also be established by taking the children to the park, zoo, ball game, or museum on a certain day of the week; having Saturday cleanup days; going out to a restaurant or age-appropriate movie on a certain day; having a family game night; or having a creative day when the family paints or does crafts together. I remember when I was in high school my best friend's big Italian family had Friday night fish dinners and big, eight-course Italian feasts every Sunday afternoon.

If you don't go to a religious service, think about having a special time each week when the family spends some "spiritual" time together. It could be as simple as a hike in the woods, a time for scripture reading and conversation, or even something creative like a puppet show featuring a spiritual theme such as stories from the Bible, the Koran, the Indian Mahabharata, or even fairy tales.

Seasonal Rhythms

Celebrate the seasons in as many ways as you can think of to help your child attune himself to the earth and the rhythms of nature. From New Year's Day until after midsummer, it is as if the earth is breathing out. It is an expansive time, when children gradually want to be unencumbered, free, and outdoors more often. It is a time for making plans, doing creative projects, taking vacations, and doing outward-focused activities.

From late summer until just before New Year's Day, it is as if the earth breathes in again. The energy is one of contraction. Animals hoard winter supplies, burrow, and hibernate. The world gets darker as there is less sunlight each day. We want to keep warm, snuggle, rest, and be indoors, and our activities will be more contemplative and inward directed.

Some ideas for these seasonal rituals include:

- Decorations and lights for the home or table that signify the seasons.
- Special holiday parties that the whole family helps to plan and prepare for.
- For preschool and young children, parents can keep their imaginative and spiritual world alive by creating magical experiences in the context of a holiday. Remember, many religious traditions have their own holiday rituals that you can use, or you may want to make up your own.

For example, my kids believed in Santa Claus until they were around twelve years old. When they came home saying, "Billy said there is no Santa!" I replied, "Do *you* think there is a Santa?" I would lead the conversation in such a way that the magic could be believed, because I knew that's what my children wanted. Without lying to them, I covertly gave them permission to believe. The magic of Christmas trees, making ornaments, sparkling lights, the smell of evergreen, fires in the woodstove or fireplace, the anticipation of Santa bringing special gifts, and leaving cookies and milk and a thank-you note for Santa on Christmas Eve all created light in our hearts at the darkest time of the year.

We had few resources when the children were small, and for a couple of Christmases Mom and Dad began in September to make toys and gifts for the children and save money for one special store-bought toy so the kids would not feel "poor" or left out when their friends showed off their store-bought loot. Later, when we could afford more, we had to work less diligently but we tried to keep the spirit of the season intact. (It is a good idea to make a family rule that a gift cannot be used, worn, or spent until a thank-you card has been sent.)

Christmas music, special cookies, and ways that the children could serve the needy were all included in our holiday celebration. For example, one year our project, from Thanksgiving until just before the holidays, was to make simple Christmas stockings for twelve children at an orphanage in the Dominican Republic. We got very inexpensive toys and candies (that to them would be amazing presents) and painted their names on the gift-filled stockings. I then sent them to the nun who was running the orphanage. Another Christmas, the children gathered up the toys, clothes, and books they had outgrown, but that were still in good condition, and sent them to an orphanage in Guatemala. Each time, we looked up the location of the orphanage on the map, and I tried to get photos of the children and their home from the orphanage so my children would know more about the kids they were helping.

One of our rituals, when both children were in preschool, was for Mom and Dad to do a puppet show on Thanksgiving Day, acting out a fairy tale that had been read to them nightly since the leaves had begun to fall. It was all prepared in secret, very hush-hush, and the children were delighted with the entire program. They then had the handmade puppets and cardboard theater to play with, and it kept them occupied through the holiday season. This linked one holiday with the other, and was a way of keeping continuity through the seasons even as we recognized each holiday separately.

On Valentine's Day, the children would find special treats in their lunches and Valentine cards from Mom and Dad under their pillows. On Groundhog Day, I would line baskets with foil and fill them with earth, and the children would plant grass seeds in their baskets. By Easter time, their baskets were full of beautiful green grass. Then the Easter Bunny would come in the night and hide the colored eggs the children had prepared and leave treats in their baskets for them. Easter morning we would greet spring and the children would scramble to find the eggs and their baskets full of treats. As an extra magic touch, the night before I would dip my fingertips in mud-colored washable paint and make bunny footprints all over the house.

Older children, who have figured out who Santa and the Easter Bunny really are, can be convinced to help keep the magic for their younger siblings. This also allows them to hold onto the magic of childhood without losing their dignity as "big kids." They might even participate in hiding eggs or other things parents would ordinarily do. My kids, even after they knew it was *me* doing all of this, wanted me to keep doing it!

We greeted summer with trips to the zoo, water parks, drive-in movies, amusement parks, or the beach. We allowed summer to bring its chaos into our lives and suspended many of our rituals. We slept in and woke up whenever we wanted, didn't follow much of a schedule, and let the children play later into the night because it didn't get dark until after nine. By the time September rolled around, we were all ready and eager to re-establish routines, rituals, and rules, and to breathe in again.

All of these ways of creating continuity for your children shift slightly and change as they grow older, but I urge you not to allow them to drift away. These are the ways in which your children feel safe, protected, nurtured, and secure. If you go through a divorce, death, illness, move, or other potentially traumatic event, these rituals help your children because they give them something to hold onto during a time of change in their outer environment.

Principle Eight with Teens

Keeping agreements and promises is an essential part of maintaining continuity. Teach your children the importance of keeping their word by demonstrating it yourself. Do not break promises to your children. There is nothing more important, barring death or disaster, than following through on a promise you made to your partner or your child. So think carefully before you make promises. To gain trust, we must be trustworthy, and there is no greater way to demonstrate trustworthiness than to follow through on agreements and promises. Our children need to know we can be counted on to keep our word, so the spirit of continuity in our relationship with them throughout life can be counted on as an absolute.

Continuity in Communication

We've looked at the need for continuity in discipline; here, I'd like to say that a key — probably *the* key — to Principle Eight in parenting is the communication of unconditional love, especially when a child needs to be disciplined. This means that you carefully let him know it is his behavior, not his *being*, that is the focus of the discipline. You wish to teach him how to be appropriately self-disciplined in the world, not to punish or shame him.

Approach behavior problems with a problem-solving attitude rather than criticizing your children for being "bad" or not remembering the rules. Use psychologist Thomas Gordon's model for "I" messages: "When you A, I feel B, because C." For example, "When you don't empty the dryer, I feel angry, because I have to spend extra time retrieving clothes and ironing them." Saying "You make me angry" is destructive because it turns the ownership of your feelings over to your child, making him responsible for your feelings and moods; he is not responsible for your feelings, you are. When you understand this, you become a far better parent — and a far more powerful person as well.

It is easier for children to respond to a complaint stated as a general idea rather than aimed at them personally. For example: "When our lawn is brown and the other lawns in the neighborhood are green, it looks like we don't care about our property. I feel embarrassed and sad, because I *do* care. Is there something you need or some way I could help you to do a better job to remember to water the lawn?" In this way, the emotional temperature of the conversation doesn't rise, and the dialogue is kept open for explanations, apologies, amends, and problem solving without anyone feeling attacked or feeling that his character, rather than his action or non-action, is being criticized.

Always ask yourself first, what needs are not getting met here? Commit yourself completely to your role as teacher, guide, and mentor for your children. Make it your top priority, and your children will feel unconditionally loved. Only you can provide the atmosphere in which the magic of childhood can be maintained and remembered. There is no greater job you can do than to fill your children with this feeling of being loved, being safe and secure, and being guided; it will remain with them throughout life. There is no greater legacy you can leave the world than people who have this love within them and can freely give it to heal and restore balance to our planet.

Exercise for Principle Eight

1. Sit comfortably, close your eyes, and relax each part of your body.
2. Take eight deep belly breaths. As you inhale repeat, "maintain," and as you exhale repeat, "continuity."

Principle Nine

BE PRESENT

───── ⟡ ─────

*Those who follow Tao reduce everything in complexity
until they reach the final, irreducible conclusion: You are
Tao. When you can be that without any contradictions,
then you have truly achieved sublime simplicity.*

— Deng Ming-Dao, *365 Tao Daily Meditations*

I n every spiritual tradition in the world you will find the key to true
enlightenment is to "be here now." That means to be in the present, in the moment, with no thought in your mind about the past, the future, or what else is happening anywhere but where you are. A simple teaching, but increasingly difficult to achieve in a world in which we are constantly bombarded by distracting stimuli. But it is only difficult because of the way we are raised and conditioned, not because it goes against the natural flow of who we are.

In older times this teaching was easier to follow because the center of life was relatively small. It must have been more natural to keep your mind in the present if you lived in a village or on a farm with no transportation except perhaps a horse or mule and no television or radio or other technology, and, in order to survive, you had to move from task to task each day. I have noticed this in my travels to India. In the country villages, not much that went on beyond the compound made any difference. Each day was concerned with what was going on at the moment, and plans for the future were rarely made. Ruminating on the old days was the pastime of the elderly, whose memories served as teachings for the young. I believe this is one reason I found it so much easier to meditate in these places — the present moment permeated all existence, and the pressure to be somewhere else was not there.

The Girl with the Pot on Her Head

There is a fable I often heard in India, in different versions but with the same ending. A simple, orphaned village girl lived in a hut, and her only possessions were a cow and a jug for its milk. Each day she took the jug full of milk to the market to sell.

One day this girl became possessed by ideas about the future, as she set the jug of milk upon her head and began to walk to the village market. In her mind, she began to plan. If she could save half the money from this jug of milk, and so on each day for so many days, she would have enough money to buy a goat. Then if she could make cheese from the goat milk, and take it with her to the market and sell both milk and cheese, she could double her money. She went on like this until, in her mind, she had enough money for a huge dowry. Then, she imagined, she could attract the most handsome and prosperous young man in the village to be her husband, and life for her would be so much easier! At that moment, she felt so much happiness she jumped for joy. The pot on her head clattered to the ground, spilling all the milk and breaking into a thousand pieces.

Being present doesn't require that we have no dreams or plans for the future, but it does require that we set aside times to make those plans in a way that involves concrete steps with reachable goals, and that we then return our minds to the present moment to experience it. We may also need to set aside appropriate time for reviewing the past in order to learn from it while remembering to return our minds to the present again, for the present is all we really have. The past and the future do not exist, so if we miss the present moment we are living in a world that does not exist and therefore does not matter and does not nourish our souls.

Process and Goal

Being present allows you to give yourself more to the *process* rather than the goal. Modern people are very goal oriented; we want machines to do all the processing for us so we can have the result to enjoy right now. That is fine if you are in such a state that you *can* enjoy the result right now. You don't need to build your own car or bake your own bread to be in the present when you enjoy having them. But because much of what we really want is not what we *think* we want, it is hard for us to enjoy the process of each day's passing. We think we want a new car, and why? It will bring us happiness, a feeling of security and accomplishment, and make our lives easier. But when we get a new car, our minds are on something else we want for the exact same reasons, and we begin to complain about the car payments and dream about the day when we no longer have to worry about them. But by the time that day comes, we will either have new car payments or something else to worry about. Most of what we worry about never happens, and when we achieve our goals, the feeling of satisfaction and joy we get only lasts a limited time, then we must have new goals and achievements to look forward to.

I learned this fairly quickly as a writer and an artist. The published book and the "Best of Show" awards have their moments of true joy, completion, and satisfaction about a job well done. But by the time those moments arrive, my mind is usually well into another project. I realized early on that the *doing* of the thing is more important to me than the result.

The process itself is a kind of meditation for me. I learn about timeless things from the concrete work that comes out of my mind, heart, and hands: patience, perseverance, faith, flow, and presence. Misery only comes when my mind takes over the driver's seat and I begin to worry about selling or showing my work, or I compare my work with that of other people, or obsess about how others will judge it. I have many examples of art pieces that I sent to juried or judged shows, and that came back with comments from the judges. On one piece, there will be comments about certain aspects "needing work" while another judge at another show will praise those very same aspects as "excellent, very fine work." I listen to them both — check out whether the criticism has any learning value — and then put them both away in favor of what I think and feel about the work.

In Tai Chi, there is no point to doing the movements at all if you are not breathing into the moment as you do them. You might as well be doing jumping jacks while you watch MTV. If you are not in the moment, all the movements will become sloppy, and you will quickly feel bored. As Tai Chi teacher Douglas Lee says,

> You must "die" totally to each form as it is completed. If you can let go of the past completely, then you can pay attention to what you are doing now at this moment and the present will be ever fresh and new.

THE OPPOSITE

If I were to summarize the opposite of Principle Nine, be present, in one word I would use the word "craving." Craving occurs when the mind becomes the master rather than the servant, and, as master, it blows its power all out of proportion and would have us believe we control or can strive to control just about everything. This causes us to worry, desire, regret, obsess, and seek endlessly for pleasure and relief. We live entirely in the past or in the future. We ruminate over and over about things we did wrong, how we were hurt, and even about good memories of what went well for us and how great we "used to be." Or we dwell in the future. We imagine how great it would be if we just didn't have this or that problem, or if we only had enough of this or that. Or we get on an even greater, more destructive mental treadmill: "What if *(something terrible)* happens?"

The Terrible What-If

Many baby boomers were brought up on the idea of "what-if" because our parents were so profoundly affected by World War II and the Great Depression. The question of "what-if" is based on an assumption of permanence, that if we just get it right, we can achieve a state of permanent peace, harmony, prosperity, security, and happiness, and we can prevent bad things from ever happening. This is a false premise, because impermanence is the stuff from which the entire universe is made. Nothing is permanent! So if we wish, we can "what-if" ourselves into the grave.

The fact is, most of our fears never occur. To dwell on and fear what could happen in the future robs us of the enjoyment of this moment. If you string all the present moments together, you have a beautiful, impermanent, constantly moving, growing, changing life. And you get to experience it while it is happening, not as a memory or a false projection of your mind. This doesn't get us off the hook in terms of taking responsibility to appropriately plan our lives, secure our futures, and tend to our family's well-being. Taking time to do that is part of being an adult, and not taking that responsibility is to insist on never growing up, which is another type of craving. But with our plans in place and a flexible attitude, we can then enjoy the present moment with all our hearts. With our children it is particularly important to understand the opposite of Principle Nine, because falling into its traps robs us of moments we can never retrieve.

BEING PRESENT

Use your controlled belly breathing time to practice being in the present for a few moments each day. If your mind drifts into the past or future, just label it "thinking" and return to your breath and the present moment. It is not good or bad, it's just "thinking." This is a Buddhist meditation that can be of great help to you.

From the moment you begin your day, put your soul, not your mind, in charge of whatever happens during the day. It can help you, when you are worried or stressed, to use the time to get back into the present moment and allow "thinking" to dissipate as you connect yourself with the ever-evolving flow of creation. Try it when you are in the doctor's waiting room, stuck on the freeway, or in the back of the grocery line. Be present in who you are, right now. You may notice that you participate more fully in what is going on around you. For example, enjoy the antics of a toddler, the gossip of the two elderly people behind you, the bizarre headlines of the tabloids, the feel of the steering wheel, or the smell of the produce in your grocery basket. You may find yourself engaging with the checkout clerk, the nurse leading you to the doctor's office, or the person in the car next to you.

As Deng Ming-Dao says,

> If you constantly regard Tao as extraordinary, then it remains unknown and outside yourself — a myth, a fantasy, an unnameable quantity. But once you know it, it is yours and part of your daily life.

PARENTING WITH PRINCIPLE NINE

Of all the principles in this book, Principle Three, empower, and Principle Nine, be present, are the most important in terms of your own life now, and in the future when you become an elder. These principles will also powerfully affect your child later in his or her adult life. They are the building blocks of self-respect. Practicing being present allows you to receive the teachings your child was born to share with you. Your memories, the greatest treasures of the elderly, are created in moments when you are able to be fully present with your partner or child.

Principle Nine in Pregnancy

Throughout your pregnancy you have one of the best opportunities in your life to live in the present moment. The miracle of a new life is growing within you, or your partner, day by day, moment by moment. If you can begin to realize that this moment will never come again, you will want to engage with it, and experience and feel it completely. Now is the time to make time for just you and your baby to be together in love with no interference. It doesn't have to be a long time, but it will help you be more present to your children throughout their lives, and it will keep you connected during difficult, traumatic, or stressful times.

Being present in the moment is a principle that your baby is a master of; it is one she can teach you, if you will relax and slow down enough to be receptive to the teaching. Babies and young children are fully present, all the time. What is happening right now is all that exists for them. Especially during pregnancy, and throughout childhood, your children will be better people if you spend twice as much time and half as much money on them as the culture expects.

Principle Nine with Young Children

When you massage your baby or change his diaper, use the opportunity to be fully present. Empty your mind, just for this short time, of anything else and be in the same space as your baby. Experience life though his eyes. Breathe deeply, relax, and allow your love to communicate through your hands, your eyes, your expression, and how you speak to and handle your baby. Using the "love bucket" concept, this is the time to fill your baby's chalice to the brim. The stress of daily life, both good and not so good, can drain that chalice. It is your job to continually fill it again to overflowing. In this way you return the favor: your baby teaches you how to be present and you give him the gift of inner security for life.

Buddhist teacher Pema Chodron gives us beautiful insight into the value of being in the present moment:

> When we cling to thoughts and memories, we are clinging to what cannot be grasped. When we touch these phantoms and let them go, we may discover a space, a break in the chatter, a glimpse of open sky. This is our birthright — the wisdom with which we were born. . . . All compassion and inspiration come from that.

Our babies have a rich gift they give to us freely and openly, twenty-four hours a day. If you have ever longed for or fantasized about going to a far-off land to sit at the feet of a spiritual master and receive the teachings that will free your soul to enlightenment, guess what? The master has decided to come to you, through your own body — indeed, *made out of your own body* — and she has nothing better to do than offer you her wisdom at any moment you choose to receive it. Remember this when your baby cries uncontrollably for seemingly no reason. Remember this when your toddler continually toddles toward danger. Remember this when, just as you fill with pride at how cute and good your child is, she bites your new friend's leg or kicks over her best vase. And remember this as you watch your baby nurse or sleep, with the total surrender of one secure in the now and empty of mental craving.

We all think our autobiographies are terribly interesting, and, most of the time, we are right. But children live now. They will be interested in your story later, when they become interested in their own, as adults. Observe your tendency to project your own experience onto your children. When you do that, you respond not to them but to a long-gone you. It doesn't help them. If that long-gone you needs attention, get it in the therapist's office. Try to see your child without that filter.

For example, when you hear your baby cry, do you analyze its meaning through your own autobiography? Perhaps you were left to cry for hours alone in a crib because a pediatrician told your mother to "let her cry it out" or not to "spoil the baby." So when you hear a baby cry, especially your own, it triggers those feelings of abandonment and fear in you. The unthinking response would be to get the baby quiet at all costs so *you* don't have to re-experience that pain. You may empathize with a feeling that is yours, not your baby's, and so your response does not fit your baby's need. True listening begins in your child's infancy, when you begin to practice removing your autobiography in order to understand your baby's language and to mirror appropriately what he tries to tell you. This requires getting into present time with your whole being.

Early childhood experts, doctors Eileen and Tom Paris say it well:

> Learning the developmental themes of bonding, mirroring,
> and separating and the skills that support them from early

on will give your baby the best possible start. These themes are ongoing and lifelong. We all need to be attached and bonded. We all need to feel understood, and we all need to be respected as individuals with experiences and feelings of our own.

Sometimes your baby may need to cry, in the warmth and safety of your presence. Your practice is to be present with him, mirror with your expression and speech what you hear, and check yourself for autobiographical projection, until you are sure your baby feels heard and can be comforted. Controlled belly breathing and relaxation can get you through this. Each time you do it, you will find it is less stressful and more interesting. You will find yourself engaged in the process of learning from your baby. You learn to accept your baby's pain in the same way you feel his pleasure, without the attachment of craving, but with the compassionate love that is true non-attachment. Practicing in this way will affect the way you love everyone else in your life as well. It will teach you how to be more truly compassionate not only with the suffering of others, but with yourself. This sets the foundation for your relationships for the rest of your life.

As your child grows older, being present with him can become as natural as breathing — or a day-to-day struggle, depending upon your commitment, your temperament, and life situation. If both parents work outside the home, it definitely requires a conscious effort. You have other needs, too — to nurture your relationship with your spouse, to have some personal time and privacy. It's hard to fit it all into one day. Return to your parenting mission statement to evaluate what is really important to you and what can be put on the back burner — and how your important, but not necessarily urgent, values and activities can be worked in through careful and conscious choice-making. When you approach life this way, though it may seem a little contrived at first, you will find that you enjoy everything much more, and that you are empowered by your choices and decisions rather than left feeling as if your life is running *you* with "shoulds" and "have tos."

Revisit Your Priorities

Being present with your children requires that their well-being is your top priority. After you have decided to be present, you will revisit that decision often and begin to find ways to do it that fit your lifestyle, and you will begin to design your lifestyle to fit this decision. Rather than just one more "should," being present for your children will become a fun, creative, and exciting endeavor that will teach you valuable lessons and bring joy to your everyday life. You will find yourself more present for everything else in your life, including your private time. One dad said, "When my wife goes away on business and I'm at home with the baby, I don't expect to get a lot done. I have learned to take a deep breath, shut off the computer, and give my baby my undivided attention. A great thing about this approach is that it gives me a rewarding break from things that only *seem* important, and I get back in touch with what really *is* important."

Another dad suggests that you spend time introducing your child to the things that you loved when you were a child. For example, if you loved model airplanes, a trip to the hobby shop to show your child its riches can be great fun. "You will be surprised," he says, "at how much bonding happens and how much you learn about your child from the things he is attracted to."

Much of the time our work requires us to be in a kind of left-brain, linear, logical, analytical mode. Being present with our children requires shifting gears. You can use the time in the car driving home from work or take some personal time after work to begin to shift and to create a ritual that helps you move into a more right-brain, creative, imaginative, non-linear mode. Music, gardening, art, meditation, exercise, dance, visualizations, even reading a good novel can help you do this because they are all right-brain activities. If you take some time to shift gears between work and home, you can prevent a lot of fussiness, both on your part and within your family. One dad told me that as he drove home from work each day, he put his favorite compact disc in the car stereo and sang with it, at the top of his lungs. The stares of people in other cars made him laugh, and by the time he got home he was relaxed and in a humorous frame of mind.

Cultivate a deep curiosity about your child, or each child if you have more than one. This curiosity opens you to the moment and allows you to discover all the things that make him unique. Your interest in turn invites your child to show you how unique and beautiful he is, because a child who has not been judged and beaten down knows he is special and wants to share himself with you. Your delight feeds his joy, like an ever-nourishing figure eight of love between you.

Principle Nine with Teens

The way you can practice being present with your adolescents is to retrieve your own teenage nature. Rather than tightening up with fear of all the "what-ifs," consciously lighten up. Remember what we learned in Principle Three, empower. Research consistently shows that 80 percent of teens go through their adolescence with little difficulty. Don't assume because your child becomes more withdrawn, silent, or secretive that he has problems. Some of this behavior is perfectly natural for teenagers. They want the basement bedroom. They want to paint the walls dark. They disappear into their womblike rooms with music blaring, for hours at a time. They are gestating. They are learning to find and be who they are apart from the family, to be born into adulthood. So, unless this behavior is excessive or destructive, don't be alarmed.

During this time, your teens may rarely come to you. Rather, it's time for you to go to them. Knock on their doors and respect their privacy and autonomy. Never, ever read their diaries or go through their things, no matter how much you want to. Remember that in just a few short years, all their belongings will be off limits to you anyway. Start getting used to them as separate beings with their own power and control. Their ability to trust you is more important than anything you may find, no matter how shocking or unacceptable. If you have raised them with respect and trust, they won't *have* things such as hard drugs or weapons. These things are popular topics for talk shows, but are not issues conscious parents need be overly concerned about.

Knock on their doors and enter their space respectfully, without criticism. Flop down on their beds and ask how it's going. Even if the communication coming back to you is less than eloquent (there was an entire year when monosyllables were the only noises my son made), don't let it turn you off, frustrate you, or prevent you from being there anyway.

Another big no-no, at this stage, is to discipline your teen in front of other people. Show respect (especially if you are disciplining them for showing a lack of respect) by asking them to step into another room with you where you can discuss the matter in private. Teen egos are very fragile, and anything remotely akin to shaming them in public, or even in front of their siblings, is a sure way to lose their trust.

Lighten Up

To get into present time with your teen, do not try to become a teenager yourself (that will only embarrass them). Rather, try to find a balance. Loosen up; start reading their magazines and listen to their music. Ask them questions with a genuine curiosity about what's "cool," what they like, and why. Let go of any attachment you may have to the styles and music of your generation. This is a great time to practice being non-judgmental, as your teen tries on different styles, ways of being, philosophies, and points of view. Allow it. I would say, *encourage* it. Give them little to rebel against. Then let them educate you and keep you young and up-to-date.

One sure sign that your own identity is too tied up with your children's is if you become extremely angry over infractions of what you consider model behavior. The more expectations you have for your teens to be poster children for your great parenting, the greater the chance they will behave in just the opposite ways. They are trying to cut loose of all those expectations and figure out what *they* want, expect, and believe. Especially if you have a boundary tester, a "spirited" child, you can expect a lot of weird ideas, clothing, music, art, and behavior from your child during this phase. Just be with it. Explore it, find out about it inquisitively, without a lot of judgment. You can challenge your child by presenting an idea that may poke holes in some of his conclusions about a subject, just as a friend might argue a different point of view with no big emotional charge on the issue, but don't try to overpower him.

I remember once, a friend of mine was visiting who was a high-powered executive type with great expectations for his children. He asked my eighteen-year-old son what he planned to do after high school, expecting to hear about all the Ivy League schools he had applied to and the great dreams he had for his future. With a twinkle in his eye that only I could see, my son replied, "I think I'll go on the road and follow a band for a while." I had to step into the bathroom to laugh into a towel, knowing my son had completely figured out my friend and had given him the reply that he was least prepared for or impressed with. My friend stood speechless, then quickly changed the subject as my son ambled away.

Another friend of mine was visiting with her fourteen-year-old son, who wore the latest in teen fashion at the time, including boxer shorts with extremely baggy jeans pulled way down almost past his butt. My friend was absolutely incensed about this, and said there was no way she was going to continue to allow *that*. My spirited boy, dressed in precisely that same costume, came ambling in and had an intelligent and humorous conversation with the mom, and then went off on a hike with her son. I told my friend, "Hey, it's *only clothes*. Remember the '60s? This too shall pass. What's important is that your son feels your love, your trust, and your respect for him. Those are the things that'll never pass, and are not worth sacrificing just because you feel embarrassed that his underwear is showing." She argued a bit, but thought deeply about it and by the time they left there was a lot less tension between them.

Try to tune in to what is cool, what everybody your child's age is watching on TV, what the latest fashions are, and what the newest slang means. You don't have to use it, just be hip enough to know about it and not embarrass your kids by acting like a "dork." Once in a while, you can use their slang, dance their dances, play their video games, and watch their shows with them, if this is something you can genuinely do without being facetious or contrived. Once when my daughter's boyfriend was visiting from the city, I said (and it wasn't planned, it just came out), "I think you'll like this dish. It's one of my specialties. It's the *bomb!*" He laughed, and I heard him later in the other room. "Your mom just said, *'It's the bomb!'* Wow. She's really cool."

On the other hand, if you try using their slang and get it wrong, and they laugh at you, just laugh along with them and ask for correction. Allow them to make fun of your "old fogyness" without taking it personally. It's just another way of separating; they aren't trying to hurt your feelings. They will respect you and enjoy being around you a lot more if you can laugh at yourself right along with them.

One of the biggest mistakes I see parents making all the time is not being present with their kids. Of course, we're not perfect; we can't do it all the time. Our own lives, problems, and relationships need attention and often distract us. But, especially during the teen years, many parents seem to think that, because they're no longer needed to physically take care of their kids anymore, they're not really needed at all. They allow the natural selfishness and ingratitude of the teen years to distance them from their children and fester into resentments that come out in fights and ultimatums.

People think it's natural for parents and teens to despise one another, but it certainly isn't. As teen expert Dr. Lynn Ponton says, "The teen years are not naturally a time of danger but of normal, even healthy, risk taking." Parents still have the responsibility to do their job and act as midwives for their kids as they enter the world of adults.

In the old days, respect was a one-way street: Children respected their elders, period. That is no longer the case. The paradigm has shifted; the map we were given no longer has any relationship to the territory we are in. So confusion often reigns, and parents often respond by either bailing altogether or clamping down so hard their teens have to run away to get air to breathe. But it's really very simple. Respect your kids, and be present with them. Realize you still have a job to do and your children still have deep needs for love, affection, validation, guidance, and the non-judging presence of witnessing parents to provide ground under their feet as they move into this big world of unknowns.

Exercise for Principle Nine

1. Sit comfortably, close your eyes, and relax each part of your body.
2. Take nine deep belly breaths. As you inhale repeat, "be," and as you exhale repeat, "present."

Principle Ten

BE ATTENTIVE

———— ⚜ ————

When listening not with the ear but the spirit,
one can perceive the subtle sound.

— Deng Ming-Dao, *365 Tao Daily Meditations*

Attentiveness in Tai Chi means using all your senses and peripheral vision, not over-concentrating. When sparring, it means being aware not just of one aspect of an opponent, but of his entire body and energy field.

Concentration and attentiveness are not the same. Concentration is focused, exclusive, ready effort. Effort dissipates energy. Attentiveness is a spontaneous and relaxed union of mind and body. When you are reading, you don't say to yourself, "I am reading, I am reading." You just do it, as your mind and body become absorbed in the ideas. The synchronization of eyes, hands, and brain are all harmonized in attentiveness.

Often, if you concentrate on something rather than bringing attentiveness to it, there is an awkwardness to the effort. You probably got your first lesson in this when you learned how to ride a bike. If you try too hard to concentrate on all aspects of what you are doing, you fall. When you allow your whole body-mind to sink into attentiveness, you go effortlessly, and, when mastered in this way, you never forget how to do it.

In *Vitality, Energy, Spirit: A Taoist Sourcebook,* master Lu Yen counsels:

Vitality is always controlled by energy. Once energy runs
outside, vitality eventually leaks out. Therefore, to stabilize
vitality one should guard the energy. How is the energy to
be guarded? This requires freedom from craving, clear
openness, and serenity, not acting impulsively.

To guard our energy, we cultivate attentiveness, a non-focused
awareness of our bodies, minds, and spirits. In Tai Chi this is how
we perceive the subtle flow of *chi* throughout the body — we don't
picture it or concentrate hard on it, but as we move, we are aware
of how the movement feels, where our balance is, where our
groundedness comes from, how our breath moves, and how our
muscles work together, and we feel energy flow through our bodies.

After a while, this feeling becomes more and more palpable.
Our peripheral vision takes in our surroundings and our subtle
mind — intuitive senses — can feel what is around us and/or coming toward us. One of the reasons for sparring, after the student has
mastered the basic forms, is to cultivate this attentiveness as she is
tested by her opponent.

Wu-Wei: The Way of Not Knowing

Attentiveness is the way of not *knowing*, which inherently has
more possibilities than the way of knowing. It allows you to be
aware yet open to whatever comes up, to shift your energy and
respond according to the changing conditions. For example, if you
ski, you may begin at the top of a run and think, "I know this run
because I've done it before." You start to ski — suddenly there's a
mogul or a tree where you don't remember one before, and you're
in trouble. If, however, you can remain attentive and open, "not
knowing," your awareness is attuned to the new elements and nego-
tiates them with ease. You are able to shift and change even with
your knowledge of this particular place.

With regard to Tai Chi as a martial art, attentiveness brings
awareness to any negative energy coming toward us, allowing us to

see it coming, not be uprooted by it, and to respond to it appropriately and calmly. Tai Chi teacher Ron Sieh says,

> In presenting ourselves as the target, we open ourselves to the intimate participation in the relationship. If someone is in a position . . . to throw a punch, you see that person. You don't see a punch and you don't behave as if a punch is happening. That way, when the punch happens, you see it as it is. . . . You are cool while you participate, you move out of the way.
>
> When I get uptight or hooked into what the other person is doing, I don't do so well. When I see "us," I am relaxed and open, and I do better.

Attentiveness is that awareness of "us" in our relationship with our kids. It is an open, responsive approach to parenting rather than a defended, reactive approach. If you stand, raise your arms in front of you, and make a circle by bringing your fingertips together, you can see the circle within your arms. If you think that space is not your body and has nothing to do with you, think again. It is part of your energy field, and if you use "sinking power," and open your field of perception, you will feel the energy within the circle as a part of your own energy.

THE OPPOSITE

The opposite of attentiveness involves not only the obvious — inattentiveness or abandonment — but it is also both over-concentration and enmeshment. In Tai Chi, the opposite of attentiveness is primarily over-concentration, trying to get each move exactly right instead of being attentive to the flow of *chi* in one's own body and/or one's opponent. In all martial arts, it is over-concentrating on the specific move, such as a kick coming at you, as opposed to an all-encompassing awareness of the energy between and around the two of you.

In the same way, attentiveness is not over-concentrating on the seemingly urgent, day-to-day business of parenting at the expense of the more important job of building a lifelong relationship of love and trust with your child. It is not abandoning your child to peer groups, the street, or her room, or letting school handle her; it is not allowing stress to take you away from your children in the fundamental ways that involve time, attention, affection, trust, mentoring, and having fun together. Aletha Solter's book, *Exercises in Self-Awareness for New Parents,* can help you and/or your partner explore your own experience of being parented and how that affects your actions and reactions with your child.

Attentiveness involves all your senses, including the intuitive or spiritual ones, and paying attention to your gut feelings and perceptions. Check them against what may be your own "inner child" projection, and follow through on feelings that continue to bother you. It is not attentive to read a book on parenting and then follow, 1-2-3, what the "expert" says your child should do or where your child should be in her development at such and such an age.

When I was a baby, I cried a lot, and my mother had a "gut feeling" something was wrong. She took me from doctor to doctor, all of whom told her she was just a worried mother, I had colic, it was nothing. Finally, she found a specialist who discovered I had a serious heart problem. If I hadn't had surgery that year, I would have died before my twelfth birthday. Her attentiveness to my cues and her intuitive senses saved my life.

Being attentive does not mean blindly reacting to fear-inducing television ads and shows or magazine articles that make you feel as if your child is in danger of being kidnapped, joining a gang, getting addicted to drugs and alcohol, using weapons, and so on. It is not being so enmeshed with your child that you are unable to stand apart and allow her to find her own solutions to problems, experience the consequences of her actions, and discover her strengths and weaknesses by exploring many different ways of being and behaving.

BEING ATTENTIVE

Being attentive, you notice what is *not* there as well as what is. As when we work with the calligraphic *t'ui sho circle,* we bring our awareness to the emptiness as well as the container. We value the important over the urgent, and that involves conscious parenting because our entire culture is based on urgency.

We often save the important things — time with our children, partners, and friends, time for ourselves and our creativity, building trust and quality into our work relationships, and living our dreams — until later, when we're done with the urgent: the phone call, the meeting, the deadline. But eventually, sometimes too late, we realize that if we continue to live this way the important things will never get done, because the urgent list never ends. Finish one thing and another takes its place.

If we put the important things first, we find the urgent list diminishes gradually. This is a principle of the universe that you don't truly understand until you commit to it. The process can be uncomfortable at first for those of us who are can-do, achieving leaders — but only for a little while. When the dust settles, you find yourself easier to be around, happier, and with more time to give to the important things and people in your life, including your children. They feel it when they are moving toward the bottom of your priority list. Acting out is a symptom of this.

PARENTING WITH PRINCIPLE TEN

In *The Seven Habits of Highly Effective People,* Stephen Covey presents the analogy of the "emotional bank account," which we have with every person in our lives. Deposits include courtesy, kindness, time, respect, honesty, keeping promises, and awareness of the other person's state and needs. Withdrawals include discourtesy, lying, disrespect, overreacting, ignoring, being arbitrary, judging, betraying trust, threatening, interrupting, and lecturing. When withdrawals exceed deposits, you are overdrawn, and the trust in the relationship becomes very low. As he explains, at this point you have no flexibility. If deposits exceed withdrawals, however, there is "extra cash." That is, there is some flexibility, some room for mistakes and amends. But in a state of overdraft, the relationship deteriorates. He says, "Suppose you have a teenage son and your normal conversation is something like, 'Clean your room. Button your shirt. Turn down the radio. Go get a haircut. And don't forget to take out the garbage!' Over a period of time, the withdrawals far exceed the deposits."

With Principle Ten, your attentiveness tells you when deposits are necessary, and you are very conscientious about making them, and making sure there is never an overdraft in your relationship with your child. Making a deposit can be as simple as taking advantage of opportunities as they arise: tucking a special appreciation card into her lunch box, bringing home a book about aquariums or whatever your child may be interested in, or keeping a promise in spite of any important or urgent things that come up, even an invitation from the President of the United States. Dag Hammarskjold, past Secretary General of the United Nations, said, "It is more noble to give yourself completely to one individual than to labor diligently for the salvation of the masses." Our children are more important than anyone else in our lives, and should be given that priority.

To apply Principle Ten, you must be as clear and up front as you can about what your expectations are, and what your child's expectations are, for any given event or task. For example, if you are a non-custodial parent and you tell your child you will pick him up on Saturday, be sure to give him an exact time and then be there on time. When you apologize for making mistakes, misunderstandings, broken promises, and bad judgments, it can be considered a deposit. But apologies don't work for the same behavior more than once. A correction (that is, an amend) must be made before a withdrawal can be forgiven and considered a deposit.

Principle Ten During Pregnancy

During pregnancy this principle can be followed by being attentive to your body (or your partner's body) and the being growing within. In addition, you can use Covey's idea of the emotional bank account and build an extra reserve of trust and flexibility with each other so that during those first sleep-deprived months, you have the ability to listen to each other, to meet both your needs and the baby's needs, and to forgive yourself and each other when you blow it.

Be Attentive to Your Partner's Needs

Pay extra attention to one another, do things that you enjoy together, and create special nourishing treats to build deposits during the pregnancy.

If you are the father, deposits can include doing things for your partner that nourish her emotionally and physically. If you don't know what those are, you are bound to give her the things *you* would want, and miss the mark. Now is the time to ask. Nourishing acts can include giving her flowers, complimenting her, taking her out for dinner and dancing, going for walks, massaging her, making meals, doing housecleaning, detailing her car, doing some chores she ordinarily does, being especially conscious about her comfort, or simply allowing her to relax and cry or complain in your arms, without trying to solve her problems or arguing, lecturing, analyzing her, or becoming defensive.

Withdrawals include many things you may not have otherwise considered: teasing her about her emotional ups and downs or about becoming "fat" or overly sensitive are high-magnitude withdrawals for most pregnant women. Learn how to listen effectively and you will have a skill that creates huge deposits in your relationship's emotional bank account. You will also be prepared and accustomed to doing this with your child, as well.

For mothers-to-be, allowing your partner time for himself and to be with his buddies is important. When he needs to watch a game on TV or go camping with his friends, unless there is some medical reason you need him to be with you at that moment, encourage him to do these self-nourishing activities. Don't go into his "cave" and drag him out. Learn how to hold your tongue until he is ready to be present for whatever talking you need to do.

Develop a support network of friends and relatives so that all your emotional and physical needs aren't centered on your partner. Work on a parenting mission statement together, and pay special attention to his input so that he feels like an indispensable team member, and not just a bystander. If necessary you, and your partner if he is willing, can seek help from a therapist to work out possible win-win solutions for situations in which you have conflicting needs. Then you can talk about how to use these win-win skills together. Now is a good time to practice, for every partnership runs into these situations at some point, and practice helps you learn the skills. Learning negotiation skills now will help you later, when you need them with your children.

Be Attentive to Your Body's Messages

Attentiveness will get you through labor and delivery; the more attuned you are to your own body and its ways, the better you will be able to cope with the natural progression of your pregnancy. Good prenatal care from a midwife can help you with this. Learn as much as you can about your body, including what is "normal," how your body differs from the norm, and what you may need in terms of preparation.

Be Attentive to Your Newborn's Cues

When your baby is born, attentiveness to his or her special cues is very important, as is the bonding process. Touch your baby skin-to-skin, make eye contact, talk or sing to your baby, and respond to his needs. These are all important elements of the attachment process. Many research studies have been done on the importance of this bonding time, whether it happens, as is ideal, from the moment of birth or, if there are problems, later. Early bonds that are close and warm help the child develop positive values and, later, positive adult behavior.

One study showed that the type of bonding a person experienced as an infant is reflected in his or her adult relationships. There are three types of bonding attachments:

- *Securely Bonded.* These adults believe it is easy to get close to others and have no problem with occasional mutual dependence (in other words, interdependence). They have happy, trusting relationships; their romances last the longest and their marriages end in divorce the least often of all the groups studied. They had close, secure relationships in infancy and were held, kissed, and "coddled."

- *Anxious-Ambivalent.* These adults want to be close to others but they tend to attract people who are unable to be close. They worry about people leaving them, tend to be very jealous, and have intense emotional ups and downs. This was the largest group — perhaps a reflection of the "don't spoil the baby" attitude of the parents of the baby boom generation. They were loved as infants but their parents were ambivalent and confused, giving them mixed messages about their worth, their safety, and the trustworthiness of the world.
- *Avoidant.* These adults feel uneasy when people get too close. They have trouble trusting or depending on others, and are afraid of intimacy. They tend to give the message, "I love you — go away." They were neglected in infancy, punished for "bad" behavior, made to be independent and "strong" too soon, and told it wasn't nice to express emotion.

Scientist Lee Salk reported studies that revealed a correlation between adolescent suicide and pregnancy or birth complications. Of the suicide victims studied, the majority had experienced complications at birth that required extensive intervention, which limited or eliminated the natural bonding time with parents. Because the parents didn't know they needed to consciously bond with their children, it never happened. Other studies have shown a high correlation between a lack of infant-parent bonding and children who lack a well-developed conscience and torture and kill animals and demonstrate other destructive, abusive, and violent behavior early in life. These children often go on to hurt others and end up in prison as adults.

Principle Ten with Young Children

Principle Ten is about being fiercely attentive to your infant's bonding needs in the early days and months of life. Because my daughter's birth was traumatic, I could not nurse her or bond with her right after birth. When I was taken back to my hospital room, I begged them to bring me my baby and the nurses, with all good intentions, condescendingly patted me and said, "No, dear, we don't allow early contact with our cesarean moms, especially after what you've been through. Wait a few days and let your body heal." My body couldn't heal, because I was in such distress about my baby. I cried and had nightmares about trying to find her at night.

Be Attentive to Your Baby's Bonding Needs

On the seventh day of my daughter's life, it was discovered she had contracted an infection in the nursery and she was rushed to Pediatric Intensive Care. Being the attentive mother I was, I forced myself out of bed and, holding my incision, went to her. I had to fight, for over a week, for every moment with my daughter.

I moved into the pediatric unit, slept in a hardwood rocking chair, kept vigil over my baby's isolette, and often took her out to hold her and talk to her. I carried her in my front pack when she was finally unhooked from all the monitoring equipment, even though I incurred the disapproval of the nursing staff by doing so. Now, close body contact — or "Kangaroo Care" — is in fashion in hospitals because an expert studied and endorsed it — but most often it is the nurse or a volunteer, rather than the parents, who carries the baby in a front pack, and this defeats the most important purpose of the practice, which is to create a bond between the parent and child.

With conscious effort, "sinking power," and attentiveness, I was able to bond with my baby in spite of a great many obstacles. I saw many young mothers give up and go home, overwhelmed by the competence of the nursing staff and under-confident about their own importance in the picture. Thank heaven, things are now changing in hospitals as researchers prove that parents who are present and attentive are important to their children's growth and well-being.

Be Attentive to Your Child's Individuality

Principle Ten can be brought into your child-raising in many small ways. It can help you discover your child's individuality and avoid reacting to her as a typical child. It can help you figure out what is *important* to you in your relationship with your child. These are the things that will create happy memories for the future and that will add deposits to your child's emotional bank account. Spend time with your child doing seemingly insignificant things such as watching a video, going to a ball game, giving a massage, listening to music, reading, throwing a ball around, swimming, going bowling, or just hanging out. This lets your child know she is your priority, and that there doesn't have to be something big, important, or life-threatening to get your attention.

By being attentive to your child's individuality, you can find ways to skirt some of the day-to-day issues that can bring on unnecessary conflict. Food issues are a good example. My son decided he absolutely hated green peppers — something I use extensively in my cooking. He wouldn't eat them, no way, no how. I soon discovered that cajoling, fighting, and making ultimatums only distanced us and didn't solve the problem. (And after all, *it's only a green pepper!*) So when making a dish that needed the peppers for flavor, I cut them in large pieces, put them in to cook, and then took them out before serving the dish; he never noticed. If I made something like stuffed peppers, I gave him the side dishes and allowed him to make himself a sandwich. Sometimes I'd throw the peppers in the blender with some tomato sauce to add flavor to a dish. It was a little sneaky but it was a way to get around the conflict.

I had to do this with some other foods, too — ones that my children thought were "yucky" but were high in protein and calcium, and important to our vegetarian diet. I'd put cottage cheese or tofu in the blender with pancake batter or smoothies and, in other ways, got these foods into their diet without a fight. It made for calmer meals and less worries for me as a mother.

Other ways to get around food conflicts include declaring one night a week to be "scrounge night," when everybody just scrounges up whatever they want to eat; on those nights, if I felt like it, I could make a dish that I liked but that my kids didn't like. Or, you can have a "buffet night," when a variety of different foods are put out and each person chooses what they want. Another solution we used for a while was to allow each child to have one night when they chose the menu and helped cook the meal. This had the added benefit of giving them the opportunity to learn how to cook.

Principle Ten with Teens

Teens need you to be attentive to their growth, their mood swings, and their body changes without making a big deal out of everything. Leave books in their rooms, such as *Our Bodies, Ourselves* for girls or the *What's Happening to My Body? Book for Boys,* to give them a chance to read up on these changes for themselves, in private. Talk casually with them about sexuality and other potentially touchy subjects while doing some other activity like playing a board game, going for a drive, braiding your daughter's hair, or messing around on the computer — anything that gives you both private time and something else to focus on so your teen doesn't feel embarrassed.

Teens need to know that you are willing to listen to them without interrupting, judging, or inserting your autobiography. They want you to communicate your concerns about their negative behavior in a respectful manner. They need to know that what they say and how they feel is important to you even when you don't agree, and that you love them unconditionally. They need to know that their well-being is as important to you as your own. Every time you look at or communicate with or touch your child, you have an opportunity to convey these messages. Look for opportunities by being attentive.

Try to avoid conversation killers that only serve to shut your teen down and turn him off. These include attempts to correct, interrupt, analyze, or lecture. Don't be sarcastic or snide, tease, use harsh or disapproving tones of voice, communicate negative judgments of his character or his friends, tell him how he feels, or demonstrate an excessive need on your part to be right or to have the last word.

If your attentiveness lets you know your child has a problem that she is having difficulty coping with, respond to it immediately. You can go to a therapist and ask for advice (before you talk to your teen), read up on the problem, or research the issue, and then listen, listen, listen — with your heart.

The parents of a thirteen-year-old boy who killed a small child said later that the signs of repressed hostility, depression, and difficulty managing anger were all there, but that they didn't engage their child enough to understand how overwhelmed he was by those feelings. The only advice he was given, when he hinted to his father that he felt angry a lot and couldn't control it, was to go beat on something in the garage. At first, the child tried to deal with his anger by hitting a tree with a baseball bat — but later he ended up beating another child to death.

To be attentive means to be aware of the types of energy your children are exposed to and, rather than trying to over-protect or smother them, to offer alternatives that affirm your own positive values. Television violence has been proven to increase aggressive behavior and anxiety in young children. One study of local news broadcasts revealed that 71 percent of the content was "helplessness invoking," and led to feelings of frustration and anxiety in both adults and children. To imitate so-called superheroes causes children to project the role of the hero's enemy onto other children. Your children probably won't talk about or even be conscious of these anxieties and other feelings. Your best remedy, if you allow your children to watch television, is to watch these shows with them and bring consciousness to bear on the violent imagery and messages they see. Talk to them about what is being done to protect them and about the difference between what is on TV and what real life is all about, and explicitly condemn actions of hatred or violence, explaining your reasons as clearly as you can.

Model Empathy

If you want to enhance your children's capacity for empathy, emphasize the things they have in common with rather than the ways they are different from other people. Get them involved in activities that help others and expose them at an early age to other cultures and races. Studies of altruism — the unselfish regard for or

devotion to the welfare of others — show that truly altruistic people have had several common childhood experiences. First, they
were raised with a lot of affection and love. Second, their parents
showed empathy with them, letting them know it was important to
the parent how the child felt and thought. And third, the parents
themselves modeled altruistic behavior by being involved in causes
they believed in. Cross-cultural studies have shown that children
who have ongoing involvement in altruistic service are kinder, more
empathic, and more helpful later in life.

  There are all kinds of ways to encourage your child to open up
to you:

- Truly listen, as we have already discussed.
- Use "I" messages about your feelings rather than "you"
  judgments about your child.
- Be interested in and kind to his friends; invite them over for
  dinner or along on outings.
- Let your teen have some parties at your home.
- Get involved and interested in the things that your teen is
  interested in, such as attending the school basketball games
  if she is on the team.
- Allow your teen freedoms that are age appropriate and not
  harmful, such as picking out his own clothes or leaving his
  room a mess.
- Offer to massage your teen's back, arms, neck, or feet.
  Especially if you have been massaging her since birth —
  but even if you haven't — touch can open her up. Kids are
  kinesthetic (body-centered) learners, so they respond more
  positively to your inquiries and talk if you touch them affec-
  tionately.

  If you are attentive to your child, she will feel it, and the message "I am loved and respected" will go to her innermost being.
What more could anyone want or need?

Exercise for Principle Ten

1. Sit comfortably, close your eyes, and relax each part of your body.
2. Take ten deep belly breaths. As you inhale repeat, "be," and as you exhale repeat, "attentive."

Principle Eleven
ACCEPT AND VALIDATE

Each day, we all face a peculiar problem. We must validate

our past, face our present, plan for the future. Those who

believe that life was better in the 'old days' sometimes are

blind to the reality of the present; those who live only for the

present frequently have little regard for either precedent or

consequence; and those who live only for some deferred

reward often strain themselves with too much denial.

— Deng Ming-Dao, *365 Tao Daily Meditations*

Acceptance is the hallmark of many Eastern teachings, including Taoism, from which Tai Chi originates. To let tension go without effort, become aware of the tension and accept it. This is an example of *wu-wei* Tai Chi, or doing by not doing. In the beginning it is helpful to just observe and accept what your body is doing.

If you worry, you tense up and restrict the flow of *chi*. Let go and breathe deeply to enhance the flow and allow yourself to accept things as they are. Author Melodie Beattie says, "Acceptance is the magic that makes change possible." You are able to make the space for change if you accept and validate what is. Accept your body as it is and breathe from the *tan t'ien* in order to regain balance and be centered. Tai Chi does exactly this. It helps you get in touch with *your* body, *your* potential, and who you really are without all the labels.

Dr. Stephen T. Chang, author of *The Integral Management of Tao*, says,

> One hundred percent perfection does not exist in the real world. The best one can do is hope to come close to it. Perfection is either in the past or in the future or in the dream world. Because inside *yang* there must be *yin* — nothing is absolute. Nothing, for example, is absolutely good or bad. Therefore tolerance is a necessary strategy.

In learning Tai Chi it is important to have teachers who are accepting and patient, who don't constantly criticize and correct their students. A good teacher spends a lot of time in the beginning helping students get in touch with the flow of *chi*, and how it feels in their own bodies, through different types of exercises (such as the calligraphic *t'ui sho circle*). If the teacher expects each student to do a movement in exactly the "correct" way, and all his or her students are in perfect unison, you can be sure that is not really Tai Chi; it is just a series of exercises that mimic Tai Chi. Real Tai Chi is intensely internal; it is a meditation on the flow of *chi* within and around you. The forms are only brought in when the student begins to feel this flow.

In the same way, with our children, we need to concentrate on teaching them self-acceptance and acceptance of others. We can help them become aware of their energy and how it flows or stops flowing, turns from slow to fast, from sticky to fluid in different situations, according to the emotions and thoughts they experience. Then we bring in the concept that they can *control* that flow, and teach them the forms and techniques that allow them to do so.

THE OPPOSITE

The opposite of acceptance and validation is judgment and denial, which make us tense up, lose our center, criticize ourselves and others, and hold impossible standards for everyone. When we are being judgmental, we invalidate ourselves and others. We deny what we feel, tell others what they feel or should feel, and consciously or unconsciously try to make others feel small and inadequate.

It is easy to accept in another person the qualities you like, or that you share. It is easy to focus on what you have in common. For both ourselves and our children, the test of our ability to accept and validate comes when differences arise. If we try to push our children to be more like us, to like the things we like, to dislike the things we dislike, and to, in essence, be little carbon copies of us, we are not in harmony with Principle Eleven.

As a child, you may not have had role models who showed you how to deal with other people's feelings and preferences in healthy, supportive ways. Many of our parents grew up in an era when it was considered "not nice" to show your feelings, and any expression of emotion was uncomfortable. When women cried, they were considered "hysterical." When men cried, they were considered "sissies." Our parents often used their emotional states to hold us hostage: "You made your father angry" or "Be quiet or you'll upset your mother." So many of us received mixed messages about emotions that we can unconsciously pass along to our children.

Even when they are stated with "I" ownership, our reactions to another person's feelings often tend to be unsupportive. We feel we have to do something about their feelings, and too often we resort to unskillful reactions that make the problem worse and make the feelings bigger. We dismiss, deny, medicate (usually with food or TV), distract, blame, fix, advise, and rescue, when all that is really called for is validation: "Yes, you feel that way. It sounds like you're having a hard time with it."

Denial prevents us from accepting what is actually there, what is happening, and what is missing. As Yoruba spiritual teacher Iyanla Vanzant has said, "By accepting what is, you become keenly aware of what isn't."

ACCEPT YOURSELF, ACCEPT OTHERS

According to yoga philosophy, self-acceptance leads to true contentment. It is not easy in our present world. The images we see every day — on TV, in magazines, at work, and in the marketplace — stare back at us with reproach. We can never be beautiful enough, wealthy enough, smart enough, or even happy enough! Acceptance means to recognize something for what it is and realize that all of our experiences are temporary. What you see in the mirror today will not be what you see tomorrow. Acceptance allows you to handle change in a calmer way, and to work for change when necessary. If people "accept" abuse from their partners and neither party gets help and commits to change, it is not true acceptance. To accept you have hurt or abused someone is to practice humility, and that gives you access to your power to change.

Our relationships are our greatest teachers, so the more intimate and committed a relationship is the more it has to teach us. Even passing acquaintances can help us practice acceptance and thus allow the light of peace to shine within us. An encounter with a police officer, a sales clerk, or a postal worker gives us a chance to bring love, acceptance, and healing to the world. In her wonderful book, *One Day My Soul Just Opened Up*, Iyanla Vanzant said,

> Accept that what is yours will come to you in the right way at just the right moment. Patiently acknowledge and accept that what is not for you is not for you, no matter what you choose to tell yourself.

To accept something about yourself or another person doesn't mean you approve of or agree with it, or that you are not affected by it. Practicing acceptance just helps you make wiser choices and respond in a healthier way. A good example of acceptance can be found by observing your pet, if you have one. Animals accept and love you no matter what. They don't withdraw their love in disapproval of a choice you make. You know they are there for you with all your imperfections.

Acceptance is what we want from that which we perceive to be God. We want God to know us and all our imperfections, and to still love us unconditionally. My spiritual teacher used to say that when you fall down and get dirty, God picks you up, brushes off all the dust, and holds you in his lap, never judging you for falling, even if you do it over and over again. As parents, we want to emulate this paradigm, and, in addition, teach our children how to avoid some of the sinkholes and other pitfalls that may be there to trip them.

PARENTING WITH PRINCIPLE ELEVEN

Many parents think it's their job to correct their kids, to "straighten them out," by pointing out what they do wrong, and what is wrong with them. Though well-intentioned, this type of parenting damages self-esteem when it is not balanced with lots of praise and acknowledgment of the good things the child has said and done and how beautiful and intelligent they are. One study showed that if praise is connected with touch, the child takes it in 85 percent of the time, while if it is only given verbally, the child accepts it only 15 percent of the time.

Negative criticism sticks like glue and your child will remember it long into adulthood — much longer than the positive things you say, if you say them infrequently. Criticism makes children self-critical and cripples their confidence. It is important to reinforce the positive by a factor of ten over the negative. Reserve "constructive" criticism for short-term situations over which the child has control — situations that can be changed by choice, and that are *outside* the personality.

Principle Eleven in Pregnancy

Accepting that you are pregnant is your first opportunity to use Principle Eleven during your pregnancy. I remember going from joy to numbness to fear to wonder to acceptance, and back again, in those first weeks. Finally accepting we were pregnant allowed my husband and I to begin planning how we wanted our lives to change, what changes we needed to make, and to begin reading up on all our choices. During both pregnancies, it was a big project. The second time, we had the added stress of a downwardly-mobile financial situation, and a two year old who was still nursing, while, at the same time, I was in the midst of writing my first book. So more accommodations, more sacrifices, and different choices had to be made. Every baby, whether it is your first or fifth, is utterly different and each requires a deeper commitment to and understanding of the concept of acceptance.

During pregnancy we imagine and fantasize what our baby will be like. We dream, we wish, we look at every baby on the street and wonder. After our baby is born, we are called upon not only to totally accept our child but to validate who she or he is as a person separate from us. We may delight in discovering Mama's eyes, Daddy's chin, or a hint of Grandmother's cheekbones in our child's face. But we must always validate this being as a separate person.

As a parent, your capacity for acceptance and validation is truly tested when so-called problems arise — when, for example, your baby is premature, has Down Syndrome, a cleft lip, or any of a myriad of differences that you may not have been prepared for. The sooner you can work through your feelings and come to acceptance, the sooner you can begin building a positive bond with your baby. Massage and holding and touching can help you with this. As you bond, soul to soul, with your baby, you will come to realize, deep within your heart, that your mission on this earth includes showering your child with love, being loved by your child, and allowing your child to teach you some of the deepest lessons you will receive in this life.

Principle Eleven with Young Children

As your child grows, he will provide you with endless opportunities to practice acceptance as he does exactly the opposite of what you wish or expect! Your challenge, beyond merely accepting the situation, is to continue to validate your child as beautiful, intelligent, and worthy even when he makes mistakes.

One way to do this is by actively exploring the ways in which you and your child are different and accepting and validating those differences. With curiosity, determine which differences bother you, and why. What do you find difficult to accept and validate? We have so many agendas for our children, it is amazing they are, for the most part, so carefree and don't seem to feel the weight of our projections, expectations, wishes, hopes, and fears for them.

Acceptance and Expectations

By accepting your children as they are right now, you can help them grow up feeling secure with lots of self-esteem and healthy personal power. Jean Liedloff, in her groundbreaking work, *The Continuum Concept*, illustrates this point in her account of the village life of the Yequana people of South America.

> I was present at the first moments of one little girl's working life. She was about two years old. I had seen her with the women and girls, playing as they grated manioc (a root vegetable) into a trough. Now she was taking a piece of manioc from the pile and rubbing it against the grater of a girl near her. The chunk was too big; she dropped it several times trying to draw it across the rough board. An affectionate smile and a smaller piece of manioc came from her neighbor, and her mother, ready for the inevitable impulse to show itself, handed her a tiny grating board of her own. The little girl had seen the women grating as long as she could remember and immediately rubbed the nubbin up and down on her board like the others.

She goes on to describe how the child lost interest in just a few minutes and ran off, but no one laughed or was surprised or saw her gestures as "cute." As Liedloff says, "That the end result will be social, cooperative, and entirely voluntary is not in question. . . . The object of a child's activities, after all, is the development of self-reliance. To give that either more or less assistance than it needs tends to defeat that purpose." It is always assumed that the child's motives are social and that whatever he or she does will be accepted as the act of an innately "right" creature.

This assumption of rightness and sociability is the keynote of Principle Eleven. But Western societies tend to take the reverse approach, and assume that children are innately impulsive and, if not anti-social, are at least asocial, and that their impulses need to be curbed — they need to be "socialized." To put the principle of acceptance into practice in a Western family, the parents can allow their small children to "help" with the housework (using child-size housecleaning tools), help wash dishes or clothes, help with grocery shopping, help cook by stirring a pot, and so on.

It is important for you, as parents, not to anticipate failure or danger or make a big scene if your child breaks a dish or burns his finger. You are teaching him that family life is the same for everyone — even Mommy and Daddy break dishes and burn fingers sometimes — and validating his importance as part of the social system of the family.

Beware of giving too many apprehensive warnings; you can thereby unconsciously program your child to hurt himself. As Liedloff says, " . . . he is more likely to do what he *senses is expected of him* than what he is told to do," because of his innate, unsatisfied longing for acceptance by his caregivers. "Mindful predominantly of playing the part expected of him in his battle of wills with his caretaker, the little challenger is out of responsible balance with his surroundings and his self-preservation system is handicapped," says Liedloff.

As parents in Western cultures, we are in a double bind, for we cannot raise our children "tribally." They will get information and messages from others — teachers, peer groups, the media — that go against our best intentions and make it nearly impossible to raise them with the natural acceptance and validation they would receive in another environment. We have traded much that is good about village life for our modern conveniences. But at least we can try to be aware of the messages we are giving our children through our expectations of them. They need to know it is assumed they will be cooperative and social, and that you are there to guide them to the information *they seek*. They need to know that, deep inside you and not just through your words, they *themselves* are always accepted, even though their *actions* may be accepted or rejected according to society's rules.

Validation means to accept that the experience of the individual is true. We invalidate our children when we argue with them about what they tell us they feel, and when we tell them they should be seen but not heard. We invalidate them when we say things such as, "Nobody asked you!" or "Don't even *think* that, it's not nice," or "If you don't have something good to say, don't say anything at all." When we invalidate our children, we set them up to be invisible, to themselves and to others, and to put other people's needs, wishes, and opinions above their own — eventually, they won't even *know* what they want or need.

Principle Eleven with Teens

A friend once told me that when she first started dating she was much more concerned about not upsetting her date than she was with honoring herself. She didn't even *know* what she thought, wanted, or preferred. She was so conditioned to be the background for the men in her life that she had lost herself. I was also raised this way, as were many in my generation, and I was surprised when my daughter behaved assertively with her boyfriends, and when my son was rejected by his girlfriends when he tried to exercise "male privilege."

Validation and acceptance are key to successful parent-child relationships during the teen years when teens are trying on different clothes, ways of behaving, and philosophical ideas. Holding them to any external standard, especially to their own past, is destructive to their growth.

I don't mean, however, that teens should not be held accountable for their behavior or expected to know right from wrong. These things can and must be emphasized, practiced, modeled, and taught from birth on. In an age when, supposedly, two-thirds of American youths surveyed say they do not believe in any rules of right and wrong, providing parental guidance and support is obviously a necessity. But I question that survey, because I know that teens have a sixth sense for what is expected of them and will intentionally tweak society's notions just to get a reaction. Psychologists know that one of the deepest impulses we have as humans is to do what is expected of us. If we expect our teens to be irresponsible, violent, and uncooperative, while we tell them verbally to "just say no," which message do you think they will act out?

In societies where children grow up as an accepted part of the social fabric and are expected to contribute to its well-being, they do so. Commands such as "Go get some water from the well" or "Give the baby some food" are simply carried out with no underlying emotional conflict. Throughout their childhood, these children live with a continuous and unwavering expectation of cooperative behavior. Nobody has to watch over them to make sure they do as they are told — there is no doubt that they want to cooperate as part of the society.

In our society, we give our children double messages all their lives by both telling them to be cooperative and expecting them not to be cooperative. The child unconsciously wages war with himself and feels unaccepted and invalidated by this assumption of guilt until proven innocent. During the teen years, when the child's body provides him with the ability to overpower his parents, it is a natural time for him to rebel, in either an outright or unconscious way, against his society's hypocrisy. The conscious parent accepts the child as he is and mentors him in whatever direction he wants to take. She offers choices and helps broaden his understanding of his choices, and she encourages him to think big, to allow his imagination to grow, and to discover his strengths.

A conscious parent encourages his child to try out a lot of different ideas, to seek and explore and think and philosophize and talk. He sees himself as an aid to his child's explorations and goes the extra mile to get information and materials for her, to make room for long talks, and to share his child's offbeat humor about the strangeness of the world.

Conscious parents allow their teens to sit in on adult conversations and begin helping with the adult household responsibilities, without burdening them with too much, too soon. Information is shared in a matter-of-fact, relaxed way, and children are celebrated at each new phase of their maturation. Conscious parents are much more concerned about the health and well-being of their relationship with their children than about what any other adult thinks of them. When parents are accepting and validating, they send their kids an important message: you are loved, you are respected, you are lovable, you are innately loving, and you are very much needed in our world.

Exercise for Principle Eleven

1. Sit comfortably, close your eyes, and relax each part of your body.
2. Take eleven deep belly breaths. As you inhale repeat, "accept," and as you exhale repeat, "validate."

Principle Twelve

HARMONIZE

———————— ⚘ ————————

Colored light, when mixed together, becomes pure,
bright light again. That is why those who follow Tao
constantly speak of returning. They unify all areas of their
lives and unify all distinctions into a whole.

— Deng Ming-Dao, *365 Tao Daily Meditations*

The *yin/yang* symbol represents everything that Principle Twelve embodies: opposites that attract, blend, encompass one another, and give birth to the middle path in which all is accepted and life is a process of mindfulness. The *yin/yang* balance includes black and white, heavy and light, tense and relaxed, up and down, right and left, and motion and stillness. Each aspect contains the seed of its opposite, and all blend into the state that acknowledges extremes while returning, always, to the middle — the gray areas, the middle weight that is easy to carry, the suffused light that makes seeing possible, the middle distance at which things come into focus, the movement that requires the least exertion while remaining grounded to the earth and continuing to grow.

To be a completely integrated person means to be whole: your energies are not fragmented here and there between work, friends, family, social obligations, play, and spirituality. It is all one thing, and you are the same person within all these situations. Decisions are made from the perspective of the whole and not just one aspect of life. It is this union of the whole, of the inner and outer, that brings harmony and peace.

Harmony is simplicity. It requires a flowing unity in all your movements in Tai Chi, and a flowing energetic pattern in all your life and relationships. It means you have only what you treasure and need, with little extra clutter. You move and speak from your heart, even when your words are difficult to form and hard to hear. As Eastern teacher Osho said, "Only a simple heart sings with God in deep harmony."

THE OPPOSITE

In order to achieve harmony, we usually need to experience discord. When we do not have harmony, we feel out of balance. We may pay too much attention to one area of our lives and neglect the rest. To neglect our bodies leads to disease. To neglect our partners leads to separation. To neglect our true mission and work leads to deep dissatisfaction. To neglect our children leads to the loss of the chance to share intimate and memory-making moments with them, and creates big problems for our children as they grow up and interact with the world. To neglect our parents leads to regret. To neglect our finances leads to endless struggle. To neglect fun leads to joylessness. To neglect our spirituality leads to a feeling of uselessness and deadness in our souls.

Traumatic events such as illness, death, disasters, crime, and divorce can disrupt both individual and family harmony. We have little or no control over most of these events. When they happen, practicing all the principles in this book will give you and your family a good foundation for coping with, and ultimately triumphing over, adversity.

Dr. Janice Cohn, author of *Raising Compassionate, Courageous Children in a Violent World,* offers good advice on how to respond to your children when distressing events occur. In the following list, I have included her ideas and added some of my own as well:

- Be honest. Imagination feeds anxiety and often leads children to believe the problem or crisis is their fault.
- Take cues from your children. Answer their questions as clearly as you can. Don't give them information they didn't ask for, and keep it simple. If you feel there is something more they want to know, something they can't express, you can use third-person or hypothetical examples to bring out their questions, or say something like, "If I was your age, I'd probably feel _____." This may encourage your children to ask for the information they want.
- Encourage communication, but don't pressure your children about their feelings. Let them know you will be there if they want to talk or have questions, and that there is no such thing as a "dumb" question.
- Validate your children's feelings. It is okay to feel angry, sad, afraid, or confused. It is also okay not to feel much of anything, or even to feel glad or happy.
- Encourage your children to think of ways they might help others in the situation who may be hurting.
- Offer a back rub. Affectionate touch can help a child release pent-up stress and talk about feelings.
- Offer hugs often and tell your children you love them.

Cohn gives many inspiring examples of young people who have responded to adversity with kindness and creativity. In *365 Tao Daily Meditations,* author Deng Ming-Dao adds a good point:

> Scars that have happened through no fault of our own may also bar us from spiritual success. Unfortunately, it is often easier to give up a bad habit than to recover from the incision of others' violence. The only way is through self-cultivation. . . . The true course of healing is up to us alone.

DISCOVERING HARMONY IN YOUR LIFE

In order to find harmony in your own life and to create harmony in your family, you must evaluate the level of discord you feel right now. You need to look at each aspect of your life and ask your-self if it is in accord with your mission. If not, ask yourself, why not? What small steps can you take over the next six months or more to bring that aspect of your life into harmony with your mission?

For some people, there just isn't enough time in the day, and they need to make a plan to decrease their workload, and thus their stress, in order to create a balanced life. The way to do this is to spend more and more time on the important things — family, recreation, spirituality, making your dreams come true — and less time on the urgent things. Eventually, the urgent list gets shorter, and more time becomes available for the important things.

Follow Your Bliss

When you begin to reprioritize your life, you may find that you lack a creative outlet, and want to take a class, begin to play a musi-cal instrument, write, paint, or sculpt. Or you may need to spend more intimate time with your partner and talk about creative ways to schedule special weekend trips or "date nights." You and your partner may want to get relationship counseling or take a class in relationship-building skills. Or you may need more one-on-one time with your children, or to change your family schedule so the whole family can be together at regular intervals to eat or play games.

Maybe you need more rest. In Western societies, we tend to wear our bodies out with constant activity. These days more car accidents are attributed to falling asleep than drunk driving. Think about how you might incorporate a nap, a yoga session, or a deep relaxation period into your day. There are lots of tapes, videos, and fun paraphernalia to help you do this. If you are missing regular exercise, try to find an activity that is fun for you — a nice walk, roller blading, hiking, or swimming — and look at it as a gift to your body rather than a chore that must be done.

If you feel alone, if you feel that no one understands your strug-gles, and, especially, if you grew up in a not-so-functional family and are trying to create a healthy one for yourself, consider going to therapy and/or joining a support group. Lingering unresolved issues from the past can hinder the process of creating harmony in the present. Consider how you might heal these issues, either by for-giving and making amends to people from your past or by express-ing your feelings, possibly in a letter that you can either send or burn (which allows you to release your feelings in a symbolic way).

Harmony is not a given in our fractured society. A conscious effort must be brought to the task of creating it, but that effort reaps great rewards as, gradually, your life begins to feel whole again, and there is room for joy to come in and take its place as an active part of your everyday experience.

PARENTING WITH PRINCIPLE TWELVE

Everyone hopes for a harmonious pregnancy and birth, and it is common to want to be able to plan the method, place, and other aspects of your new parenthood. But things don't always go accord-ing to the plan, and those first months can be stressful as you try to adjust what you *thought* your life was going to be to what the Tao has ordered. Your best course is to surrender, release your old plans, and get involved in the interesting and exciting prospect of a new life.

Principle Twelve in Pregnancy

From the beginning, commit yourself to finding win-win solu-tions for every instance of opposition that comes your way, whether it is a difference between your own and your partner's parenting style, your mother's birthing experience, your employer's expecta-tions of time off, or your friends' desires for involvement and input.

Win-win doesn't mean compromise. It is deeper than that. Win-win means that both parties consciously want the other to have whatever they want and are willing to spend the time to find extra-creative solutions. It doesn't mean saying, "I'll give up this if you give up that." It means asking, "How can we structure this so that the whole is greater than the sum of its parts? How can we arrive at a scenario that allows everyone to get everything they want?" You will discover that most of the time conflict doesn't really exist. It is just a call for more creative thinking.

Principle Twelve with Young Children and Teens

The win-win strategy can also be used in your relationships with your children. Creating harmony through conscious parenting requires you to loosen up, think more creatively, and question your assumptions. It requires that you yield when you know your children are right, and that you remember what it was like to be a child and occasionally allow yourself to step into that place of limitless security, in-the-moment awareness, and joyful playfulness.

To harmonize with your children and teach them about Principle Twelve, arrange for them to spend time on a regular basis with their extended family — biological and otherwise. Make sure each child has at least two special adults he or she can relate to and enjoys spending time with. Talk to your children about the importance of developing support networks as they grow up, so that when difficult times come, they have more than one or two people to lean on. Encourage healthy friendships, sleep-overs and parties, and make your home a haven for your children's friends.

Help your children learn that they are an important part of a larger community by involving your family in community events such as a "Walk Against Violence in Families" or an environmental clean-up project. Discuss the news with them and find out what they think and feel. Talk together about what world news has to do with your daily lives and how they might get involved in issues they are concerned about. In a recent example, a teacher in Denver, Colorado, discovered that slave trading still occurs in the African country of Sudan, and she helped her students get involved in a project to save Sudanese children from being sold into slavery. As the issues arise, make time with your children to discuss racism, sexism, and other problems that affect your community, and talk about how you and your child, in your own small way, can help stop their negative impact.

Chinese master Huai-Nan-Tzu said it beautifully:

> Human nature is developed by profound serenity and lightness; virtue is developed by harmonious joy and open selflessness.

When we work with these twelve principles, we create serenity and lightness, joy and selflessness. What is more important than that? And as we commit ourselves to this kind of inner work, our joyful actions have a definite, wonderful affect on our children and on the whole world as well.

Exercise for Principle Twelve

1. Sit comfortably, close your eyes, and relax each part of your body.
2. Take twelve deep belly breaths. Be silent as you inhale, and repeat "harmonize" as you exhale.

Summary

—⟡—

Practicing these two simple exercises can help you absorb and integrate the wisdom of the twelve principles of the path of parenting:

Controlled Belly Breathing

Early in the morning, and whenever you feel a need during the day, relax and take several deep breaths into your belly. Relax deeply as you breathe and let go of your tension and your thoughts.

Find that moment of peace and serenity that comes when you simply let thought go and relax into the moment, into the Tao.

Twelve Breath Exercise

Sit comfortably, close your eyes, and relax each part of your body.

Take a deep breath, inhaling far down into your belly. As you exhale, say the word *Relax* to yourself.

Take another deep breath; as you exhale, say *Slow down*.

Take another deep breath; as you exhale, say *Empower*.

Take another deep breath; as you exhale, say *Be yourself.*
Take another deep breath; as you exhale, say *Be responsive.*
Take another deep breath; as you exhale, say *Avoid extremes.*
Take another deep breath; as you exhale, say *Flow and let go.*
Take another deep breath; as you exhale, say *Maintain continuity.*
Take another deep breath; as you exhale, say *Be present.*
Take another deep breath; as you exhale, say *Be attentive.*
Take another deep breath; as you exhale, say *Accept and validate.*
Take another deep breath; as you exhale, say *Harmonize.*

Repeat this exercise as often as necessary to remind you of these principles as you progress on your path of parenting. May every step you take bring you closer to health, harmony, fulfillment, and deep and lasting serenity.

BIBLIOGRAPHY

———— ❦ ————

Allen, Marc. *A Visionary Life.* New World Library, 1998.

Baldwin, Rahima. *You Are Your Child's First Teacher.* Celestial Arts, 1989.

Berrends, Polly Berrien. *Gently Lead: How to Teach Your Children about God While Finding Out for Yourself.* Crossroad Publishing, 1998.

Byng-Hall, John. *Rewriting Family Scripts.* Guilford Press, 1998.

Callan, Dawn. *Awakening the Warrior Within.* Nataraj, 1995.

Chang, Stephen T. *The Integral Management of Tao.* Tao Publishing, 1991.

Chopra, Deepak. *The Seven Spiritual Laws for Parents.* Harmony Books, 1997.

Cleary, Thomas, ed. *Vitality, Energy, Spirit: A Taoist Sourcebook.* Shambhala Publications, 1991.

Cohn, Janice. *Raising Compassionate, Courageous Children in a Violent World.* Longstreet Press, 1996.

Covey, Stephen R. *The Seven Habits of Highly Effective People.* Simon and Schuster, 1989.

Elkind, David. *The Hurried Child.* Perseus Press, 1989.

————. *All Grown Up and No Place to Go: Teenagers in Crisis.* Perseus Press, 1997.

Elgin, Suzette Haden. *The Gentle Art of Communicating with Kids.* John Wiley and Sons, 1996.

Hallett, Elisabeth. *Soul Trek: Meeting Our Children on the Way to Birth.* Light Hearts Publishing, 1995.

Henkart, Andrea and Journey Henkart. *Cool Communication.* Perigree, 1998.

Hinze, Sarah. *Coming from the Light: Spiritual Accounts of Life Before Birth.* Pocket Books, 1997.

Hood, Helen. *Awakened Heart Parenting: Relating to and Raising Children as Spirit Beings.* Dancing Hearts & Co., 1997.

Huang, Chungliang Al. *Embrace Tiger, Return to Mountain.* Celestial Arts, 1987.

Lee, Douglas. *Tai Chi Chuan.* Santa Clarita, Calif: Ohara Publications, 1976.

Liao, Waysun. *T'ai Chi Classics.* Shambhala Publications, 1990.

Liedloff, Jean. *The Continuum Concept.* Addison-Wesley Publishing, 1985.

Magid, Ken. *High Risk: Children without a Conscience.* Bantam Doubleday Dell, 1990.

McClure, Vimala. *Infant Massage: A Handbook for Loving Parents.* Bantam Doubleday Dell, 1989.

———. *The Tao of Motherhood.* New World Library, 1997.

———. *A Woman's Guide to Tantra Yoga.* New World Library, 1997.

Ming-Dao, Deng. *365 Tao Daily Meditations.* Harper San Francisco, 1992.

Montague, Ashley. *Touching: The Human Significance of Skin.* HarperCollins, 1986.

Montague, Ashley, and Ronald Goldman. *Circumcision, the Hidden Trauma: How an American Cultural Practice Affects Infants and Ultimately Us All.* Vanguard, 1997.

Ni, Hua-Ching. *8,000 Years of Wisdom, Book I.* Santa Monica, Calif.: Seven Star Communications, 1993.

Palladino, Grace. *Teenagers: An American History.* HarperCollins, 1997.

Paris, Eileen and Tom. *I'll Never Do to My Kids What My Parents Did to Me: A Guide to Conscious Parenting.* (out of print).

Peterson, C., Maler, S., and M. Seligman. *Learned Helplessness.* Oxford University Press, 1995.

Ponton, Lynn. *The Romance of Risk: Why Teenagers Do the Things They Do.* Basic Books, 1998.

Pratt, Jane. *For Real: The Uncensored Truth about America's Teenagers.* Hyperion, 1995.

Sears, William. *The Baby Book.* Little, Brown & Co., 1993.

———. *The Fussy Baby: How to Bring Out the Best in Your High-Need Child.* Signet, 1989.

———. *Nighttime Parenting: How to Get Your Baby and Child to Sleep.* New American Library, 1995.

Sieh, Ron. *T'ai Chi Ch'uan: The Internal Tradition.* North Atlantic Books, 1992.

Solter, Aletha. *The Aware Baby: A New Approach to Parenting.* Shining Star Press, 1998.

———. *Exercises in Self-Awareness for New Parents.* Shining Star Press, 1998.

Stoltz, Paul G. *Adversity Quotient: Turning Obstacles into Opportunities.* John Wiley and Sons, 1997.

Swets, Paul W. *The Art of Talking with Your Teenager.* Adams Publishing, 1995.

Vanzant, Inyala. *One Day My Soul Just Opened Up.* Simon and Schuster, 1998.

Verny, Thomas. *The Secret Life of the Unborn Child.* Delta, 1994.

———. *Nurturing the Unborn Child: A Nine Month Program for Soothing, Stimulating, and Communicating with Your Baby* (out of print).

Verny, Thomas, and Sandra Collier. *Love Chords: Music for the Pregnant Mother and Her Unborn Child.* In cassette or CD. Children's Book Store Distribution, 1998.

Wu, John. *Tao Te Ching.* Shambhala, 1989.

RECOMMENDED WEBSITES

⁘

Here are some of my favorite websites that I return to again and again:

ADOL: Adolescence Directory On-Line
http://education.indiana.edu/cas/adol.html

ADOPT
http://www.adopting.org/pads.html

Babies Today: The First Year
http://babiestoday.com/resources/articles/babymassage.htm

Baby Center
http://www.babycenter.com

Baby.Com
http://www.baby.com

Baby Place
http://www.baby-place.com

Childbirth.Org
http://www.childbirth.org

Healthy Touch: Infant Massage for Teen Parents
http://www.in4y.com/pm/healthy/touch.htm

International Association for Infant Massage
http://www.iaim.net

Infant Massage
http://www.com.edu/html/infant_massage.html

Infant Massage: A Holistic Approach to Infant Health
http://www.angelfire.com/ms/infantmassage

Infant Massage! Homepage
http://www.bouncingback.com

The InSite (Teens)
http://www.talkcity.com/theinsite

Life Before Birth
http://www.birthpsychology.com

Maria Mathias Infant Massage Programs
http://www.infantmassageprograms.com/html/what.html

Massage: Infant Massage
http://www.infantmassage.com

Mothers Who Think
http://salonmagazine.com/80/mwt/feature

The Natural Family Site
http://bygub.com/natural/massage.html

New World Library
http://www.nwlib.com

PACT: An Adoption Alliance
http://www.pactadopt.org/press/articles/taking.html

ABOUT THE AUTHOR

———— ⚜ ————

Vimala McClure has studied, practiced, and taught yoga and meditation for over twenty-eight years. She is the author of *Infant Massage: A Handbook for Loving Parents* and the founder of the International Association for Infant Massage, which is a parent education organization with over twenty-seven chapters worldwide. She is credited with bringing the art of infant massage to the United States and supporting its dissemination throughout the world. She is an award-winning art quilt maker, the mother of two grown children, and the author of several books and numerous magazine articles and essays. Vimala resides in her "ancestral home" of Boulder, Colorado.

BOOKS BY VIMALA MCCLURE

꙳

The Tao of Motherhood (New World Library)
A Woman's Guide to Tantra Yoga (New World Library)
Infant Massage: A Handbook for Loving Parents (Bantam, Doubleday, Dell)
Bangladesh (Simon & Schuster)
Teaching Infant Massage: A Handbook for Instructors
(Self Published)

Essay:
"Parenting in the New Millennium,"
in *The Fabric of the Future: Women Visionaries*
Illuminate the Path to Tomorrow (Conari Press)

These books can be found at your local bookstores, or on
the World Wide Web through Barnesandnoble.com or
Amazon.com, which also features an interview with Vimala.